Library of
Davidson College

Applications of Operations Research Models to Libraries

Applications of Operations Research Models to Libraries

A Case Study of the Use of Monographs
in the Francis A. Countway Library of Medicine,
Harvard University

Ching-chih Chen

The MIT Press
Cambridge, Massachusetts, and London, England

Copyright © 1976 by
The Massachusetts Institute of Technology

All rights reserved. No part of this book may be reproduced in any form or by any means, electronic or mechanical, including photocopying, recording, or by any information storage and retrieval system, without permission in writing from the publisher.

This book was set in IBM Composer Century by Technical Composition, printed on R & E Book, and bound in Holliston Amerspun Buckram by The Colonial Press Inc. in the United States of America.

Library of Congress Cataloging in Publication Data

Chen, Ching-chih, 1937-
 Applications of operations research models to libraries.

 Based on the author's thesis, Case Western Reserve University, 1974.
 Bibliography: p.
 1. Francis A. Countway Library of Medicine, Boston. 2. Operations research—Case studies. 3. Library use studies—Boston. I. Title.
Z733.F784C47   1976   025.6   75-28210
ISBN 0-262-03056-X

To
My Mother, Mrs. May-ying Liu
Sow-Hsin
Anne, Cathy, and John

Contents

List of Figures   x

List of Tables   xii

Foreword by Philip M. Morse   xv

Introductory Note by Harold Bloomquist   xvi

Preface   xvii

Chapter 1. Introduction   1

Part I.   Theoretical Models   5

Chapter 2. Morse's Theoretical Models   7

Basic Assumptions of the Book-Use Models   8
Procedure Used by Morse to Develop His Models   9
Properties of Probabilistic Models   10
Morse's Book-Use Models and the Markov Process   10
The Transition Probabilities   16
The Geometric Distribution for the First-Year Circulation   17
Morse's Modified Model on Book Use   18

Chapter 3. Extension of Morse's Theoretical Models   22

First-Year Circulation Distribution   22
Estimating the Sample-Year Circulation Distribution   26
Estimating the Total Annual Circulation   31
The Geometric Distribution   31
Analyzing Relative Numbers of High-Circulation Books   32
Analyzing the Inactive Books   32
Predicting the Future Circulation   33
Predicting Fraction of Books Not Available on Shelf   35

Part II.   Testing the Theoretical Models   37

Chapter 4. The Francis A. Countway Library of Medicine—a Sample Library   39

The Collection   39
The Arrangement of the Collection   40
Rules Governing the Borrowing of Books   42
Procedures for Charging and Discharging a Book   42

The Users of the Library   44
Library Hours   44
Current Status of Countway and Its Book Acquisition   44

Chapter 5.   Samples and Methodology   50

The Collection of the Book-Use Data   50
  Types of Book Use   50
  Methods Used for Collecting Book-Use Data   50
  Evaluations of the Methods Used for Collecting Book-Use Data   51
Samples and Methodology of the Study   52
  Major Objectives of the Study   52
  Methodology Used in the Study   53
  Samples   53
    Defining the Scope of the Sample   53
    Sampling Unit   54
    Deciding the Sampling Period   54
    Determining the Sampling Size in Each Sampling Period   56
    Selecting Specific Classes for Detailed Study   58
    Types of Data Collection   59
    Difficulties and Problems of Data Collection   65
  Limitations of the Study   66

Chapter 6.   Experimental Results and Testing of the Theoretical
              Models   67

The Simple Markov Process   67
Analyses of the Data and Experimental Results   67
Verifying the Models   73
  The Simple Markov Model   73
  The Correction Models   81

Part III.   Interpretation of the Results   97

Chapter 7.   Budgetary Considerations   99

Chapter 8.   Book Selection and Duplication Policy   110

Book Selection Policy   110
Duplication Policy   114

Chapter 9.   Weeding Policy   119

Chapter 10.   Further Illustrations   127

Contents ix

Loan Period   127
Nonuse of the Library   129
Browsing and Linear Arrangement of Library Books   129

Chapter 11.   Conclusions   131

Appendixes

1. Detailed Book Circulation Statistics   135
2. Mean Loan Period   145
3. Browsing, Search Models, and the Linear Arranging of Library Books   153
4. Users of the Countway Library   157
5. Additional Analyzed Circulation-History Results for Checking Markov Models   161
6. Additional Results for Checking the Extended Theoretical Models Discussed in Chapter 3   171
7. The Most Frequently Circulated Books in the Countway Library   183

Glossary of Symbols   197

Bibliography   199

Index   209

List of Figures

2.1 Mean Circulation $N(m)$ for Year $t + 1$ as a Function of Circulation m for Previous Year t 15

3.1 Fraction of Books That Have m Circulation(s) during the Year   25

3.2 Uncorrected and Corrected Circulation Distributions for Class WM at Countway (January 1973 Data)   30

4.1 A Sample Completed Circulation Charge Card   43

5.1 Circulation and Attendance Distribution at the Allen Library of the Cleveland Health Sciences Library   55

5.2 Countway Library Circulation Distribution   57

5.3 A Sample Date-Due Slip   62

6.1 Part of a Sample Year-Pair Entry Form   69

6.2 A Sample of Final Table of Circulation-History Results Prepared Manually for Each Sample Studied   70

6.3 A Sample Figure for $N(m) = \alpha + \beta m$ Prepared Manually for Each Sample Studied   71

6.4 Mean Circulation $N(m)$ for Year $t + 1$ as a Function of Circulation m for Previous Year t—WM Books.
1968-1973 Pairs—January 1973 Data   74

6.5 Mean Circulation $N(m)$ for Year $t +1$ as a Function of Circulation m for Previous Year t—WM Books.
1963-1968 Pairs—January 1973 Data   75

6.6 Uncorrected and Corrected Circulation Distribution for QZ Books   90

6.7 Uncorrected and Corrected Circulation Distribution for WM Books   91

6.8 Uncorrected and Corrected Circulation Distribution for WS Books   92

A2.1 Loan-Period Distribution of W Book Classes—April 1973 Data   150

A2.2 Loan-Period Distribution of All Countway Books Returned in October 1973   152

A5.1 Mean Circulation $N(m)$ for Year $t + 1$ as a Function of Circulation m for Previous Year t—WM Books

A5.1a 1968-1973 Pairs—April 1973 Data   162
A5.1b 1968-1973 Pairs—July 1973 Data   163
A5.1c 1968-1973 Pairs—October 1973 Data   164

A5.2 Mean Circulation $N(m)$ for Year $t+1$ as a Function of Circulation m for Previous Year t—WM Books
A5.2a 1963-1968 Pairs—April 1973 Data   165
A5.2b 1963-1968 Pairs—July 1973 Data   166
A5.2c 1963-1968 Pairs—October 1973 Data   167

List of Tables

2.1 Values of $M(m)$, N_{mn}, and $N(m)$ for Different Values of m and n (WM Books Returned to Countway in January 1973—1968-1972 Pairs)   14

3.1 Examples of Book-Circulation Histories   23

3.2 Summary of Circulation History of a Sample of 126 WM Books Returned to Countway in January 1973   24

3.3 Values of $1/[1 - (1-\rho)^j]$ and $1/(1-e^{-j})$ 29

4.1 Outline of the National Library of Medicine Classification Schedule (Used for Books Published since 1960)   41

4.2 Outline of the Boston Medical Library Classification Schedule (Used for Books Acquired and Cataloged before 1960)   42

4.3 Countway Library Expenditures   46

4.4 Summary of Some Statistics of the Countway Library   47

4.5 Total Number of Monographs Cataloged at Countway   48

4.6 Number of Selected New Countway Acquisitions Listed in Both the Countway and NERMLS Newsletters   48

5.1 Estimated Total Number of Book Volumes at Countway   64

6.1 Values of $M(m)$, N_{mn}, and $N(m)$ for Different Values of m and n for WM Books Returned to Countway 1968-1973 Pairs—January 1973 Data   74

6.2 Values of $M(m)$, N_{mn}, and $N(m)$ for Different Values of m and n for WM Books Returned to Countway 1963-1968 Pairs—January 1973 Data   75

6.3 Values of $M(m)$, N_{mn}, and $N(m)$ for Different Values of m and n for WM Books with Theoretical Values of $N(m)$ and N_{mn} Obtained by Using Eqs. 2.3, 2.4, and 2.9   76

6.4 Values of α's and β's of the Eight Selected Classes of Books in Countway   78

6.5 Mean Yearly Circulation $\overline{R}(t)$ of WM, WA, and WS Books at t Year after Accession   80

6.6 Uncorrected and Corrected Circulation Distributions for QZ Books Returned in 1973   84

6.7 Uncorrected and Corrected Circulation Distributions for WM Books Returned in 1973   86

6.8 Uncorrected and Corrected Circulation Distributions for WS Books Returned in 1973   88

6.9 A Summary of Equations Used to Measure the Total Yearly Circulation and to Predict the Future Use   93

6.10 Predicted Following-Year Circulation for the Same QZ Books Circulated in 1972-1973   93

6.11 Predicted Following-Year Circulation for the Same WM and WS Books Circulated in 1972-1973   94

6.12 Comparison of the Estimated Total Yearly Circulation ($\overline{R}_a N_a$ or $\overline{R}_\ell N_\ell$) with Actual Circulation Data   94

7.1 Distribution of Countway Users in January 1973   103

7.2 Minimal Nucleus of Countway Users   104

7.3 Distribution of Countway Book Circulation in 1973   107

7.4 Minimal Nucleus of Countway Books   108

7.5 Comparison of the Countway Circulation Distribution Data by Date of Publication with Two Earlier Studies   109

A1.1 Circulation Frequency Distribution by Subjects (during the Four Sample Months at Countway)   136

A1.2 Countway Circulation Frequency Distribution by Book Publication Dates   138

A1.3 Number of Books Circulated j Times in Countway during the Sample Months   139

A1.4 Subject Distribution of Books Circulated in Countway   140

A1.5 Number of Countway Books Circulated in Both January and April 1973 (Selected NLM Classes)   142

A1.6 Request Distribution by Subjects (during the Four Sample Months)   143

A1.7 Circulation Distribution by Day of the Week   144

A2.1 Renewal Distribution by Subjects   147

A2.2 Loan-Period Distribution of Books of W Classes in Countway   148

A2.3 Loan-Period Distribution of All Countway Books Returned during the Four Sample Months   151

A3.1 Connectivity of Interest among Subject Books as Measured by the Frequency of Pair Circulations to the Same User   155

A4.1 Circulation Distribution among User Groups of the Countway Library—January 1973 Data   158

A5.1 Values of $M(m)$, N_{mn}, and $N(m)$ for Different Values of m and n for WM Books Returned to Countway
A5.1a 1968-1973 Pairs—April 1973 Data   162
A5.1b 1968-1973 Pairs—July 1973 Data   163
A5.1c 1968-1973 Pairs—October 1973 Data   164

A5.2 Values of $M(m)$, N_{mn}, and $N(m)$ for Different Values of m and n for WM Books Returned to Countway
A5.2a 1963-1968 Pairs—April 1973 Data   165
A5.2b 1963-1968 Pairs—July 1973 Data   166
A5.2c 1963-1968 Pairs—October 1973 Data   167

A5.3 Values of $M(m)$, N_{mn}, and $N(m)$ for Different Values of m and n for WM Books with Theoretical Values of $N(m)$ and N_{mn} Obtained by Using Eqs. 2.3, 2.4, and 2.9
A5.3a 1968-1973 Pairs—April 1973 Data   168
A5.3b 1968-1973 Pairs—July 1973 Data   169
A5.3c 1968-1973 Pairs—October 1973 Data   170

A6.1 Uncorrected and Corrected Circulation Distributions for QU Books Returned in 1973   172

A6.2 Uncorrected and Corrected Circulation Distributions for WA Books Returned in 1973   174

A6.3 Uncorrected and Corrected Circulation Distributions for WG Books Returned in 1973   176

A6.4 Uncorrected and Corrected Circulation Distributions for WO Books Returned in 1973   178

A6.5 Predicted Following-Year Circulation for the Same QU and WA Books Circulated in 1972-1973   180

A6.6 Predicted Following-Year Circulation for the Same WG and WO Books Circulated in 1972-1973   180

A7.1 Publication-Date Distribution of the 163 High-Circulation Books   184

A7.2 Subject Distribution of the 163 High-Circulation Books   185

Foreword

This book is a welcome addition to the growing literature that analyzes the collective use of library books. Previous work on probabilistic models for measuring the effectiveness of book-lending procedures and for predicting future book use were developed from a rather narrow base of data. The models turned out to fit data gathered from a university science library. It was expected that the resulting formulas, with modified parameters, should hold for other book collections and other book-user populations, but it was anticipated that more data, from other libraries, would be needed to extend and clarify the model.

This volume reports an important step in this extension. The data analyzed here show that the formulas that worked for a science library also work for a medical library, in conformity with expectation. Moreover, the differences in the parameters for the two libraries illuminate the different ways in which the two collections are used. In addition, new ways of processing the data are developed—ways necessitated by the different circulation records used in the medical library.

One can now hope that data similar to those reported here can be collected and analyzed for some large, heavily used collection of literary and historical books to round out the picture and to illuminate the statistical differences in behavior of the three user populations. This completed picture will be needed if circulation computerization is to provide the librarian with the cost-user-benefit measures he should have to control his library's effectiveness.

Philip M. Morse
Professor of Physics, Emeritus,
Massachusetts Institute of Technology

Introductory Note

This book is the result of a happy set of circumstances: institutional, individual, and temporal. In the late 1960s and early 1970s, the faculty of the library school at Simmons College was affirming its interest in research in librarianship. Ching-chih Chen, Associate Science Librarian at the Massachusetts Institute of Technology, became familiar with the work of MIT Professor Philip M. Morse, who had turned his considerable experience in operations research to libraries. Mrs. Chen and Professor Morse met, and he encouraged her to cultivate her interest in operations research. As her interest developed, she embarked on a study of physics journals at MIT that appeared in the literature.

In 1971 Mrs. Chen was invited to join the faculty of the Simmons Library School to strengthen the school's expertise in library research. Shortly thereafter she conceived of a study to apply Morse's theoretical models to the use of monographs in the field of medicine. She therefore approached me at Harvard University's Countway Library of Medicine, which was located a scant two blocks away from Simmons, and which had both a strong interest in research in librarianship and a large and active user population.

Mrs. Elaine Ciarkowski, Countway's Chief of Circulation, and I studied the Chen proposal and enthusiastically offered her access to the necessary records and two pairs of critical ears as the study progressed.

The indefatigable Professor Chen began a unique form of commuting between Boston and Cleveland, where colleagues at the library school of Case Western Reserve University urged her to use her Countway study as her doctoral thesis, with Professor Morse as her thesis adviser. This book is based on that doctoral thesis.

To comment on the purpose and usefulness of the book would be redundant here. Let me say that several of the models and products that are suggested by the book's content can and should be replicated in other libraries. The library community will profit from these sophisticated new tools.

Harold Bloomquist
Librarian,
Francis A. Countway Library of Medicine,
Harvard University

Preface

About a decade ago the first attempt to use probability theory and modern analytical techniques to predict the future use of the library was made by Professor Philip M. Morse of the Massachusetts Institute of Technology. He and his students in a laboratory course in operations research began by developing suitable models. In 1968, his authoritative book *Library Effectiveness* (MIT Press) was published. It contains specific objectives to bring operations research experts and librarians together, to break new ground for further research for these two groups, and in an experimental sense, to extrapolate and formulate theoretical models, and to discuss their potential applications.

Almost all of his models are basic and simple, with only a very small number of parameters and variables in order to facilitate the actual applications of these models in libraries. This is probably why, after a decade, his book is still considered to be one of the most authoritative publications on the subject.

Morse's book focuses on the pattern of book use, its change over time, and the problems of evaluating and estimating the degree to which the library does or does not satisfy the seeker of information. The models developed by Morse were tested by using quite limited experimental data obtained at the MIT Science Library in the early 1960s. In order to test the validity and accuracy of his probabilistic models, further research in a different library environment was necessary, and more up-to-date and comprehensive data were needed. To fulfill these needs, I completed a Ph.D. research study in 1974. This book is mainly a revised publication based on the doctoral thesis for the Case Western Reserve University.

This is a case study of the use of monographs in the Francis A. Countway Library of Medicine, Harvard University, the country's largest medical research library, with the exception of the National Library of Medicine. In this study, Morse's probabilistic models on book use are adopted as the general theoretical basis. The experimental data base consists of approximately 12,000 circulation records collected in four selected complete months of 1973, and these records have been manipulated in a dozen or more ways. Furthermore, because of the availability of much more complete and comprehensive data, some earlier models have been modified and extended, and certain new models have also been developed.

It should be stressed that this study is concerned only with the testing of Morse's Markov models. It does not imply that this type of model is the only technique for predicting future library use. In order to make realistic forecasts, either the experience or the subjective judgments of librarians or of other knowledgeable people are always needed to add to any predictive model. There are ways of enriching hard data with knowledgeable judgments regarding the future within one and the same model with inputs obtained by using various consensus-seeking techniques. It is, however, not the purpose of this study to explain how and to what degree librarians' experience, intuition, judgment, and knowledge can be combined with the Markov model in the process of decision-making. For these problems, the readers should refer to various texts on decision theory.

This book is presented with the following objectives in mind: (1) to test Morse's probabilistic models on book use in a library entirely different from the MIT Science Library; (2) to broaden and update the base of these models; (3) to modify, extend, and develop new models; (4) to demonstrate the importance and usefulness of operations research techniques in various library decision-making processes; and (5) to facilitate and promote librarians' appreciation of operations research applications in libraries.

To fulfill these objectives, this book is divided into three parts, with one introductory chapter.

Part I deals with the theoretical models. It contains two chapters: Chapter 2 discusses mainly Morse's Markov models of book use, which are to be tested in this study; Chapter 3 presents the new and extended models developed for the most part because of the biased nature of the Countway data base. These models can be used to correct the biased circulation data gathered from book charge cards and thus to obtain unbiased operating data such as the estimated yearly circulation of books of a given class, the identification of active books and those of some or of little potential use, and the prediction of future circulation.

Part II deals with the testing of the theoretical models presented in Part I. It consists of three chapters: Chapter 4 describes the sample library of this study—its collection, its users, its policies, and its services—with specific emphasis on the background information on the Countway book collection. I hope that this will provide an adequate picture of the sample library in order to better the reader's understanding in later discussions. Chapter 5 explains the methodology used in this study, the selection of the samples used, the types of data collected, and the problems in-

volved in this study. Chapter 6 analyzes the experimental results in
great detail and discusses how these analyzed data have tested the
validity of the theoretical probabilistic models described in Part I.
Because of the large scope of this study, the huge data base, and
the enormous multitude of generated results, it is too confusing
to include all available results in a single chapter. In this chapter,
only those major and necessary sample results for the testing of
the theoretical models are presented. The rest of the results are
grouped together in Appendixes 1 to 6. It should be specifically
noted here that a large number of tables and figures presenting
both analyzed circulation-history results and summarized circulation-history data of various chosen samples were available as
Appendixes 5 and 6 in the original thesis[1] but were deleted from
this book. Similar representative results are available in Chapter 6
and Appendix 5 of this book.

Finally, Part III deals with the interpretation of the results. I
have tried to demonstrate, in simple and nontechnical language,
how an operational study such as this, employing analytical
techniques, can yield valuable results for aiding librarians in making decisions about such things as the planning of budget allocations, the determining of book selection, duplication, weeding,
and other operational and administrative policies, and the establishing of various library activities and services to meet their users'
needs. In this part, little mathematics is involved. All chapters are
written about real day-to-day library problems, with numerous
references to pertinent sources that are familiar to most librarians.
While all library operations, activities, planning, and problems
are interrelated and thus should be treated together, for the purpose of clearer and simpler illustrations, the interpretations are
divided into four chapters: Chapter 7 discusses library budget allocations, with emphasis on book budgetary allocation; Chapter 8
is on book selection policy (both single and duplicate copies);
Chapter 9 devotes its discussions to weeding policy; and Chapter
10 offers other illustrations, such as loan policy. Although some
discussions may be redundant, they are considered necessary and
helpful.

The final chapter, Chapter 11, is a brief conclusion to this
study. Recommendations for areas of further research are given.
This author feels strongly that a library is a complex service orga-

---

[1] Ching-chih Chen, "Applications of Operations Research Models to Libraries," Ph.D thesis, School of Library Science, Case Western Reserve University,
September 1974, Appendixes 5 and 6, 230-284.

nization, and in order to provide the most effective services to satisfy the needs of its users at minimum cost, librarians must learn to employ analytical techniques to aid them in planning for tomorrow.

Appendixes 1 to 6 provide additional results of this study. They are frequently referred to in Parts II and III. Appendix 7 is a by-product of this study, which lists 163 Countway books circulated four or more times during the sample periods. After these appendixes, there is a glossary of symbols used in this book. It is worth noting that since one of the main objectives of this study was to test and to extend Morse's Markov models, for the readers' convenience in relating this book to Morse's *Library Effectiveness* and his other publications, every possible effort has been made to use symbols like those in Morse's book and publications.

Finally, the Bibliography provides a comprehensive list of materials pertinent to this study. It can also be used as a valuable bibliography on operations research in libraries.

I wish to express my deepest gratitude to Professor Philip M. Morse for the encouragement, guidance, and valued assistance offered during the course of this study, and for his generosity in giving me time and advice whenever I needed it. Permission generously granted by Professor Morse and The MIT Press to summarize and paraphrase some of the models presented in Professor Morse's *Library Effectiveness*, in particular Chapter 2 of this book, is greatly appreciated. I am also greatly indebted to Mr. Harold J. Bloomquist, the Librarian of the Francis A. Countway Library of Medicine, for his enthusiasm and support of this investigation. Because of his gracious interest in analytical approaches to library operations, he and his staff have provided me the ideal laboratory for this study—his library, without which this research would not have been possible. Last but certainly not least, special thanks are due to all members of my family—my mother, Mrs. May-ying Liu, my husband, Sow-Hsin, and my children, Anne, Cathy, and John. Each of them, in his or her own way, has given me graciously and unselfishly the support, understanding, encouragement, and love that have helped me to complete this book.

Ching-chih Chen
Boston, Massachusetts

Applications of Operations Research Models to Libraries

Chapter One
Introduction

During World War II the term "operations research" was applied primarily to the study of military operations, with the aim of improving their effectiveness. It was defined as a scientific method of providing executive departments with a quantitative basis for decisions regarding the operations under their control (Morse, 1951). It was felt then that the systems approach to the difficult problems of waging war could mean the difference between winning and losing (Bellomy, 1968). Because of the great success of its applications in the military field, operations research has developed rapidly since its origin. It is now applied not only to the problems of military operations but also to the activities of commercial organizations, notably railroads and other public transportation systems, manufacturing and industrial companies, and sales organizations. These commercial organizations, motivated by the desire for greater profits and the necessity to battle for bare subsistence budgets, have discovered the benefits of adopting operations research techniques (Bellomy). For these private firms,

"wherever systems are so large or changes so rapid that the manager does not have time to learn by traditional empirical methods, these teams of analysts can bring improvements in system design, operational efficiency, and effectiveness."[1]

Public institutions, like hospitals and schools, which lack the urgency of military operations and the profit motive of business organizations, are slower in employing operations research approaches to their operational problems. In the past ten years, however,

"an increasing number of experts have become persuaded that the procedures of operations research would be effective in solving some of the problems of the public sector, such as those in urban operations, in public health, and in education. . . . At the same time a growing number of managers of public operations became aware of O.R. and began to be interested in trying out its techniques."[2]

[1] Alvin W. Drake, Ralph L. Keeney, and Philip M. Morse, eds., *Analysis of Public Systems* (Cambridge, Mass.: MIT Press, 1972), 2.

[2] Philip M. Morse, ed., *Operations Research for Public Systems* (Cambridge, Mass.: MIT Press, 1967), v.

A quick check of the table of contents of recent issues of *Operations Research* reveals the wide range of interests in operations research applications from the public sector. More insights into operations research in public systems can be gained from monographs such as Morse's *Operations Research for Public Systems* (MIT Press, 1967) and Drake, Keeney, and Morse's *Analysis of Public Systems* (MIT Press, 1972).

Libraries have been found to be even slower than some other public institutions in adopting operations research approaches to their problems. Prior to the late 1960s, libraries in general did not adopt quantitative management with any enthusiasm. Although Ralph Shaw advocated scientific management in libraries in 1947, it was not until 1954 that a whole issue of *Library Trends*, edited by Shaw, was devoted to the subject. The first book on the subject, Dougherty and Heinritz's *Scientific Management of Library Operations*, did not appear until 1966 (Heinritz, 1970). T. F. Parker described the situation well:

"Librarians are long on practical knowledge of their work but short on systematic analysis of the tasks they perform. As a result, traditional tasks go unanalyzed, inefficient methods go unsurveyed, personnel training is almost entirely oral and user needs are estimated by intuition and flawed memories of past experience."[3]

Some librarians, because of their background in traditional approaches and their unfamiliarity with scientific management, even object to having their work quantified. The majority of librarians are not aware of the great value and potential of the operations research techniques, and consequently they are unwilling, and to a certain extent unable, to follow the operations research arguments.

In the past decade, a few publications of merit have appeared in the literature showing how and under what conditions an operations research study can be conducted in a library environment. Some of these were prepared by librarians, but most of them have been written in a highly technical language by individuals whose credentials are in fields other than library science. These operations researchers have successfully discovered and used the library as an ideal laboratory for their studies and in doing so have given the library profession some of its most substantial contributions

---

[3]T. F. Parker, "Missing Stream: Operations Management in Libraries," *Library Journal*, 94 (January 1969), 42-43.

(Burns, 1971). Yet most of the operations researchers or systems analysts have little knowledge of the day-to-day library operations and problems. They tend to model library problems on a theoretical basis, and thus their arguments tend to be remote, incomprehensible, unrealistic, and sometimes inapplicable to libraries. On the other hand, librarians, when confronted with these highly technical publications, generally find themselves unable to grasp the essential points and are easily frustrated by the mathematical presentations of the probabilistic models that have been worked out mostly by operations research experts.

The operations research approach to any system involves the use of interdisciplinary teams. In libraries, the operations research potential can be fully realized only with the intensive involvement and dedicated efforts of both the librarians and operations researchers involved. The operations research models can be validly established and properly tested only when both the librarians' knowledge, experience, and sensitivity to their library needs and problems and the operations researchers' interests in library problems and expertise in systems analysis are joined. Leimkuhler (1970) suggested that libraries need system engineers as permanent members of their staffs, along with other research and development personnel.

It should be stressed that the greatest potential of the techniques of operations research lies in predicting the future by employing the mathematical models developed rather than in knowing the present by analyzing the past experimental data. As Leimkuhler stated,

"At the heart of most O.R. work is the development of analytic models which describe in a meaningful way the behavior of man-machine systems operating in natural environments and predict how the system can be regulated or improved upon through the manipulation of certain control variables."[4]

As for the mathematical models, some librarians seem to have the notion that the models will tell them what they should do and will make decisions for them. Actually, quite to the contrary, the librarian must never allow a mathematical model to replace him or her as the ultimate decision-maker. This implies that the respon-

---

[4] F. F. Leimkuhler, "Mathematical Models for Library Systems Analysis," *Drexel Library Quarterly*, 4 (July 1968), 185-196.

sibility for decisions must rest with the person, not the tool. The model has no magic. It is just a tool to be used as a guide and an aid to the decision-maker. In other words, knowing what will result in the future, if certain decisions are made now, will enable an administrator to make wiser decisions for the future.

Since the output of an operations research study is quantitative, the input must therefore be quantitative too. The standard techniques of data collection and reduction, such as methods based on sampling theory and statistics, will be used. Probability theory must often be used to obtain and express the results of the study and to formulate the probabilistic models. One should keep in mind that probability theory is a quantitative means of prediction in the face of uncertainty. Therefore, models can be utilized to demonstrate only the average behavior of the samples studied. Furthermore, the models should be as simple as possible, with only a very small number of parameters and variables, so that the data collection will not be cumbersome and impossible.

Although library literature has revealed many quantitative studies on library problems and uses, Morse's *Library Effectiveness* (MIT Press, 1968) is still one of the most comprehensive and authoritative books ever published on operations research in libraries. His probabilistic models are generally basic and simple and should be applicable to all types of libraries without much difficulty. Because of this, they are adopted as the theoretical base of this investigation.

Part One
Theoretical Models

Chapter Two
Morse's Theoretical Models

A survey of library literature reveals that there have been abundant use studies undertaken by various researchers. Davis and Bailey (1964) provided a list of 438 studies up to 1963, Deweese (1967) added 109 to supplement Davis and Bailey's list, and Atkin (1971) provided a bibliography of some 700 titles of such surveys during the period 1950-1970. The value of many of these studies is limited by the fact that they were essentially census-taking in nature (Pings et al., 1969), and there is a lack of systematic treatment of the interaction of the variables (Gomes, 1970). Also, many of them were of limited scope, and quite outdated. Most of the statistical data collected have been described as redundant, essentially descriptive, and not amenable to analyses for predictive purposes, and so are of minimal utility (Rees, 1966). As to book usage, however, several studies, such as those of Shaffer and Ernst (1954), Rothkopf (1962), and Dawson, Aldrin, and Gould (1962), did develop some deterministic mathematical models for the description and prediction of the average use of books. These models were classified as exponential, logarithmic, and square-root classes by Jain (1967).

Morse's Markov model (1968) was the only significant probabilistic model on book use presented at that time. Jain also developed a new mathematical model, called *Pn* model, but the presentation of that model was rather complicated and not easily comprehensible to an average librarian.[1] It should be kept in mind that Jain developed the *Pn* model mainly to accommodate the "zero-use" books, because he found that the use distribution of these books did not follow the same Poisson distribution as was suggested by Morse.

Morse further developed and extended his basic Markov models in 1972. These later extensions simplify the computation processes of the original Markovian models. In these newer models, he separated the use of active books (used one or more times during a given period) from the use of "zero-use" books. Therefore, these models amended that part of his original Markovian models which was criticized by Jain.

In this chapter, Morse's Markov models, together with his extended ones, will be summarized. Since they have been described carefully and fully in Morse's book *Library Effectiveness* and at his presentation at the thirty-fifth Annual Conference of the

---

[1] For the detailed discussion of the *Pn* model presented by Jain, see his Ph.D. thesis (1967), 24-84.

Graduate Library School of the University of Chicago in 1971 (Swanson and Bookstein, 1972), readers should go to these publications particularly for detailed information on how these models were developed. Unless specifically quoted, references to Morse's publications will not be made in this chapter.

Most of the simple models presented in Chapters 2 and 3 could undoubtedly be developed much more intricately. These complex models might produce more accurate but not necessarily better predictions on which to base administrative decisions. They could, however, increase considerably the computations required to make the predictions and the amount of data needed to obtain values of the appropriate parameters. Since the purpose of a model is to represent an operation as accurately as needed and in sufficient detail to account for the important aspects of its behavior, I have tried to keep all models as simple as possible, with only a very small number of parameters and variables.

Basic Assumptions of the Book-Use Models

There are three basic assumptions of Morse's book-use models.
1. It is assumed that the process of book circulation is a *random* one. In other words, the use of a library, including the use of books, by its clientele is the result of a large number of random occurrences. The behavior of an individual user, or the degree of use of a given book, cannot be predicted with any degree of certainty. There is no way to tell whether Book A is to be used seven times next year while Book B is to be used zero times. Nevertheless, the average use behavior of a class of books *can* be predicted. The accuracy of the prediction is proportional to the number of samples or the time span included in the prediction.
2. On the average, book circulation drops off exponentially with time. This was found to be true from the studies of Trueswell that appeared in *College and Research Libraries* (1964) and Fussler and Simon (1961).
3. There is a time correlation from one time period to the next, or "memory," involved in book use. In other words, although book circulation, on the average, decreases year by year exponentially, there are many exceptions. Books could suddenly become popular after having been in a library for several years. Once such a book becomes popular, the circulation history thenceforward is as though it had been popular all along. Likewise, if a book happens suddenly to lose popularity, its future circulation history is as

though it had always been neglected. This basic assumption disagrees with that of Fussler and Simon's study. Fussler and Simon assumed a random model of book use, but they considered the book use as a function of age. They took the past use to be the best single predictor of the future use of that book. For example, they said:

"The model underlying the entire study treated books as if each had a random probability of use within a specific time period . . . but . . . the amount of use during one year *does not* influence the amount of use in any subsequent year."[2] [Italics added.]

Procedure Used by Morse to Develop His Models

Morse used the probabilistic approach. Furthermore, he followed the measurement-model procedure. In other words, data taken from actual library operations were examined carefully. Probabilistic models of the operation were then devised. With the basic assumptions of the library use and operation in mind, the models, with their random elements, should correspond reasonably well to both the observed data and the basic structure of the operation. The models developed can never be claimed to be the ideal and absolute ones. This is simply because our knowledge of any library operation and of library-use behavior can never to totally complete, and the data taken on any specific type of library operation or library use are generally on a limited scale (either in time or in scope within the time limit). Because of these limitations, Morse said:

"We will find these models imply other properties of the operating system, predict other characteristics which can be checked by taking *more* data. If the actual system behaves as the theoretical model suggests, it strengthens our trust in its predictive value; if the measured data do not fit, we look for another, more appropriate model."[3] [Italics added.]

This is the reason why Morse's book-use models were modified and extended in his later publication of 1972. The following chap-

[2] H. H. Fussler and J. L. Simon, *Patterns in the Use of Books in Large Research Libraries* (Chicago: University of Chicago Press, 1961), 142.

[3] Philip M. Morse, *Library Effectiveness: A Systems Approach* (Cambridge, Mass.: MIT Press, 1968), 19.

ter will discuss how Morse and this author together were able to extend further some of his book-use models using a broader and different kind of data base.

One of the main advantages of using this measurement-model procedure is that it saves the collection and analysis of large quantities of data. A proposed model includes certain variables and parameters, which suggest the type of useful data necessary to be collected. In other words, the properties of the model could be either checked out or not checked out with relatively little effort.[4]

Properties of Probabilistic Models

Many criticisms have been voiced by librarians of using mathematical models to describe the library's use and operation. Some feel that the systems analysts and library operations researchers deliberately turn simple and easy library operations into fancy, complicated, and incomprehensible models. Some say critically that the models generally do not work because their predictive results are seldom correct. For example, a certain model predicts that the next year's average circulation of physics books is likely to be about one per book, yet a year later, some books are found in fact to circulate six or more times. These types of criticisms are made by those who are not familiar with the properties of a probabilistic model. It should be stressed again that the models can predict only the average behavior of a group of books, a collection of events, and so on, but they need not predict the use of a particular book or a specific event. Furthermore, even these average predictions need not be exceptionally precise. As indicated in Morse's *Library Quarterly* article (1972), it is much better to use a model which requires few data and predicts within a possible error of 25 percent than to use one which predicts with great accuracy but requires man-years of effort to acquire the data for its implementation. Some library models, though theoretically sound, are unnecessarily complicated and too mathematically oriented, and therefore are of little use to librarians.

Morse's Book-Use Models and the Markov Process

Since by assumption the process of book circulation is a random one, the distribution of circulation in a year can be taken to be

---

[4] For more detailed discussion of this, see Chapter 2 of Morse's *Library Effectiveness*.

the Poisson distribution. For events occurring randomly in time, the number of events n occurring in a time interval t is distributed according to

$$P_n(m) = \frac{m^n}{n!} e^{-m}, \tag{2.1}$$

where m is the average number of events occurring in that interval of time. This distribution law is equivalent to the statement that the time interval distribution between successive events follows an exponential law

$$dP_t = \lambda e^{-\lambda t} \, dt, \tag{2.2}$$

where λ is the expected arrival rate of the events and is equal to m/t. The probability, then, of another event occurring between $(t, t + dt)$, given that an event had occurred at $t = 0$, is dP_t.

In order to take into account the fact that circulations in successive years are correlated, one has to inject "memory" into the random process. The Markov process is the simplest class of stochastic process that exhibits a time correlation (Bharucha-Reid, 1960).[5] In the Markov process the state of the system at a given time period is determined only by its state at the last period. This means that it has only indirect memory to states of even earlier periods. In this process, a quantity of central importance is the transition probability T_{mn}. This is conditional probability and can be written in another form, $P(n|m)$. In other words,

T_{mn} = Transition probability $\begin{pmatrix} \text{Transit from } m \text{ circulation (year } t) \\ \text{to } n \text{ circulation (year } t + 1) \end{pmatrix}$

= Probability $\left(\begin{matrix} \text{Having } n \text{ circulation} \\ \text{during } (t+1)\text{th year} \end{matrix} \middle| \begin{matrix} \text{Given } m \text{ circulation} \\ \text{during } t \text{ th year} \end{matrix} \right).$

Morse took a simple form,

$$T_{mn} = \frac{(\alpha + \beta m)^n}{n!} e^{-(\alpha + \beta m)}, \tag{2.3}$$

which satisfies the normalization condition

$$\sum_{n=0}^{\infty} T_{mn} = 1.$$

---

[5] For a complete theoretical treatment of the theory of the Markov process, see Bharucha-Reid (1960).

Equation 2.3 can then be used to compute an experimentally measurable quantity $N(m)$, which is the average number of circulations in the $(t + 1)$th year, given that the sample has m circulation in the tth year. We have, by using Eq. 2.3,

$$N(m) = \sum_{n=0}^{\infty} T_{mn}\, n$$

$$= \alpha + \beta m. \qquad (2.4)$$

This means that the average circulation behavior of a class of books $N(m)$ in its $(t +1)$th year depends on its previous year's (year t) circulation m. The mean circulation of $(t +1)$th year—$N(m)$—does not depend explicitly on the book's age or on the circulation earlier than the tth year. The parameters α and β are to be determined for each class of books studied. Generally, β seems to stay constant throughout the life of the book, independent of time t, and α diminishes slightly with age.

This kind of model takes into account the following two things, as stated earlier: On the average, book circulation decreases as book age increases. Also, if a book becomes popular again, the circulation history thenceforward is treated as though the book had been popular all along. Likewise, if a book happens suddenly to lose popularity, its future circulation history is regarded as though it had always been neglected. For example, if $N(m)$ is replaced with $\overline{R}(2)$, and m with $\overline{R}(1)$, where $\overline{R}(1)$ is the mean first-year circulation, and $\overline{R}(2)$ is the mean second-year circulation, given that the first-year average circulation is $\overline{R}(1)$, we then obtain

$$\overline{R}(2) = \alpha + \beta \overline{R}(1).$$

During the third year, the mean circulation of a book or a class of books will then be

$$\overline{R}(3) = \alpha + \beta \overline{R}(2)$$

$$= \alpha + \beta[\alpha + \beta \overline{R}(1)]$$

$$= \alpha(1 + \beta) + \overline{R}(1)\beta^2,$$

and therefore, during the $(t + 1)$th year, the mean circulation will be

$$\overline{R}(t + 1) = \alpha(1 + \beta + \beta^2 + \ldots + \beta^{t-1}) + \overline{R}(1)\beta^t$$

$$= \frac{1-\beta^t}{1-\beta} + \overline{R}(1)\beta^t$$

$$= \frac{\alpha}{1-\beta} + \left[\overline{R}(1) - \frac{\alpha}{1-\beta}\right] \exp\left[-t \ln\beta^{-1}\right]. \tag{2.5}$$

Equation 2.5 accounts for the exponential decrease of book circulation in time if $\beta < 1$.

Several book-use studies, such as those of Trueswell (1964 article) and Fussler and Simon (1961), have assumed that on the average, book circulation drops off exponentially over time. Many of them arrived at the result

$$\overline{R}(t+1) = A + [\overline{R}(1) - A]e^{-\gamma t},$$

which is equivalent to Eq. 2.5. Or more generally, they used the Poisson distribution, $P_n[C_s f(t)]$, to account for the mean of the actual circulation of a given class of books. Here $C_s f(t)$ is the expected circulation rate of the sth class of books in its tth year, $f(t)$ is a monotonically decreasing function of t, and C_s is the first year's circulation. Any one of these models is not detailed enough to take into account automatically the surge of interest in books in the class studied. Book use generally does not monotonically decrease in time. Many books were not used much during their first few years after library acquisition, but became quite popular afterward.

Thus Morse's Markov model is much more detailed and powerful than any of those described. It is not formulated and based on convenient assumptions alone but is a composite result of assumptions, thoughtful modelings, measurements, and fittings of analyzed data. I shall further elaborate on the experimental process used in arriving at the basic relation, Eq. 2.4.

First, the meaning of the following quantities will be defined:

M = Total number of examples (year-pair) in the sample
m = Number of circulations in the tth year
$M(m)$ = Number of examples with m circulations in the tth year
n = Number of circulations in the $(t+1)$th year
$N_{mn} = M(m)T_{mn}$
= Number of examples that have m circulations in year t and n circulations in year $t+1$
$N(m)$ = Mean number of circulations during year $t+1$ given that the sample has m circulations in year t.

Table 2.1 Values of $M(m)$, N_{mn}, and $N(m)$ for Different Values of m and n (WM Books Returned to Countway in January 1973—1968-1972 Pairs)*

m	$M(m)$	N_{mn}												$N(m)$	Theoretical
		$n=0$	1	2	3	4	5	6	7	8	9	10	11	12		
0	91	22	26	17	13	9	2	0	1	0	0	1	0	0	1.78	*1.58*
		18	*29*	*23*	*12*	*4*	*1*	*0*	*0*	*0*	*0*	*0*	*0*	*0*		
1	109	22	33	22	16	6	7	2	0	1	0	0	0	0	1.87	*1.95*
		15	*30*	*29*	*19*	*9*	*6*	*3*	*1*	*0*	*0*	*0*	*0*	*0*		
2	116	15	32	22	22	16	3	4	1	1	0	0	0	0	2.24	*2.31*
		11	*26*	*30*	*23*	*13*	*6*	*2*	*0*	*0*	*0*	*0*	*0*	*0*		
3	83	8	18	19	20	11	2	3	1	1	0	0	0	0	2.45	*2.68*
		5	*15*	*20*	*18*	*12*	*6*	*2*	*1*	*0*	*0*	*0*	*0*	*0*		
4	73	5	7	18	15	12	10	1	2	2	1	0	0	0	3.16	*3.05*
		3	*10*	*16*	*16*	*12*	*7*	*3*	*1*	*0*	*0*	*0*	*0*	*0*		
5	32	2	3	4	8	6	2	1	1	2	3	0	0	0	3.91	*3.41*
		1	*3*	*6*	*6*	*5*	*4*	*2*	*1*	*0*	*0*	*0*	*0*	*0*		
6	22	1	2	5	1	9	1	0	2	0	0	1	0	0	3.64	*3.78*
		0	*1*	*3*	*4*	*4*	*3*	*2*	*1*	*0*	*0*	*0*	*0*	*0*		
7	9	0	3	2	0	1	2	0	0	1	0	0	0	0	3.22	*4.14*
		0	*0*	*1*	*1*	*1*	*1*	*1*	*0*	*0*	*0*	*0*	*0*	*0*		
8	14	0	3	1	0	2	2	2	2	1	0	0	0	1	4.93	*4.51*
		0	*0*	*1*	*2*	*2*	*2*	*1*	*1*	*0*	*0*	*0*	*0*	*0*		
9-13	11	...														
$M = 560$																

*The experimental data are in roman type, while the theoretical results are italicized. This table is part of the same sample (WM books returned to Countway in January 1973—1968-1972 pairs) presented in Table 6.1. The theoretical numbers are generated by computer and contain some rounding errors.

In order to illustrate the relationships among these quantities, some of the actual experimental data collected in this study are presented in Table 2.1, which represents the combined circulation history of the WM (Psychiatry) class of books circulated during one sampling period, January 1973. The past-use data of these books, between 1968 and 1972, are included. At the most, books with a complete circulation history between 1968 and 1972 would contribute four year-pair entries to the table, that is, 1968-1969, 1969-1970, 1970-1971, and 1971-1972, while others would contribute either a one year-pair entry or two year-pair or three year-pair entries to the table.

For all four years, from 1968 to 1972, in this WM class of books in the sample, there were M examples. As shown in Table 2.1,

Morse's Theoretical Models

$M = 560$ examples. Some of the relationships can be summarized as follows:

$$M = M(0) + M(1) + M(2) + \ldots = \sum_{m=0}^{\infty} M(m)$$

$$M(m) = N_{m0} + N_{m1} + N_{m2} + \ldots = \sum_{n=0}^{\infty} N_{mn}$$

$$N(m) = \frac{1}{M(m)} \sum_{n=0}^{\infty} n N_{mn}. \tag{2.6}$$

Table 2.1 gives both experimental and theoretical results of N_{mn} and $N(m)$. The experimental data are in roman type, while the theoretical ones are in italics.

Plots of $N(m)$ against m for year-pairs from 1968 to 1972 can be found in Fig. 2.1. It demonstrates a linear relationship as formulated in Eq. 2.3. The parameters, α and β, can be determined either by the weighted least-square-fit method or by direct graph observation. In the case of samples represented in Table 2.1, the values of

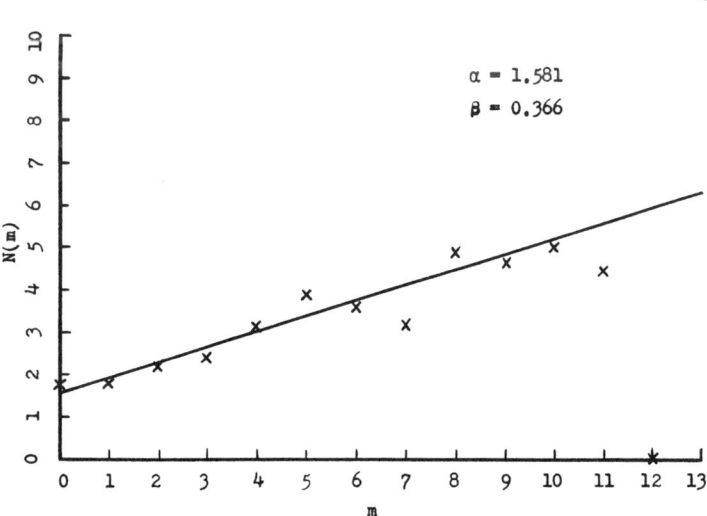

Figure 2.1 Mean Circulation $N(m)$ for year $t + 1$ as a function of circulation m for previous year t (data of Table 2.1)

α and β were found to be 1.581 and 0.366, respectively, by the weighted least-square-fit method. Once the values of α and β are known, given m, one can easily calculate the theoretical values of $N(m)$ by using Eq. 2.4, $N(m) = α + βm$. A comparison of both the experimental and theoretical values of $N(m)$ in Table 2.1 seems to show that Eq. 2.4 is checked out remarkably well.

In the case of several samples of the same class of books used during different sampling periods, average values of α and β can be computed easily by using the following equations:

$$\alpha = \frac{M_1 \alpha_1 + M_2 \alpha_2 + \ldots}{M_1 + M_2 + \ldots}$$

$$\beta = \frac{M_1 \beta_1 + M_2 \beta_2 + \ldots}{M_1 + M_2 + \ldots} , \qquad (2.7)$$

where M_1 books of Sample I have parameter values α_1 and β_1, and M_2 books of Sample II have values α_2 and β_2. Since Eq. 2.4 is linear in α, β, and m, average values of α and β can be worked out with similar computational advantage, by following equations of the same form.

As stated earlier, if, for a class of books, α and β stay constant throughout the life of the books, or in other words, α and β are independent of time t, then Eq. 2.5 can predict the mean circulation of that class of books at year t or $t + 1$. Nevertheless, experimental results do show that α diminishes slightly with age. After T years, the value of α changes to $α'$, and the mean circulation for year t, greater than T, is

$$\overline{R}(t+1) = \frac{\alpha' + (\alpha - \alpha')\beta^{t-T+1} - \alpha\beta^t}{1 - \beta} + \overline{R}(1)\beta^t , \qquad (2.8)$$

where β^t can be obtained either by calculation or by graphic determination.[6]

The Transition Probabilities

We have discussed the transition probability in Equation 2.3 and shall elaborate on it further in this section. We know that the values of N_{mn} are related to the transition probability T_{mn} by

$$N_{mn} = M(m)T_{mn} . \qquad (2.9)$$

[6] See Fig. 5.2 in Morse's *Library Effectiveness*, 96.

Morse's Theoretical Models   17

By using the experimental values of $N(m)$ as given in Table 2.1, together with Eqs. 2.3 and 2.9, the theoretical values of all N_{mn} were computed as were the italicized ones in Table 2.1. Particularly when considering the smallness of the sample, the theoretical data do seem to correspond quite well with the experimental ones.

We can also use Eq. 2.3 to obtain the transition probability that one of the books will have circulation n in the second year, the third year, and so forth. The probability that one of them has a circulation n in year $t_0 + t$ if it had circulation m in year t_0 is independent of t_0 and is given as

$$(T^t)_{mn} = (T^{t-s})_{m0}(T^s)_{0n} + (T^{t-s})_{m1}(T^s)_{1n} \\ + (T^{t-s})_{m2}(T^s)_{2n} + \ldots, \qquad (2.10)$$

where s can be any integer greater than zero and less than t. The transition probability T_{mn}, which we discussed earlier, should be written as $(T^1)_{mn}$ in the present notation. Furthermore, it can be shown that as $t \to \infty$,

$$(T^t)_{mn} \to P_n^\infty,$$

which means that the book collection has reached a statistical *steady state*. Every book in the collection has the same probability distribution at this time. The collection of books at this time, then, tends to "forget" what its initial circulation was.

From this discussion, one is clear about the usefulness of the transition probability T_{mn}. Nevertheless, unless the values of T_{mn} have been made available for different values of α and β, as those given in the Appendix of Morse's *Library Effectiveness*, the computation of the individual values of T_{mn} is a tedious task.

The Geometric Distribution for the First-Year Circulation

Taking a class of books, all having the same values of α and β, and all bought during the same year, Morse found that the first-year-circulation distribution was geometric with parameter γ. (This assumption will be tested further in my study.)

In other words, the fraction of these books that circulated m or more times in their first year, $P_1(\geqslant m)$, was

$$P_1(\geqslant m) = \gamma^m, \qquad (2.11)$$

and the fraction that circulated exactly m times was

$$P_1(m) = P_1(\geqslant m) - P_1(\geqslant m+1)$$

Theoretical Models   18

$$= (1 - \gamma)\gamma^m, \qquad (2.12)$$

where γ was found to be approximately equal to $\overline{R}/(1+\overline{R})$, with $\overline{R}$ the mean circulation for the first year. Thus γ^m represents the popularity of the accession of the particular class.[7] Furthermore, we can derive the following relationships by using Eqs. 2.3 and 2.10:

$$P_2(n) = P_1(0)T_{0n} + P_1(1)T_{1n} + P_1(2)T_{2n} + \ldots$$
$$= (1 - \gamma)(T_{0n} + \gamma T_{1n} + \gamma^2 T_{2n} + \ldots)$$
$$P_3(n) = P_2(0)T_{0n} + P_2(1)T_{1n} + P_2(2)T_{2n} + \ldots.$$

Then, the probability that the circulation in the tth year is m or greater is the sum

$$P_t(\geqslant m) = P_t(m) + P_t(m+1) + P_t(m+2) + \ldots. \qquad (2.13)$$

It is obvious, then, that once the values of the parameters α, β, and γ are known, the expected fraction of a class of books that circulates m or more times in the following years can be predicted. Of course, as suggested by Eq. 2.13, values of T_{mn} should first be obtained.

Morse illustrated clearly that although the first-year-circulation distribution is geometrical, the distributions for later-year circulations are somewhat curved (not geometrical).[8]

Furthermore, although the first-year circulation behavior depends on the judgment of the book selector, the circulation behavior in later years depends much more on the users' use behavior (as represented by α and β). If α and β remain more or less constant, then the drop of popularity (as represented by γ) gradually ceases and the book circulation reaches a steady state.

Morse's Modified Model on Book Use

Both Morse's own data collected at MIT and those gathered at the Countway Library of Medicine seem to suggest that the fraction of the "nonuse" books (that is, the $m = 0$ case in Eq. 2.12), unlike those of the circulated books, deviates considerably from the geometric distribution. Jain, in his book-use study of homogeneous groups of books from Chemistry, Physics, and Pharmacy Libraries at Purdue University (1967), also found that the "zero-use" class does not follow the same probability law as the remaining classes.

[7] See Fig. 5.3 in Morse's *Library Effectiveness*, 102.
[8] Ibid.

Morse's Theoretical Models

This is understood, for example, whenever a library has a fair number of older books in its collection, since many of these older books have a much reduced value of α and tend to constitute a large "zero-use" part of the collection. Within the Markov model of book use, this can be taken into account by slightly modifying the formulation to allow for a special treatment of the "zero-use" class. This modified model also simplifies the steps and processes of computation.

In this modified model, one separates the total collection of N books into circulated (or active) and noncirculated (or inactive) books of N_a and N_0, respectively. One has then

$$N = N_a + N_0 \tag{2.14}$$

or, in terms of fractions,

$C(t) = N_a/N$ and $P_0(t) = N_0/N$,

$$P_0(t) = 1 - C(t), \tag{2.15}$$

Both $C(t)$ and $P_0(t)$ are measurable quantities when N is known.

For the year t where the circulation data are taken and the probability that a book is circulated m times, a quantity denoted as $P_1(m)$ in Eq. 2.12 is written here as $P_m(t)$ and has a form

$$P_m(t) = C(t)[1-\gamma(t)][\gamma(t)]^{m-1} \quad \text{for } m \geq 1. \tag{2.16}$$

This modified geometric distribution is seen to satisfy the normalization condition

$$\sum_{m=0}^{\infty} P_m(t) = P_0(t) + \sum_{m=1}^{\infty} P_m(t) = 1, \tag{2.17}$$

with the mean circulation given by

$$\overline{R}(t) = \sum_{m=0}^{\infty} m P_m(t)$$

$$= \sum_{m=1}^{\infty} m P_m(t)$$

$$= C(t)/[1-\gamma(t)]. \tag{2.18}$$

In order to predict the circulation in future years, we need the transition probability T_{mn}, which is taken to be the same form as in Eq. 2.3. We can then calculate

$$P_m(t+1) = \sum_{m=0}^{\infty} P_m(t) T_{mn}$$

$$= [1 - C(t)] T_{0n} + \sum_{m=1}^{\infty} P_m(t) T_{mn}. \quad (2.19)$$

We can obtain the expected fraction of the noncirculated books for the year $t + 1$, for example, by setting m equal to 0 in Eq. 2.19 and calculating

$$P_0(t+1) = [1 - C(t)] T_{00} + \sum_{m=1}^{\infty} P_m(t) T_{m0}$$

$$= [1 - C(t)] e^{-\alpha} + \sum_{m=1}^{\infty} C(t)[1 - \gamma(t)][\gamma(t)]^{m-1} e^{-(\alpha + \beta m)}$$

$$= e^{-\alpha} [1 - H(t)], \quad (2.20)$$

where

$$H(t) = \frac{C(t)}{1 + J(t)} \quad (2.21)$$

$$J(t) = \frac{1 - \gamma(t)}{e^\beta - 1} = \frac{C(t)}{\overline{R}(t)(e^\beta - 1)}. \quad (2.22)$$

Thus once the values of α, β, and γ ($\gamma = 1 - C/\overline{R}$) are determined from the circulation data at year t, we can then use the modified Markov model to predict the expected active fraction $C(t + 1)$ of the following year by using

$$C(t+1) = 1 - P_0(t+1) \quad (2.23)$$

and Eq. 2.20. The values of $H(t)$ and $J(t)$ can be either calculated by using Eqs. 2.21 and 2.22 or obtained graphically (Morse, 1972). Similarly, graphic determination of $C(t + 1)$ and $P_0(t + 1)$ can also be made. (See Morse, 1972, for details.) The expected mean circulation for the year $t + 1$ and the following years can be easily predicted by employing Eq. 2.5:

$$\overline{R}(t+1) = \alpha + \beta\overline{R}(t). \tag{2.24}$$

The value of γ for the next year and the following years can then be calculated by using

$$\gamma(t+1) = \frac{\overline{R}(t+1)}{[1+\overline{R}(t+1)]}. \tag{2.25}$$

Chapter Three

Extension of Morse's Theoretical Models

Chapter 5 of this book will present in great detail the methodology used in gathering data at the Countway Library of Medicine and the conditions imposed upon the special method of data collection. The discussions there should point out clearly that not all Countway data are compatible with those used by Morse to formulate his models. The book-use data of this study are based on the circulated books returned by the borrowers during the selected sampling months. These books were not selected randomly. Thus the use data are prejudiced toward the used or active books, because they exaggerate the effect of the higher-circulation books and leave out entirely the books that have not been borrowed and returned.

It seems reasonable, then, to expect that in order to test some of Morse's models, certain correction factors should be considered and used to counteract the bias in the collected data, such as those gathered at Countway. The following discussion and illustration on first-year-circulation distribution by using the Countway data will demonstrate clearly the need for having such a bias correction factor.

First-Year-Circulation Distribution

As discussed in Chapter 2, the first-year circulation is generally geometrically distributed, with a single parameter, γ. To determine γ for one of the book classes, one can use the mean circulation $\overline{R}$ of the class. From Eq. 2.12, we can compute $\overline{R}$ by using

$$\overline{R} = \sum_{m=0}^{\infty} m P_1(m) = \sum_{m=1}^{\infty} m(1-\gamma)(\gamma)^m = \frac{\gamma}{1-\gamma}. \tag{3.1}$$

Therefore

$$\gamma = \frac{\overline{R}}{1+\overline{R}}, \tag{3.2}$$

and Eq. 2.12 can be rewritten as

$$P_1(m) = (1-\gamma)\gamma^m$$

$$= \left(\frac{1}{1+\overline{R}}\right)\left(\frac{\overline{R}}{1+\overline{R}}\right)^m$$

$$= \frac{(\overline{R})^m}{(1+\overline{R})^{m+1}}. \tag{3.3}$$

Extension of Morse's Theoretical Models   23

From the measured value of the mean circulation and Eq. 3.3, we can then easily plot a theoretical curve of $P_1(m)$, the fraction of books in the class circulated m times during the first year.

Morse tested Eq. 3.3 quite satisfactorily, even though he used a small sample of 300 new books (1968). Morse's experimental data plotted on a semilog chart followed a remarkably straight line in light of the smallness of the sample size. The reason for this agreement was that these 300 new books were selected randomly and thus the data collected on first-year circulation were biased toward neither the nonuse nor the active books.

As for the nonrandomly collected and therefore biased circulation data available to the researcher of this study, it was expected that the experimental data would not correspond well theoretically with Eq. 3.3. To test this conjecture, three classes of books, WA, WM, and WS, were chosen for more detailed study of the t-year (after book acquisition) circulation distributions. For WA and WM books, those returned during both January and April 1973 sampling months were studied, while for WS books, only those returned in the month of January 1973 were studied. Among these three selected classes, the WM class has the largest sample size.

During the process of data collection, only books with complete circulation histories (from the beginning of their accessions) were

Table 3.1 Examples of Book-Circulation Histories

	Number of Times the Given Book Circulated during Year t*									
	$t=1$	2	3	4	5	6	7	8	9	10
Book 1	0	2	0	0	1	—				
Book 2	1	2	1	4	1	0	0	0	—	
Book 3	0	1	2	2	2	—				
Book 4	2	4	2	2	2	2	—			
Book 5	3	2	3	2	4	1	4	—		
Book 6	6	4	5	7	5	—				
Book 7	4	3	0	3	—					
Book 8	9	6	4	5	—					
Book 9	0	1	3	3	0	1	0	0	2	1
Book 10	2	3	4	2	3	1	4	8	1	0

*The year after accession of each book is t, and the dash indicates the current year. For a few older books, the current year may be beyond the end of the table.

Table 3.2 Summary of Circulation History of a Sample of 126 WM Books Returned to Countway in January 1973*

m	Number of Books Having Circulation m during Year t											
	$t=1$	2	3	4	5	6	7	8	9	10	11	12
0	27	22	17	8	8	10	6	6	4	1	1	
1	10	20	19	24	16	16	11	8	7	5	1	
2	22	21	18	21	15	14	9	5	3	1	1	2
3	21	25	21	23	16	4	2	7	1			
4	19	21	20	6	8	5	6			1		
5	10	4	13	8	3	2	1					
6	8	5	2		1	1						
7	1	2	2	3								
8	3	5	2	2					1			
9	2		1	1								
10	2	1			1							
11	1											
12			1									
$\bar{R}$	2.94	2.66	2.81	2.55	2.31	1.77	1.83	1.74	1.07	1.38	1.00	2.00

*t = Year of accession
m = Number of circulation
R = Mean circulation of the tth year

included in the samples studied. The complete circulation history of each book is shown in Table 3.1.

The collected data were then analyzed and summarized for each respective sample. For the purpose of better illustration, only results of the January 1973 sample of WM books are presented in this chapter (Table 3.2).[1] In this table, the experimental data of the tth year circulations of the samples (here t denotes the year of book acquisition) are displayed. The expected mean circulation, $\bar{R}_t$, for the years from first year of acquisition ($t=1$) to the tenth year ($t=10$) is also computed for each of the samples studied. Furthermore, data from this table for $t=1$ to $t=4$ are also plotted in Fig. 3.1. Equation 3.3 is used to compute the theoretical points for each respective figure, since $\bar{R}_t$ is known. These graphs show

[1] All other results of the April 1973 sample of WM books, both the January and April samples of WA books and the January sample of WS books, can be found in Appendix VI of my Ph.D. thesis (1974). Results similar to those shown in Table 3.2 and Fig. 3.1 were found with all other samples.

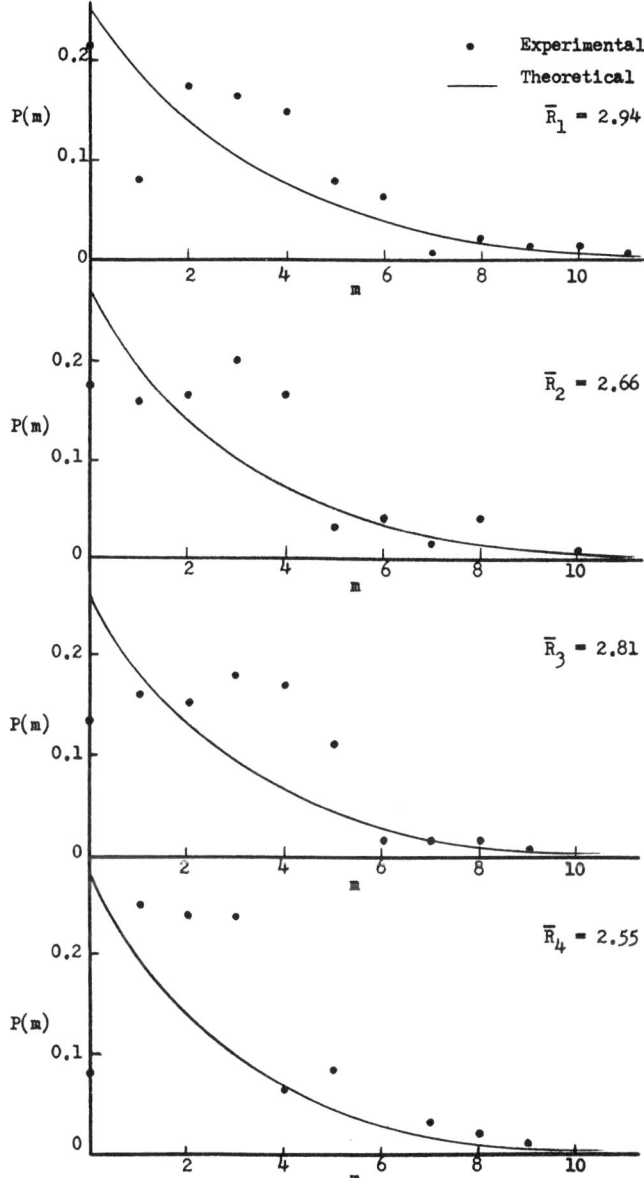

Figure 3.1 Fraction of books that have m circulation during the year. The parameter $\overline{R}_t$ denotes the expected mean circulation of books after t year of acquisition (data taken from Table 3.2—WM books—January 1973)

clearly that most of the experimental points are not geometrically distributed. The experimental data collected at Countway do not correspond to Eq. 3.3.

As already pointed out, this lack of correlation between the experimental and theoretical circulation distributions of the classes of book samples studied is due to the biased circulation data collected. Therefore it seems natural and logical for the researcher to raise the following questions:

1. If the available data are biased, is there any way to correct these biased data?
2. If so, can this correction be made relatively easily by using a certain correction factor?
3. Is there any way that the circulation distribution of a class of books in a given period (quarterly, yearly, and so on) can be predicted by using a small amount of biased circulation-history data?

An attempt to explore possibilities and to answer the questions raised above has led to the following extension of Morse's theoretical models. These extended models will be tested further in Chapter 6.

Estimating the Sample-Year Circulation Distribution

The following consideration will be presented, with the unit of the circulation-distribution period being a "year."

In a library, there are N books of a given class (such as WM of the National Library of Medicine Classification Scheme). In the case of the Countway study, we have a knowledge that among the N books of a given class, $M(a)$ of them were returned during the month of sampling, because the circulation data that were collected were based on books returned during the sampling month. Of these $M(a)$ books, there were $M(1)$ of them that had only one circulation during the previous twelve months. In other words, of the $M(a)$ books returned during the January 1973 sample month, $M(1)$ books had only one circulation during the year from February 1972 to January 1973 inclusive, and the one circulation was completed during the month of January 1973. Similarly, there were $M(2)$ of the $M(a)$ books that circulated twice during the previous year, with at least one circulation completed during the sampling month. Thus, more generally, $M(j)$ of the $M(a)$ books circulated j times during the year preceding the end of the month of sampling. Of course, j includes the return(s) during the month of sampling, thus j cannot be zero. In other words, there is no $M(0)$, because

Extension of Morse's Theoretical Models 27

each book had to circulate at least once in order that its circulation card be kept at the circulation desk. Therefore we have a relation

$$M(a) = \sum_j M(j) \quad \text{for } j = 1, 2, 3 \ldots \quad (3.4)$$

Correction Factor
Next, assuming that the j returns of a book are randomly spaced, we can calculate the fraction of the books that circulated j times during the year that did not happen to be checked out during the month. Probability theory says that within a given fraction of a time period ρ (one month out of a year would be $\rho = 1/12$), the chance that one of the returns[2] will *not* occur is $(1 - \rho)$, and the probability that all j circulations will fail to occur during the interval is $(1 - \rho)^j$. Such books would not be counted during the sampling period. Thus the fraction of the books that circulated j times during the previous year and that also were checked out one or more times during the sampling period is $[1 - (1 - \rho)^j]$. In other words, the true number of books that circulated j times that year, the expected number $N(j)$ books with j circulation(s), is related to the number $M(j)$ of such books that were counted during the interval ρ by the equation

$$N(j) = M(j)/[1 - (1 - \rho)^j] \quad \text{for } j = 1, 2, 3, \ldots, \quad (3.5)$$

and the sum N_a, the expected number of books of the given class that circulated at least once during the year (whether they were counted during the sampling period or not), is

$$N_a = \sum_j N(j) \quad \text{for } j = 1, 2, 3 \ldots \quad (3.6)$$

By using the correction factor $1/[1 - (1 - \rho)^j]$, the value of ρ can be adjusted for each individual library depending on its average circulation behavior and the length of sampling period. For example, if the monthly circulation rate of a class of books is roughly constant throughout the year, then ρ for a month would be $1/12$ of a year. However, in a real situation, a library generally has low and

---

[2] They can also be withdrawals. To avoid excess verbiage, I shall use either the word *return* or the more general word *circulation* since this study is based on books returned to the circulation desk. It should be understood, however, that the word *withdrawal* may be alternatively used, if it turns out to be easier to record book withdrawals than returns.

peak periods of both library and circulation activities. The monthly circulation rate is not uniformly equal throughout the year. The Countway Library of Medicine, like many university and research libraries, has historically had less circulation activity during the three summer months than in the other nine months of the year. Figure 5.2 of Chapter 5 shows that the general circulation rate at Countway during the three summer months drops to about two-thirds of that during the rest of the year. Thus $\rho = 2/33$ for the three summer months, and $\rho = 1/11$ for the other nine months, since roughly $2/33$ of the $N(1)$ circulations will occur during each of the three summer months and roughly $1/11$ of them will occur during each of the other nine months (the sum of all 12 fractions equaling unity).

Similarly, different values of ρ can be determined for various lengths of sampling period if the circulation rate is roughly constant during the year. For example, if the sampled period is a week, which is roughly $1/50$ of a year, then $\rho \approx 1/50$, and $\rho \approx 1/25$ if there are two sampled weeks.

Thus it is clear that we can estimate the number of books in a class that circulate j times, $N(j)$, in the sample year from $M(j)$ books that were returned in the sample month and had circulated j times in the previous year by using Eq. 3.5. To facilitate the computation of $N(j)$, we can use Table 3.3 when $\rho = 1/12$, $1/11$, and $2/33$.

It is worth mentioning that in the case of Countway, each book does not have a permanent book card. Values of $M(j)$'s are obtained by checking the number of due dates that fell during the previous twelve months and appeared on the date-due slips of the returned books. It is expected, then, that some books of high circulation could not be located for data collection because they were in circulation again. Some returned books, though available on the shelves, did not have circulation records extended over the entire preceding year. Some of these books could be new library acquisitions during the past year, while some others could have had the earlier date-due slips filled up and therefore discarded. In other words, of the $M(a)$ books returned during the sample month, there are U books for which the value j is unknown. Thus Eq. 3.4 can be rewritten to

$$M(a) = \sum_j M(j) + U \quad \text{for } j = 1, 2, 3 \ldots \quad (3.7)$$

In order to obtain a more accurate N_a and $N(j)$, it is advisable to correct the $N(j)$'s by uniformly multiplying by a correction factor

$[\Sigma M(j) + U]/\Sigma M(j)$. Here we assume that the circulation histories of these U books were roughly similar to those of the recorded $M(j)$'s, though it is possible that these U books have a higher fraction of high-circulation books than do the recorded $M(j)$'s.

Equation 3.5, the extended model, is expected to remove the bias from the sample studied. In Chapter 6, we shall test this model fully by using the circulation data of Countway books of eight selected classes. In this section, we shall present only data obtained from a count of all the books of the WM class (Psychiatry) that circulated from and were returned to Countway during the month of January 1973 (Fig. 3.2). A comparison of Fig. 3.2 with Fig. 3.1 makes it clear to us that Eq. 3.5 is adequate to remove the bias from the sample. As expected, we note that the circles, the $N(j)$'s, on the semilog plot of Fig. 3.2 follow a straight line, with a certain amount of fluctuation more noticeable with the small numbers. This means that after correction, the circulation distribution of $N(j)$'s is geometrical.

Table 3.3 Values of $1/[1-(1-\rho)^j]$ and $1/(1-e^{-j})$

j (Times of Cir.)	$1/[1-(1-\rho)^j]$			$1/(1-e^{-j})$
	$\rho = 1/12$	$\rho = 1/11$	$\rho = 2/33$	
1	12.0000	11.0000	16.5000	1.5820
2	6.2609	5.7619	8.5078	1.1565
3	4.3526	4.0211	5.8472	1.0524
4	3.4021	3.1547	4.5195	1.0186
5	2.8347	2.6380	3.7250	1.0067
6	2.4588	2.2961	3.1970	1.0025
7	2.1923	2.0541	2.8213	1.0009
8	1.9941	1.8744	2.5409	1.0003
9	1.8416	1.7364	2.3238	1.0001
10	1.7209	1.6275	2.1512	1.0000
11	1.6234	1.5396	2.0109	1.0000
12	1.5432	1.4676	1.8948	1.0000
13	1.4764	1.4078	1.7974	1.0000
14	1.4200	1.3575	1.7145	1.0000
15	1.3720	1.3147	1.6433	1.0000
16	1.3307	1.2782	1.5817	1.0000

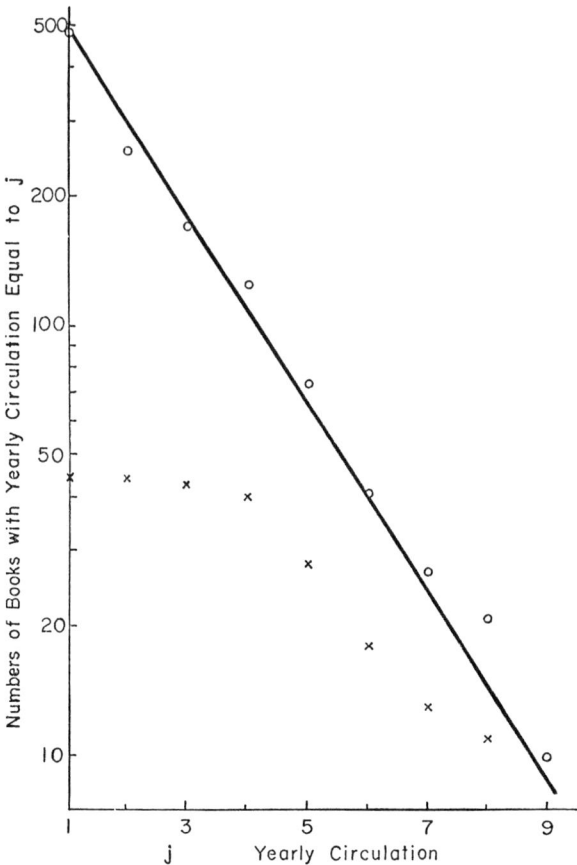

Figure 3.2 Uncorrected and corrected circulation distributions for class WM at Countway (January 1973 data). (Crosses are biased numbers $M(j)$ from circulation desk data, circles are corrected figures $N(j)$ obtained from Eq. 3.5, and straight line is the theoretical geometric distribution.)

Extension of Morse's Theoretical Models

Estimating the Total Annual Circulation

It has been shown that $N(j)$'s can be obtained from biased circulation data by using Eq. 3.5. Knowing $N(j)$'s, we can estimate the annual total circulation of the books of the given class readily, that is,

$$\text{Total annual circulation of the class} = \sum_j j \cdot N(j). \tag{3.8}$$

If the yearly total circulation of each of the classes of books in a library is known, then the library's annual total book circulation would be the sum of the class totals, for example,

$$\text{Total library book circulation} = \sum_{\text{class}} \sum_j j \cdot N(j). \tag{3.9}$$

The Geometric Distribution

We have shown in the previous sections that the bias can be removed from the circulation data. In this section, we shall demonstrate how other probabilistic techniques can be used to evaluate other aspects of circulation behavior. One can, for example, analyze both the high-circulation and the inactive books.

We have demonstrated in Fig. 3.2 that the corrected circulation data $N(j)$ follow the geometric distribution, as already noted by Zipf (1949) and Morse (1968). We can thus take

$$N(j) = N_a(1-\gamma)\gamma^{j-1}, \quad j \geq 1. \tag{3.10}$$

We can obtain an estimate of γ by setting j equal to 1 in Eq. 3.10, and then

$$\gamma = 1 - \frac{N(1)}{N_a} = 1 - \frac{N(1)}{\sum_j N(j)}. \tag{3.11}$$

We can also obtain the average yearly circulation of the active books, $\overline{R}_a$, by the definition

$$\overline{R}_a = \sum_j j \left(\frac{N(j)}{N_a}\right) = \frac{1}{1-\gamma}. \tag{3.12}$$

If we combine Eq. 3.11 and Eq. 3.12, we see that

$$\overline{R}_a = \frac{N_a}{N(1)}. \tag{3.13}$$

Once $\overline{R}_a$ is known, the total circulation for the given year is just $\overline{R}_a N_a$.

Analyzing Relative Numbers of High-Circulation Books

From the point of view of library operation, it is useful to estimate, for example, the fraction of the books in each class that have circulated more than a given number of times during the preceding year, and thus to obtain the fraction of the total circulation of the class that these more popular books represent.

First, the number of books of the class that circulated more than m times is just the sum

$$N(m+1) + N(m+2) + N(m+3) + \ldots.$$

Denoting the sum by $N(>m)$, and using Eq. 3.10, we obtain

$$N(>m) = N_a \gamma^m. \tag{3.14}$$

Thus the total circulation that these $N(>m)$ books have is given by the sum

$$(m+1)[N(m+1)] + (m+2)[N(m+2)]$$
$$+ (m+3)[N(m+3)] + \ldots,$$

and since the total circulation for the given year is $\overline{R}_a N_a$, we can obtain the fraction of the total circulation that these popular books represent by dividing the above sum by $\overline{R}_a N_a$. Denoting this fraction by $F(>m)$, we obtain the following by using again Eq. 3.10:

$$F(>m) = [m(1-\gamma)+1]\gamma^m. \tag{3.15}$$

Analyzing the Inactive Books

We have stated that book circulation is assumed to occur randomly in time. Therefore N_a, the total number of books that circulated at least once during the year, does not represent the total population of potentially useful books, N_ℓ (which we call *live* books). This population, N_ℓ, should be larger than N_a, since in addition to the active books there are a number of books that can circulate but did not happen to circulate in the last twelve months.

Moreover, in every collection of books, there are unavoidably some titles that have not circulated for quite some time and are not likely to circulate in the future. One calls these books *dead books*, N_d. Therefore

$$N_\ell = N - N_d, \qquad (3.16)$$

where N is the size of the total collection of a given class of books. The live but inactive books would be $N_\ell - N_a$. The sum of all $N_\ell(j)$'s is N_ℓ, the number of books which had the potential of circulating j times. It can be represented by

$$N_\ell = \sum_j N_\ell(j). \qquad (3.17)$$

Here, $N_\ell(j)$ could be estimated by using an argument similar to that which led to Eq. 3.5. Since the number of book circulations in a given time period follows the Poisson distribution, as was assumed from the beginning (see Eq. 2.1), the fraction of books that had the potential of circulating j times but happen not to circulate during the year is e^{-j}. We can then obtain the total number of books that had potential of circulating j times by dividing $N(j)$ by a factor $(1 - e^{-j})$, that is,

$$N_\ell(j) = N(j)/[1 - e^{-j}]. \qquad (3.18)$$

Values of $1/[1 - e^{-j}]$ can be found in Table 3.3.

Once N_ℓ is known, we can compute the value of C, the fraction of active to live books, by

$$C = N_a/N_\ell. \qquad (3.19)$$

This is a very useful parameter of a given class of books in terms of predicting the future circulation and will be elaborated on in the following section. Once C is known, $\overline{R}_\ell$, the mean circulation of live books, is known:

$$\overline{R}_\ell = C\overline{R}_a. \qquad (3.20)$$

Thus the total annual circulation of the class of books can be estimated to be

$$\overline{R}_\ell N_\ell = \overline{R}_a N_a. \qquad (3.21)$$

Predicting the Future Circulation

We have previously defined $C(t)$ as the fraction of books in the sample that circulated one or more times during the year. Thus

$C(t)$ should be N_a/N_ℓ. Then, $C(t+1)$, the next-year fraction of active books for the same collection of books, can be derived as in Eq. 2.20:

$$C(t+1) = 1 - P_0(t+1)$$
$$= (1 - e^{-\alpha}) + C(t)e^{-\alpha}\left[1 - \frac{1-\gamma}{e^\beta - \gamma}\right]$$
$$= 1 - e^{-\alpha}\left[1 - \frac{C(t)}{1 + J(t)}\right], \qquad (3.22)$$

where

$$J(t) = \frac{1-\gamma}{e^\beta - 1}.$$

Since $\overline{R}_\ell(t)$ is known, the mean circulation of the same collection of books next year, $\overline{R}_\ell(t+1)$, can be obtained by using Eq. 2.4 (see Eqs. 2.5 and 2.24):

$$\overline{R}_\ell(t+1) = \alpha + \beta\overline{R}_\ell(t). \qquad (3.23)$$

Note that the α obtained in Countway is really that of the active books, α_a. Therefore, in order to obtain α_ℓ, one should use

$$\alpha_\ell = C \cdot \alpha_a. \qquad (3.24)$$

Once $\overline{R}_\ell(t+1)$ is known, then $\overline{R}_a(t+1)$ can be calculated by using Eq. 3.20:

$$\overline{R}_a(t+1) = \frac{\overline{R}_\ell(t+1)}{C(t+1)}. \qquad (3.25)$$

Thus we have separated the "zero-used" books (we call them dead books) from the live ones, as was discussed in Jain (1967). We have shown that correction factors such as $1/[1-(1-\rho)^j]$ and $1/(1-e^{-j})$ are necessary in order to correct the biased $M(j)$'s and obtain unbiased $N(j)$'s, C, $\overline{R}_\ell$, and $\overline{R}_a$. This kind of correction is not needed, however, when we calculate the values of α's and β's, since, as discussed in Chapter 2, α and β are not derived from the numbers $M(j)$.

Morse (1972) has pointed out that parameters such as α, β, C, $\overline{R}_\ell$, and $\overline{R}_a$ are important measures of library effectiveness. Equations 3.22 to 3.25 have shown how circulation predictions can be made easily when these values are known.

Predicting Fraction of Books Not Available on Shelf

Of the $N(j)$ books of a given class which circulate j times per year, there is a certain fraction of them out in circulation at any time of inspection. This fraction can be estimated as follows: We define μ as the average fraction of the year a book of the class is off the shelf per circulation, which can be calculated as

$$\mu = \frac{\text{Mean withdrawal time in days}}{365 \text{ days in a year}}. \tag{3.26}$$

Then, since the occurrence of circulation is random in time, we can take the product μj as a good estimate of the fraction of the books in circulation. Or equivalently, the fraction on the shelf at any given time is $(1 - \mu j)$. From Eqs. 3.10 and 3.12 we can derive the probability that an active book would be circulated j times per year as

$$F_j = N(j)/N_a = \frac{1}{\overline{R}_a}\left(1 - \frac{1}{\overline{R}_a}\right)^{j-1}. \tag{3.27}$$

We can therefore calculate the fraction of the active books on shelf at any given time by the average $(1 - \mu j)$ over the distribution F_j, that is,

$$\sum_{j=1}^{\infty} (1 - \mu j) F_j = 1 - \mu \overline{R}_a. \tag{3.28}$$

Then the fraction of all live books of a class on shelf at a given time is

$$P_0 + C(1 - \mu \overline{R}_a) = 1 - \mu \overline{R}_\ell, \tag{3.29}$$

and $\mu \overline{R}_\ell$ is therefore the fraction of all live books of the class circulating. Since books can be off the shelf for many other reasons, such as in-library use, being at the bindery, or missing, the actual fraction of books off the shelf is generally much higher than $\mu \overline{R}_\ell$. To accommodate the fraction of those books which are off the shelf for purposes other than actual recorded circulations, we can simply use $(\mu \overline{R}_\ell + A)$ to denote the total fraction of all live books off the shelf at any one time. It is not unusual to find that A can sometimes be larger than $\mu \overline{R}_\ell$.

Part Two

Testing the Theoretical Models

Chapter Four

The Francis A. Countway Library of Medicine—a Sample Library

In order to facilitate a better understanding of the use patterns for monographs in the sample library of this study, the following pertinent information is provided.[1]

The Francis A. Countway Library of Medicine, which was opened in June 1965, houses two of the most extensive collections of medical literature in the United States: the Harvard Medical Library and the Boston Medical Library. In an agreement signed in January 1960, these two venerable institutions undertook to combine their resources, staffs, and services in a new building to be located on the grounds of the Harvard Medical School.

Seven years were spent in planning the Countway Library, but more than 180 years had gone into the development of the Harvard Medical Library, a library of one of the world's great centers of medical education, research, and patient care. Ninety years were behind the Boston Medical Library, a medical library of national importance, in size and in the richness of both its historical and contemporary collections ranking with the great American medical libraries, such as those of the New York Academy of Medicine and the College of Physicians of Philadelphia.

Since June 1967 the Countway Library has also been designated and funded by the National Library of Medicine (NLM) as the New England Regional Medical Library Service (NERMLS), the first of the eleven regional medical libraries (RML's) throughout the United States created by federal legislation and administered by NLM. The operations of the NERMLS began in October 1967.

The several Countway RML activities include document delivery service to health sciences libraries in New England, regional reference service, consultation service, and library training institutes for untrained personnel in charge of small health sciences libraries. Each year, about 50,000 requests for books and journal articles are received.

The Collection

The Countway Library ranks eleventh among libraries in the United States that are in possession of early and rare books related to the history of medicine. There are also strong collections of manuscripts and archives, historical collections in many subject

---

[1] The information is extracted extensively from *The Francis A. Countway Library of Medicine—Library Guide*, revised in 1973 (No. 9 in the series Guides to the Harvard Libraries).

areas, medical medals and portraits, and so on. These excellent older collections are generally noncirculating, and therefore will not be touched upon in the present study.

Of the modern collections, the Countway possesses books, reports, government documents, and many runs of medical periodicals. The Countway has current collections in all areas of the health sciences, largely excluding ophthalmology and otorhinolaryngology, which are collected intensively at Harvard's Lucien Howe Library, located at the Massachusetts Eye and Ear Infirmary. Areas of particular strength lie in cardiovascular disease, neoplastic disease, aerospace medicine, legal medicine, demography and human ecology, and modern medical history and biography.

The collections of the Countway Library exceed 445,000 volumes, and the building has a capacity of 750,000 volumes. The periodicals received regularly number 5,500, and each year about 100 new periodicals are added to the subscription list. In 1971, it was estimated that approximately 3,000 books are acquired annually.

The Arrangement of the Collection

The library has six floors above the ground and two below, Lower 1 Floor and Lower 2 Floor. The readers enter the library on Floor 1, and they go down for periodicals and up for books.

The periodicals older than five years are located in Lower 2 Floor, and the current issues of periodicals and the latest five years' periodicals in Lower 1 Floor.

Books are shelved by classification numbers found through the card catalog. More recent books (published or acquired since 1960) were cataloged according to the NLM Classification Schedule (Table 4.1). These books are located on the second floor. The older books (acquired and cataloged before 1960) were cataloged according to the Boston Medical Library (BML) Classification Schedule (Table 4.2) and are shelved on both the third and fourth floors.

Reference books are shelved near the card catalog on the first floor. Reserve books that are used in Harvard course assignments and generally with limited circulation in the library are kept in a special area near the circulation desk. Special collections (rare books, manuscripts, and archives) are on the fifth floor. Recreational reading is provided in the Aesculapian Room, located on the second floor.

Table 4.1 Outline of the National Library of Medicine Classification Schedule (Used for Books Published since 1960)

Preclinical Sciences:
- QS Human Anatomy; Embryology
- QT Human Physiology; Hygiene
- QU Biochemistry
- QV Pharmacology
- QW Bacteriology and Immunology
- QX Parasitology
- QY Clinical Pathology
- QZ Pathology

Medicine:
- W   Medical Profession
- WA   Public Health
- WB   Practice of Medicine
- WC   Infectious Diseases
- WD100 Deficiency Diseases
- WD200 Metabolic Diseases
- WD300 Diseases of Allergy
- WD400 Animal Poisoning
- WD500 Plant Poisoning
- WD600 Diseases Caused by Physical Agents
- WD700 Aviation and Space Medicine
- WE   Musculoskeletal System
- WF   Respiratory System
- WG   Cardiovascular System
- WH   Hemic and Lymphatic System
- WI   Gastrointestinal System
- WJ   Urogenital System
- WK   Endocrine System
- WL   Nervous System
- WM   Psychiatry
- WN   Radiology
- WO   Surgery
- WP   Gynecology
- WQ   Obstetrics
- WR   Dermatology
- WS   Pediatrics
- WT   Geriatrics; Chronic Diseases
- WU   Dentistry; Oral Surgery
- WV   Otorhinolaryngology
- WW   Ophthalmology
- WX   Hospitals
- WY   Nursing
- WZ   History of Medicine

Other Fields:
- A   Encyclopedias
- B   Philosophy; Religion
- BF   Psychology
- C, D, E, F Directories; History
- G   Atlases
- GN   Anthropology
- HA   Statistics
- HB   Population Statistics
- HC   Economic History
- HM   Sociology
- HQ   Family; Marriage; Woman
- HV   Social Welfare; Criminology
- J   Political Science
- K   Law
- L   Education
- P   General Language Dictionaries
- Q   Science
- QA   Mathematics
- QC   Physics
- QD   Chemistry
- QH   Biology
- QK   Botany
- QL   Zoology
- QP   Physiology
- S   Agriculture
- SF   Veterinary Medicine
- T   Technology
- U   Military Science
- V   Naval Science
- Z   Bibliographies and Bibliographic Methods

Table 4.2 Outline of the Boston Medical Library Classification Schedule (Used for Books Acquired and Cataloged before 1960)

1. Reference—Dictionaries, Directories, History of Medicine, Medical Education
2. Biology
3. Anatomy
4. Physiology
5. Physiological Chemistry
6. Medicine—Theory and Practice
7. Medicine—Clinical
8. Pathology
9. Bacteriology
10. Parasitology
11. Diseases Due to Specific Infection
12. Diseases Due to Specific Infection
13. Disorders of Metabolism
14. Blood, Lymphatics, Ductless Glands
15. Circulatory System
16. Digestive System
17. Genito-Urinary System
18. Locomotor System
19. Nervous System
20. Respiratory System
21. Medical Geography
22. Therapeutics
23. Surgery
24. Gynecology
25. Obstetrics
26. Pediatrics
27. Dermatology
28. Ophthalmology
29. Otology
30. Dentistry
31. Statistics
32. Public Health
33. Military Medicine
34. Medical Jurisprudence: Toxicology
35. Veterinary Medicine
36. Science

It should be pointed out that the present study is focused exclusively on the monographic use of books in the general collection of the Countway Library. Therefore only monographs housed on the second, third, and fourth floors are included in the study.

Rules Governing the Borrowing of Books

Books in the general collection may be borrowed by those holding library identification cards. The standard loan period is two weeks, although this may be varied for certain classes of materials. Renewal will be granted upon application, provided the item is not needed by another reader. Readers who return books after the due dates have not been charged with overdue fines.

Procedures for Charging and Discharging a Book

The Countway users may charge books out at the circulation desk. To borrow a book, a reader must fill out a three-part charge form and present it to the circulation-desk assistant together with the book and his own library identification card. The circulation-desk assistant then retrieves the user information from the library ID card by using an imprinter. The borrower's ID card and the charged

The Francis A. Countway Library of Medicine   43

book are then given back to the reader with the appropriate due date stamped on the slip attached on the inside of the book's back cover. The completed charge form (Fig. 4.1) is finally dropped in the charge-card box. All charge cards of the day will be sorted for proper statistics-taking and filed in call number order in the circulation file during the day or the following morning.

To return a book, the user can return it at the circulation desk in a slot provided for the purpose. An after-hours book depository is located near the front door of the library.

To discharge a book, the circulation-desk assistant pulls the appropriate circulation charge form (Fig. 4.1) for that book from the circulation main file. The charge form is matched against the call number of the returned book for current volume, number, or copy number. If properly matched, the last due date stamped on the book's date-due slip will be crossed out, and the book is then placed on a book truck to be reshelved. The completed charge card for this circulation is then discarded.

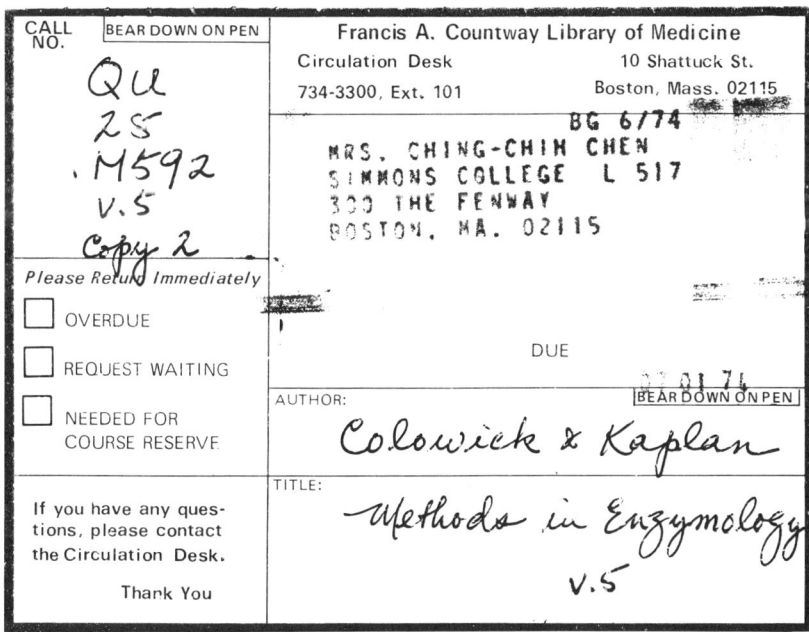

Figure 4.1 A sample completed circulated charge card

If a wanted book is not found on the shelves, the circulation-desk assistant will determine if it is charged to another reader. A reserve can be placed at the desk for a book in circulation, so that it can be held for the requester when returned or be called back if it is overdue. Books so held should be claimed within three days.

The Users of the Library

The Countway Library is intended primarily for the use of students, faculty members, and research investigators associated with the Harvard Schools of Medicine, Public Health, and Dental Medicine, for members of the professional staffs of the Harvard Affiliated Teaching Hospitals, for members and Fellows of the Boston Medical Library (BML), including members of the Massachusetts Medical Society, for medical students of Boston University, Tufts University, and the University of Massachusetts, and for certain visiting scholars. Courtesy cards are available for visiting reseachers upon request.

The following categories of persons may borrow materials from the library:
1. Students, faculty members, and researchers (and their assistants) in the Harvard Schools of Medicine, Public Health, and Dental Medicine
2. All officers and students of Harvard University as listed in the annual directory
3. House staff of the Harvard affiliated hospital services
4. Members and Fellows of the BML, including members of the Massachusetts Medical Society.

Library Hours

Monday through Thursday	8:00 A.M.-11:30 P.M.
Friday[2]	8:00 A.M.-5:00 P.M.
Saturday	9:00 A.M.-5:00 P.M.
Sunday	2:00 P.M.-11:30 P.M.

The library is closed all day on New Year's Day, Independence Day, Labor Day, Thanksgiving Day, and Christmas Day.

Current Status of Countway and Its Book Acquisition

The Countway Library has been under serious financial pressure, as have many other libraries in this country. In a recent front-page

---

[2] Prior to April 1973, the Countway Library was closed at 11:30 P.M. on Friday instead of 5:00 P.M.

write-up entitled "Making-Do" appearing in *The Francis A. Countway Library of Medicine Newsletter*, the following statement appeared:

"The Countway Library's budget for 1973/74 is slightly larger in dollar amount than it was in 1972/73. These dollars, however, will buy a great deal less this year than last. Inflation and the general shrinkage of federal government support have created a crisis in medical libraries in this country.
In order to whittle down Countway's expenditures by some 15 percent this year, we have done the following things:
1. *Eliminated five staff positions.* . . .
2. *Shortened library hours.* Since April 1973 the Countway has closed at 5:00 P.M. Friday evenings rather than 11:30 P.M. as in the past.
3. *Reduced purchasing of books.* The library's acquisition of textbooks and monographs will consist of the following classes: gifts, journal review books, new editions of basic texts, books in support of curricular needs, books requested specifically by members of the community. The library's long-standing goal of attempting to anticipate users' needs cannot be met.
4. *Suspended journal subscriptions.* . . . Since 1971, almost 1,000 subscriptions have been suspended in the Countway. . . .
Most of these economy measures have taken place behind the scenes, and most library users will not be aware of them or will be affected only in minor ways. Further economy measures, if needed, will unfortunately become more and more obvious to users. We hope that the community will bear with us during this difficult period."[3]

These Countway difficulties were also reiterated in the 1972-1973 *Dean's Report* of the Harvard Medical School:

". . . Inflation, high costs, and the scarcity of funds have made necessary drastic reductions in staff and services. Five staff positions were eliminated during the year; the Serials Department was abolished; acquisitions were restricted to gifts, essential materials for curricular needs purchased with federal funds, and books purchased with restricted endowed books funds. More than 1,000

[3] "Making-Do," *The Francis A. Countway Library of Medicine Newsletter*, No. 4 (September 1973), 1-2.

Table 4.3 Countway Library Expenditures*

Year Ending June 30	Annual Expenditures
1964	$351,989
1965	389,554
1966	639,190
1967	680,670
1968	902,175
1969	968,269
1970	945,822
1971	771,384
1972	775,214
1973	753,625

*Data taken from Harvard University, Medical School, *Dean's Report—1972/73*, 56.

journal subscriptions were suspended, and the binding of periodicals was permitted only to the extent that costs were covered by the Boston Medical Library funds. The Countway has decreased the number of hours it is open, and professional reference service on evenings and weekends, available since 1965, was eliminated. Greater use is being made of loans from other libraries, and charges are being made for optional, individual services requested by users."[4]

Table 4.3 shows that Countway's annual budget for 1972-1973 was approximately 22 percent smaller than that for 1968-1969. It is obvious that, because of this kind of drastic cut of the annual expenditures, the economic measures just described have been not only necessary but also mandatory.

Table 4.3 also suggests that the Countway Library has felt the budgetary squeeze since 1969, and the situation has greatly worsened since the second half of 1970. Further statistics of Countway on the growth of collections, the use of collections, and its personnel strength are available again in the *Dean's Report* of Harvard Medical School,[5] and are reproduced in part in Table 4.4. It is clear that with the shrinking budget during an inflationary period, Countway has been expected to provide the usual library services

[4] Harvard University, Medical School, *Dean's Report—1972/73* (Boston: Harvard Medical School, 1973), 4.

[5] Ibid., 61.

with a shrinking staff since 1969. As to the Countway collection building, the acquisition plan has been far from liberal, and the collection is certainly far from an ideal and optimum one. With the limited book budget available, as discussed earlier, book acquisitions have been restricted to gifts and essential materials for curricular needs. Table 4.4 shows that the total net increase in volumes during the year has steadily decreased since 1969-1970 (there was a slight increase in 1971-1972). Although the statistics shown in Table 4.4 include all types of library materials, a similar growth trend of the book collection can be seen in Table 4.5. It is apparent that the number of book titles cataloged by the Countway cataloging department has decreased sharply since 1969. It should be noted, however, that figures shown in that table are not all of the newer biomedical books. Many of them are gifts that could be quite old in terms of their dates of publication. Since Countway's yearly new-book accession data are not available, it is difficult to establish a fixed percentage of older materials cataloged each year. Nevertheless, it seems safe to assume that the fewer the new book titles processed during a given year, the higher the percentage of older books that would be processed, since the cataloging staff would have more time to do that.

Table 4.4 Summary of Some Statistics of the Countway Library*

	1969-70	1970-71	1971-72	1972-73
Growth of Collections:				
Net increase in volumes during the year	8,787	4,194	5,563	3,230
Total number of volumes at year end	441,399	446,844	452,407	454,378
Personnel Strength:				
Number of full-time library staff at year end	64	56	59	50
Number of part-time library staff at year end	13	14	13	13
Number of casual hours employed during the year	26,327	11,023	11,803	11,635
Use of Collections:				
Total circulation outside the library	163,538	199,676	215,213	225,849
Number of individuals entering the library	173,446	167,942	193,719	179,467
Number of courtesy cards issued	6,663	7,338	6,190	5,398

*This is part of Table XVI in Harvard University, Medical School, *Dean's Report—1972-73*, 61.

Table 4.5 Total Number of Monographs Cataloged at Countway*

Fiscal Year	Number of Titles	Number of Volumes
1963-1964	2,517	2,742
1964-1965	2,731	3,137
1965-1966	2,566	3,309
1966-1967	3,431	3,866
1967-1968	3,808	4,384
1968-1969	3,242	3,859
1969-1970	3,628	3,863
1970-1971	2,515	2,878
1971-1972	2,153	2,404
1972-1973	1,965	2,124
1963-1973	28,556	32,566

*Data obtained from the annual reports of the cataloging department of Countway. Materials acquired and processed for the Aesculapian Room (mainly for recreational reading) are not included.

Table 4.6 Number of Selected New Countway Acquisitions Listed in Both the Countway and NERMLS Newsletters

Month	1969-70	1970-71	1971-72	1972-73
September	—	297	224	116
October	—	241	231	129
November	—	207	163	108
December	—	151	118	125
January	138	109	140	128
February	198	110	109	84
March	186	101	134	90
April	221	144	161	96
May	210	124	157	89
June	199	140	160	90
Total	1,152*	1,624	1,597	1,055

*This is the second half-year total for 1969-1970; therefore the total for 1969-1970 is approximately $1,152 \times 2 = 2,304$. Newsletters are not issued during the months of July and August each year.

The Francis A. Countway Library of Medicine Newsletter and *The New England Regional Medical Library Service Newsletter* are issued by Countway every alternate month, except the months of July and August. They both attempt to list almost all of Countway's new-book acquisitions and leave out the older titles currently processed. Thus they should provide a fairly good approximation of Countway's yearly new-book acquisitions. An attempt was made to check all issues of these two newsletters from January 1970 to June 1973, and the results are shown in Table 4.6. Again, we see a steady and quite considerable drop of new Countway acquisitions since 1970.

Chapter Five
Samples and Methodology

The Collection of the Book-Use Data

Types of Book Use
In his study of book demand, Lazorick (1970) identified two major kinds: known and unknown. Similarly, the book use in a library can also be both known and unknown, or rather, as this investigator has identified it, "recorded book-use" and "nonrecorded book-use."

The "recorded book-use" is similar to what Jain (1967) called "checked-out use," which is a more appropriate term than "home-use." This type of book use consists of all uses of books that were checked out at the library circulation desk (a small fraction of them could be the limited checked-out uses of reserve books and the uses of those books which were intended for home use but returned before the borrowers left the library).

On the other hand, the "nonrecorded book-use" is generally considered to be in-library use, although a small portion of it could be out-of-library use of books that were not properly checked out.

Methods Used for Collecting Book-Use Data
Jain (1967) in his discussions of the book-usage studies indicated that the data for almost all such studies were collected in one of the following two common ways:
1. "Check-out sample." This consists of all books checked out during a specified period of time. This method has been more popularly and frequently adopted by investigators conducting user studies. The Johns Hopkins University study (1968), Trueswell's thesis (1964), Newhouse and Alexander's book (1972), and many other use studies followed this type of sample.
2. "Collection sample." This method involves choosing a sample, not necessarily random, of the total collection of books in the library or of the collection of the selected subsets of books in the library, and collecting information on either past or present use, or both, of the books in the sample. This method was used in Fussler and Simon's comprehensive study of the University of Chicago's book usage (1961).

Besides these two common ways, there is Jain's "relative use method," in which three independent samples of monographic titles are obtained from the total collection (S), the home-use materials (H), and the in-library use materials (I). These samples are divided into a certain number of groups on the basis of the following characteristics of the title: language, country of publication, year of publication, and year of accession. The frequencies of titles in these groups are computed for each of the three samples. Relative usage R is then defined as

$$R_i = \text{percent relative use of } i\text{th group} = \frac{H_i + I_i}{S_i} \times 100,$$

where S_i is the number of titles in sample S that belong to the ith group, H_i is the number in sample H that belong to the ith group, and I_i is the number in sample I that belong to the ith group. The magnitude of relative use R_i depends on the relative sizes of the samples S, H, and I.

Evaluations of the Methods Used for Collecting Book-Use Data
It is impossible to point out a better method since none of the previously mentioned methods is perfect. Jain's "relative use method" was developed, as he put it, to take advantage of the favorable characteristics of both the "check-out" and "collection" methods and to minimize their disadvantages. Nevertheless, the data collection of that method is complex and tedious. In Appendix C of Jain's thesis, he indicated twenty-seven different tables used for data collection. Obviously, his project involved much staff and computer time. Few libraries or researchers could possibly afford that without grant support. Perhaps that is why few studies to date have adopted the method.

The "collection method," although it does provide information on usage over a long period of time and the sample results are theoretically valid for the whole library collection, is generally difficult to design and operate in a truly random fashion (Jain, 1967). It also has problems regarding missing data and the interpretation of recorded usage histories because of different circulation rules in operation at different periods of time in the library. Furthermore, even if a good random sample is possible, there are many other practical problems. Many libraries do not usually keep circulation records. Some provide no book card, and the circulation card filled out by the user is generally discarded when the book is discharged. Some other libraries have a book card kept in a pocket attached to the inside back cover of a book; a patron on checking out a book will sign his name on the card, and a date is written or stamped on the book's date-due slip. This kind of use record should theoretically provide a good circulation history of the book. However, the amount of space provided for names or dates is finite. The cards and date-due slips are generally thrown out when they are filled up with signatures and dates. Thus, in this case, the book's circulation history would be lost. Furthermore, even when there are use records, it is sometimes difficult to determine whether the first date stamped on the date-due slip is the first recorded use of the book or is the first recorded use appearing on a new date-due slip (Lazorick, 1970).

What about the "check-out method"? Many investigators have considered that actual circulation is the simplest and most straightforward measure of book use and satisfied demand in a library. The planning of the sample is generally much simpler than that of other methods, and the time involved in data collection is much more economical. Yet using actual circulation records of the sample collection to measure its total use also creates problems. One cannot draw inferences about the whole collection by using this method because the sample does not include in-library use, and the sample is biased toward used materials.

Despite these difficulties, circulation volume is generally considered by many libraries to be an index of general library activity, and it can be obtained easily (Johns Hopkins University Study, 1968). Of itself circulation volume represents one important aspect of library activity. But its usefulness as an index of general activity is predicated on the basis of the existence of high correlation between circulation volume and the intensity of other activity, particularly the use of material within the library. This has been substantiated in Fussler and Simon's study (1961). Fussler and Simon concluded that generally those types of books having high-circulation use also had high in-library use. Thus recorded use is a relatively objective measure of library effectiveness (Evans, 1970).

Realizing that data on circulation are not a complete measure of the use of a portion or total of the library's collection, Morse nevertheless also feels that circulation records, in fairly compact form, supply a circulation history of each part of a library collection, which can be analyzed and from which probabilistic models can be devised (1968). As stated in Part I, he was able to develop many useful probabilistic models with the availability of very limited measurements made by his students at the MIT Science Library.

Samples and Methodology of the Study

Major Objectives of the Study
The major objectives of this study have been listed clearly in the Preface. Since this is a book-use study, several areas related to the

book-use pattern and behavior in the Countway Library will be touched upon, and attempts will be made to answer the following related questions:
1. Who uses the Countway library books?
2. How do they use the Countway Library?
3. Can a Markovian model reasonably predict the general use pattern of a collection of library books with defined characteristics?
4. What kinds of statistical procedures, when converted into practical working rules, can effectively predict the library book use?
5. How can we interpret the experimental results and provide a decision-making basis for library managers?

Methodology Used in the Study
In order to adopt a methodology that is most suitable for achieving the outlined objectives of the study, it is necessary to reflect on the advantages and disadvantages of the methods used for collecting book-use data as discussed in an earlier section. Furthermore, this is not a Countway Library project. It is a research project undertaken by the investigator alone; therefore no Countway staff time should or could be involved in any data-collection process.

The "check-out method" was then the most reasonable choice. Under the present system, the Countway circulation staff discards book-circulation slips when books are returned and discharged. Instead of discarding the circulation records in wastebaskets, the circulation assistants throw them in a designated box under the circulation desk, and bundle them up at the end of each day. Thus only a slight change of routine but no staff time is involved in data collection, and the process is simple. This method also makes it relatively easy for the investigator to design a sampling scheme (it will be elaborated on in the following section).

Circulation history data of Countway books are very important to this study. The "check-out method" is most suitable for avoiding many of the problems related to this type of data collection, as was discussed earlier.

Samples
DEFINING THE SCOPE OF THE SAMPLE This study excludes the in-library book use. Reference books and special collections do not normally circulate; therefore their uses are not studied. Reserve books are excluded because they are charged under a different system and their charge cards are kept with the books. Reading materials in the Aesculapian Room are for recreational reading.

They are mostly light reading material and usually nonbiomedical. These books, though circulated in the same manner as books from the Countway general collection, are not included in the study mainly because of the subject matter of the books and the nature of reading.

SAMPLING UNIT The finest basic unit for the collection of circulation history data is the *copy* of a book title. For example, if two charge cards of the sampling period are of the same book title, same volume and/or number, but of different copy number (as shown in the call number), then they are recorded separately, and the circulation-history data for both copies of the same book are checked. But if the call numbers of the two charge cards are completely identical, including the copy number, then they are recorded as two uses of the same book, and the circulation-history data for this book would be searched only once and recorded on the back of one of these two cards.

DECIDING THE SAMPLING PERIOD Since, as stated in Chapter 4, the Countway Library is intended primarily for the use of students, faculty members, and researchers affiliated with the Harvard Schools of Medicine, Public Health, and Dental Medicine, for members of the professional staffs of the Harvard Affiliated Teaching Hospitals, for members and Fellows of the BML, it is reasonable to assume that patterns of use in the fall and spring terms could be quite different from those during the summer months. Use data collected in one specific period of time during the academic year could be quite biased. It appeared that the use data would be more reliable if they could be collected in several sampling periods spaced throughout the year.

It was decided that four of the twelve months should be selected as sampling periods. This would cover most of the high- and low-use periods, and data gathered during these four sample months would be representative enough to cover the various book-use patterns in four seasons.

The selection of the four specific months was not an easy one. Past book-circulation data at Countway were used as a guide, and comparison with these Countway past-use data, where compatible, was also made to those of another similar institution, which was made available to the investigator. Through the generosity of the director of the Cleveland Health Sciences Library (CHSL) of Case Western Reserve University, the circulation and attendance records of its Allen Library for a period of seven years were made available (Fig. 5.1). We find excellent correlation between the circulation

Samples and Methodology 55

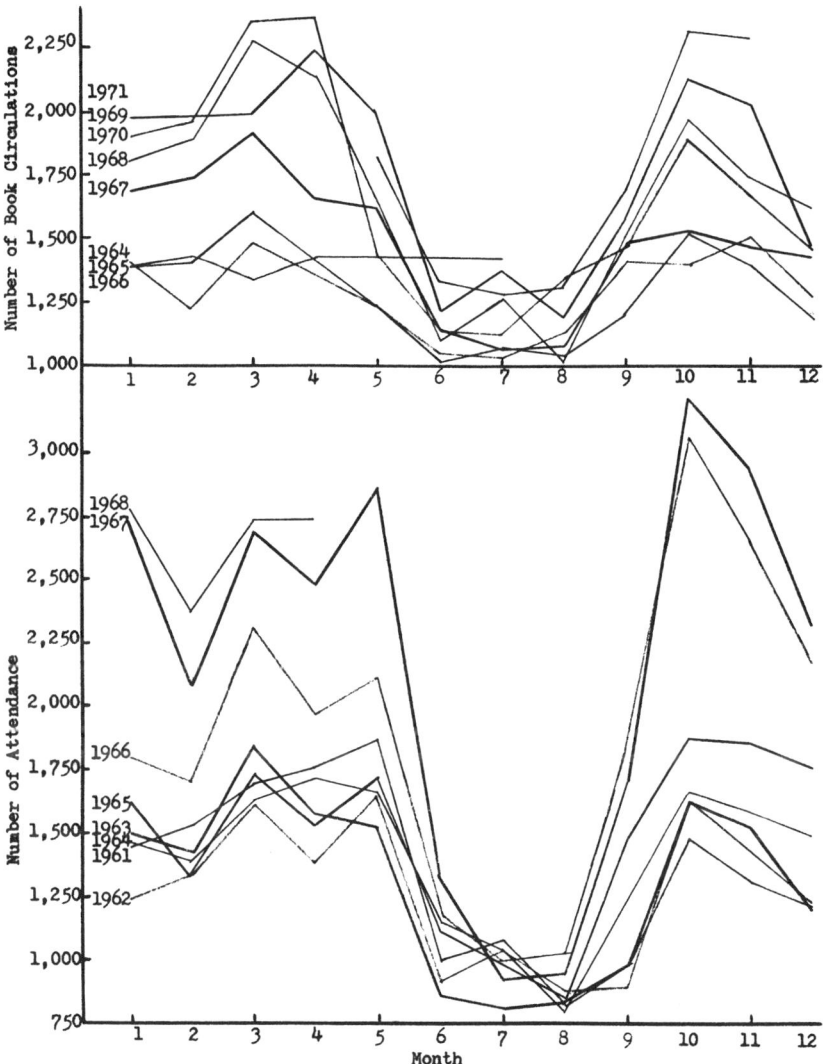

Figure 5.1 Circulation and attendance distribution at the Allen Library of the Cleveland Health Sciences Library.
This figure is taken from Robert Cheshier's Ph.D. thesis (School of Library Science, Case Western Reserve University, in process) with his kind permission.

volume and the attendance at the Allen Library. The figure also shows clearly both the low- and high-use periods, which are quite consistent over about seven years. June, July, and August have had the lowest volume of circulation and number of attendance; December, January, and February are the winter low-use period; while February to April and September 15 to November are the high-use spring and fall periods. It is also interesting to note that as time goes on, both circulation and attendance increase more rapidly in spring, fall, and winter than during the summer period.

The Cleveland Health Sciences Library is a library of the Medical School of Case Western Reserve University and the Cleveland Medical Library Association. Its clientele is very similar to that of the Countway Library. It seemed to the investigator that although the CHSL is smaller than Countway in terms of its collection size, it should be compatible with Countway in types of services offered, and therefore the use patterns of the library should be relatively similar to those of the Countway Library.

Fortunately, the Countway circulation department has also kept monthly circulation statistics for some time. Figure 5.2 shows the month-to-month book-circulation volume during the last twelve years. There is a striking resemblance between the book-use patterns at Countway and those at the CHSL. Similar lowest-, low-, and high-use periods during a year are also found at Countway. It is apparent, then, that the four sampling months could be selected at a three-month interval. They are the months of January, April, July, and October. In this way, the total sample would cover the books used at Countway in at least one of the lowest-, low-, and high-use periods.

DETERMINING THE SAMPLING SIZE IN EACH SAMPLING PERIOD In order to reduce the magnitude of sampling error and to broaden the data base of the tested models, it is necessary to take a large sample. For the purpose of analyzing the circulation histories of Countway books by classes, and of studying and predicting the patterns of book use and their changes over time, it is also necessary to have sufficiently large amounts of data so that when they are subdivided by classes, there are still statistically significant numbers of samples in each class studied.

Thus it was decided that the total circulation records of each of the four selected sample months would be used. Figure 5.2 shows the approximate circulation volume by month. In the year of 1972 the total circulation during the four months of January, April, July, and October was about 13,000, of which approximately 10

Samples and Methodology 57

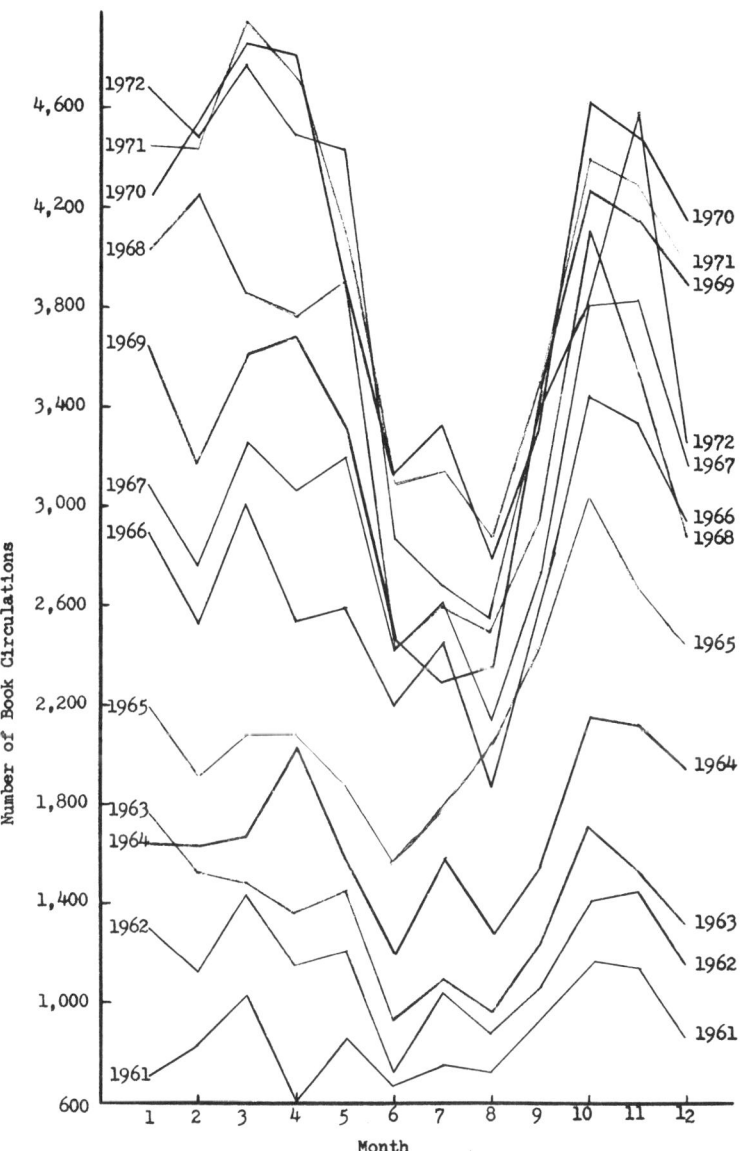

Figure 5.2 Countway Library circulation distribution. (Prior to June 1965, only data of the Harvard Medical Library are presented.)

percent were circulations of recreational reading materials from the Aesculapian Room. It is reasonable, then, to expect that the total sampling size of this study would be about 12,000 circulation records. Our final results show that the total number of records is 11,656 (Table A1.1 in Appendix 1).

SELECTING SPECIFIC CLASSES FOR DETAILED STUDY
All subject books returned during the sampling periods are included in this study. Table 4.1 lists more than forty broad subject classes; those listed under "Other Fields" are much less significant and therefore smaller classes to Countway users than those listed under "Medicine" and "Preclinical Sciences." Since the main purpose of this research is to test the Markovian models described in Part I, it is felt that there is no need to test them with every class of books circulated at Countway. A selection of a few significant classes for close and detailed study of the models should be more than sufficient. This selection would also reduce considerably the time required in both the circulation-history data collection and the data analysis.

The experience of the Countway circulation staff showed that the use of books classified by BML classification schedule (hereafter referred to as either Old Boston or BML classed books) consisted of a very small portion of the total book use at the Countway Library. Since these are books acquired prior to 1960, it was decided that they should be grouped as one class, and this class of books should be one of the selected classes for close observation. It was expected that the use patterns of older books would differ considerably from those of the newer ones.

Further selection of seven additional classes was made after the circulation records for January 1973, the first sample month, were collected and tabulated by classes. They are QU (Biochemistry), QZ (Pathology), WA (Public Health), WG (Cardiovascular System), WM (Psychiatry), WO (Surgery), and WS (Pediatrics). The selection was not made prior to the collection of January 1973 data for several reasons: First, the Countway circulation department does not keep circulation statistics by subject breakdown; thus the identification of those classes which carry high circulation volume cannot be made readily. Second, there was no immediate need to select the classes for close study since the routine in initial data collection for the total sample of each sample month would have been followed in either case.

After having the January 1973 circulation data tabulated by classes (Table A1.1 in Appendix 1), the seven classes just listed

Samples and Methodology 59

were chosen for the following reasons: First, they all have a relatively high volume of circulation, which is essential since significant amounts of circulation-history data are required to test the Markov models. Table A1.1 shows that books of these classes seem to have circulated actively throughout the year. The four-month total suggests that of the total 11,656 records, these seven classes accounted for 3,557 (or 30.5 percent of the total). All BML classed books accounted for 574 circulations in the four sample months (or 4.9 percent). Thus all eight classes selected for close study would account for more than one-third of the total records of this study. Second, it is essential to cover a diversity of subject fields in order to test the differences of use behavior, if any, among various classes of books. Two of the seven selected classes, QU and QZ, are of preclinical sciences, while the other five classes, WA, WG, WM, WO, and WS, seem to cover a wide range of medical fields. Because of this, several high-circulation classes, such as WL (Nervous System), were not chosen because a closely related subject class had already been selected. For example, WL is more closely related to WM (Psychiatry) than WG (Cardiovascular System) would be.

TYPES OF DATA COLLECTION After having obtained the samples of each sampling period, various types of data collection needed to be made. Some could be made on a daily or weekly basis before the month's records were completed, while the others would be more efficient when samples were complete at the end of each sampling period. These types of data collection will be discussed briefly in the sequential order that was normally followed by the investigator. Therefore the order to be explained in the following paragraph could, in a sense, be regarded as a general data-collection procedure.

Data on Loan Period A quick check was made of each day's circulation records in order to retrieve those for the Aesculapian Room's recreational reading materials. These records were counted, recorded, and then discarded. Next, the loan period of each returned book was computed and marked on the circulation record (see Fig. 4.1 for a sample circulation card). Since the circulation charge card had only due-date information, the loan period of each book was computed as follows: (a) each day's three-part charge cards were arranged by due dates, (b) the checkout date of each book returned, which would be two weeks before the due date, was determined, and the loan period was computed by counting the number of days between the checkout and the returned dates.

Circulation Data by Classes The three-part charge cards were then separated after the information on loan periods was determined. The third copy of the three-part card, a buff card of good paper quality, was kept for the master data file, while one of the first two thin copies was put aside in another file for user information. The buff circulation cards discharged each day were then arranged by call-number order first and recorded by classes each day on the master data sheets for number of circulations and loan periods. Furthermore, renewals were indicated on each charge card, if any, by having several crossed-out due dates and a final one. This information on renewals was also recorded. Finally, information on book requests was available on the back of the buff circulation cards if any, and it was also recorded. Summarized results of these data collections are given in Appendixes 1 and 2.

After having taken the daily statistics, all buff cards of the same sampling period were integrated in one big master file by call numbers. Those circulation cards with identical complete call numbers were clipped together.

Data on Countway Book Users Information on "user groups" is very important for this type of research. Although this study does not focus on the users of the Countway Library, an attempt was made to collect some useful data. Without the help of computer facilities, the collection of user data is an extremely time-consuming and tedious task. Thus it was decided that user data would be gathered by using circulation records of only one sample month, January 1973. The first copies of all circulation records discharged in January 1973 were arranged alphabetically by borrowers' last names. These names were further checked against appropriate directories, such as the 1972-1973 *Directory of Officers and Students* of Harvard University, for affiliations and status if not already known. The results on the Countway users are presented in Appendix 4.

Data on Subject Books Borrowed by the Same User The established user file could be used to identify various combinations of subject books of different classes checked out by the same user(s), since the cards were arranged by users' last names. Data on the frequency of different class-pair appearance were taken. For example, if user A checked out three books of WL, WM, and WS classes, the information would be recorded as WM and WL $-$ 1, WL and WS $-$ 1, and WM and WS $-$ 1. This type of information is essential in the discussion of the search theory and browsing in Appendix 3.

Circulation History Data At the end of each sampling period, all buff circulation cards for books of the eight selected classes were pulled out from the master circulation file. They were checked against the book stacks for the corresponding book copies. This is necessary because the circulation history of a given book is available only on the date-due slip affixed to the inside back cover of that book. From the date-due slip (Fig. 5.3), it is obvious that it is possible to record the number of times a book was checked out during each of the past years. For example, if the located book had a date-due slip with information such as that shown on Fig. 5.3, the circulation-history data for that book would be recorded on the back of the buff circulation card as follows:

1964-65   1 (as of May 5, 1965)
1965-66   0
1966-67   0
1967-68   0
1968-69   1
1969-70   2
1970-71   9
1971-72   0
1972-73   5

Since "May 5, 1965" was the first due date located on the slip, it was specifically noted, so that, in comparing the due date with the accession date of a given book, the researcher could determine whether this was likely to be the first due date of the book or whether there was more circulation-history data prior to May 5, 1965.

Beside the recording of the circulation-history data of those books returned during the sample month (of eight selected classes), the circulation histories of different copies of the same book titles checked were also recorded for the sake of possible use in data analysis.

Last, as stated earlier, the accession date of a book is helpful in determining whether the circulation history shown on the date-due slip of a book is complete or not. Therefore, whenever possible, the accession date of a book was recorded on the upper right corner of the buff charge card for that book.

Estimation of Book Collection Size by Classes The total number of books in a given class, N, appears frequently in the equations. It is an important quantity. Unfortunately, the Countway Library does not have detailed statistics of numbers of books by classes held in that library. A count of the library shelf-list cards could be

Testing the Theoretical Models 62

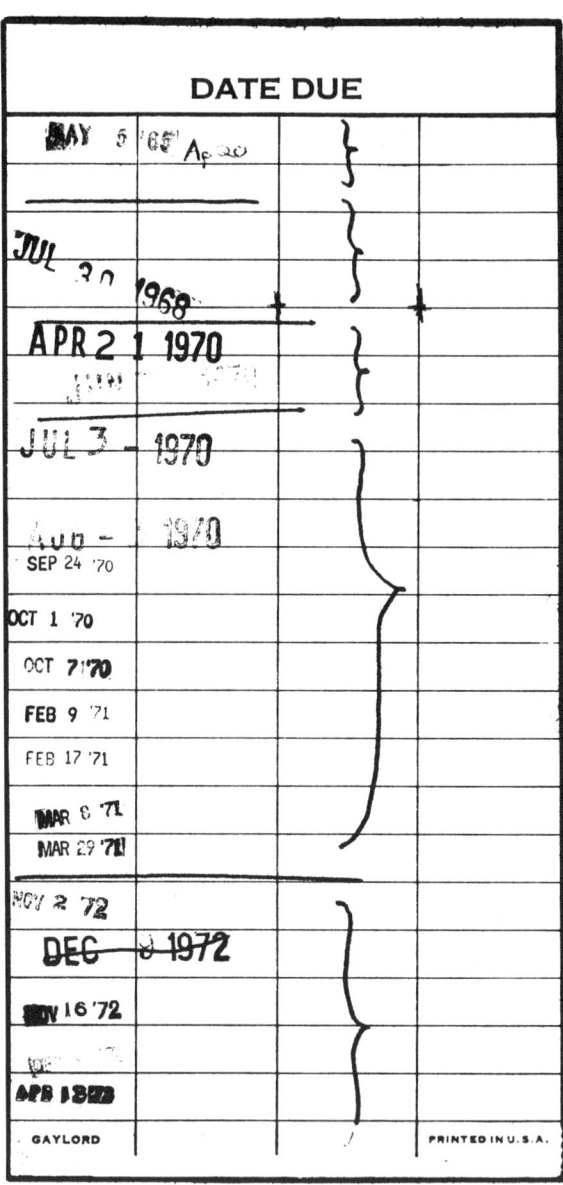

Figure 5.3 A sample date-due slip

one way to obtain an estimate; yet because of the following two reasons, a close approximation is not very likely.
1. Missing items would not be excluded from the shelf-list count if shelf-list cards were not pulled and discarded.
2. In the case of Countway, many serial publications, such as the "advances," "progress in," and "annual reviews" series, and institutional and government publications, are cataloged as monographs. Many of these are large sets containing over 100 volumes. Holdings of these publications generally are recorded numerically by volume number or number number on the shelf-list cards. Thus a set of a 100-volume series could all be recorded on less than ten shelf-list cards.

It was felt, therefore, that an easy but reliable way to approximate the collection size of each class of books at the Countway Library would be:

Total number of books in a class = $A + B + C$,

where
A = Number of volumes of the class on shelf
B = Number of volumes in circulation
C = Number of volumes off shelf for uses other than actual circulation and for other unknown reasons.

In determining the number of volumes on shelves, an actual count of the physical volumes was made. Results were recorded by subject classes as indicated in Table 4.1. As for the Old Boston (or BML) books, since their use accounted for only about 5 percent of the total library circulations during a given period, no effort was made to count them by classes, as is shown in Table 4.2. Only one sum was obtained. It was realized that it was not possible to learn the actual size of the library book collection by this kind of counting, so efforts were made to establish the closest approximation of the total number of books in a given class. To facilitate the counting process, no effort was made to differentiate duplicates of a book title or volumes of a book title except for those of the seven selected NLM classes.

Circulation cards of a given class filed at the circulation desk were either counted by number of cards if not many or measured by number of inches of the card bunch to determine the number of volumes in circulation. Generally, one inch of cards was considered to be approximately seventy-five circulations.

It is impossible actually to count the number of books off shelf for reasons other than actual circulation. In most cases, they are being used in the library. However, they could be temporarily missing, or removed for photocopying, repair, binding, and other purposes. To simplify our process of approximation, the number of volumes off shelf was estimated to be roughly the same as that of books in circulation. A check with the Countway circulation staff confirms the estimate to be reasonable.

The final results of this process of approximation are given in Table 5.1. Each number presented is an approximate sum of A, B, and C of that class of books. From Table 5.1, we know that the Countway Library's book holdings are approximately 150,000 volumes, of which about one-third are NLM-classed books, acquired and cataloged since 1960. As mentioned in Chapter 4, the total Countway collections exceed 445,000 volumes, including both book and periodical collections. Thus one-third of the total collections are monographs.

Table 5.1 provides an estimated number of book volumes of each of the classes listed. However, in order to test the models presented in Part I, it is necessary to know the total number of book titles, not book volumes. Additional checks were made to determine the

Table 5.1 Estimated Total Number of Book Volumes at Countway

Book Class	Number of Volumes	Book Class	Number of Volumes	Book Class	Number of Volumes
BML Classed	101,785	QH	1,200	U	195
		QK	65	V	15
NLM Classed Books		QL	300	W	1,725
A	175	QP	112	WA (1,700)*	2,300
B	1,070	QS	780	WB	1,950
C-G	385	QT	700	WC	670
H	1,875	QU (990)*	1,450	WD	450
J-P	600	QV	1,600	WE	1,000
Q	510	QW	850	WF	600
QA	180	QX	160	WG (1,780)*	2,000
QB	17	QY	400	WH	570
QC	350	QZ (925)*	1,300	WI	620
QD	1,200	S	325	WJ	600
QE	30	T	390	WK	690

*Estimated total number of book titles.

Samples and Methodology   65

estimated number of titles for the seven selected NLM classes, and these results are included in Table 5.1 also.
DIFFICULTIES AND PROBLEMS OF DATA COLLECTION
Most difficulties of data collection involve the collection of circulation-history data. The following four are those most frequently encountered.

First, not all books returned during the sampling month could be found on library shelves. Many of them were checked out again by other users or used in the library at the time of searching, while some others could have been removed for other reasons. Several searches at different time intervals were required in order to locate as many books of the eight selected classes for each sample month as possible. For all four monthly samples, more than one-third could not be located during the first search. This is to be expected since Eq. 3.29 tells us that the fraction of all books off shelf at any time is $\mu\overline{R}$ ($\mu \cong 1/10$, $\overline{R} \cong 3$, then $\mu\overline{R} \cong 0.3$).

Second, as has already been discussed, the circulation history of a book obtained from the book's date-due slips is often incomplete. The data collected tend to be biased toward use records of more recent years because earlier circulation records of many books

Book Class		Number of Volumes	Book Class	Number of Volumes
WL		1,800	WZ	1,350
WM	(2,160)*	2,500	Z	2,370
WN		1,100	ZQ-ZQZ	150
WO	(990)*	1,080	ZW-ZWZ	830
WP		450	*Summary*	
WQ		400	BML Books	101,785
WR		300	NLM Books	47,279
WS	(1,050)*	1,250	A-P	4,105
WT		350	Q-QZ	11,204
WU		880	S-V	925
WV		240	W-WZ	27,695
WW		600	Z-ZWZ	3,350
WX		2,000	Grand Total	149,064
WY		220		

were lost permanently after the old date-due slips were filled up with dates and therefore discarded. This problem was found particularly serious with BML-classed books; a much smaller percentage of these books had complete circulation histories than the other seven NLM classes. Furthermore, the data collected tend to discount the popular books that would often be found with either very short or no circulation history.

Third, for the study of first-year circulation distribution as described in Part I, it is necessary to identify the first year after acquisition of the book. The unavailability of information on accession dates for some books created difficulty.

Fourth, as stated earlier, an attempt was made to record circulation-history data for all copies of a same book title. However, the exact number of copies of a given book could not easily be determined, since some of them could be off shelf and in circulation. Therefore the circulation history data on duplicate copies were collected for the purpose of comparison only. They should be used very cautiously.

Limitations of the Study

This study, like other use studies, has its inherent and fundamental limitations. It can give only quantitative evaluation rather than qualitative (Chen, 1972). The study assumes that all uses are equally important, and this obviously is not an ideal assumption. There are many factors determining "value," "worth," or "usefulness" of a given book. Since other factors are difficult to measure in a quantitative way, this study and all other use studies take "frequency of use" as an index of the "value," "worth," or "usefulness" of a book.

As stated earlier, this study includes only the "recorded use" of monographs in the Countway Library. Thus it excludes the "nonrecorded use," mostly in-library use. Furthermore, this study cannot account for user convenience, frustration, and satisfaction (Kraft and Hill, 1973). The recorded use of a book is considered a measure for determining whether the book has met a need (Evans, 1970) in this kind of study.

Finally, this study is limited in one specific area of research. As with all other theses, it cannot be comprehensive in scope. The best this investigator can do is to attempt to cover some important related areas, to offer illustrations on some interesting results of areas not focused upon in this research project, and to point out potential areas of interest for possible further research.

Chapter Six
Experimental Results and Testing of the Theoretical Models

In this chapter, only experimental results related to the testing of the theoretical models found in Chapters 2 and 3 will be presented. The models described in Chapter 3 have not been tested elsewhere since they were developed only after this research was undertaken, while those included in Chapter 2 were tested earlier by Morse (1968).

In the following sections, the presentations and discussions of various statistical data and results will follow as closely as possible the same order in which the theoretical models are presented in Chapters 2 and 3. In most cases, tables and figures will be used extensively to summarize the experimental results.

The Simple Markov Process

The basic assumption of the Markov model is Eq. 2.4,

$N(m) = \alpha + \beta m$.

This means that all books of a given class that circulate m times in a given year should have an average circulation $N(m)$ the next year, and the value of $N(m)$ depends solely on m, with the parameters α and β.

For most books, $N(m)$ is smaller than m, since on the average, the circulation for a given year (call it year $t + 1$) tends to be less than that of the previous year (year t). Parameter α measures the asymptotic circulation, the value that the mean circulation of older books of the class eventually reaches. Although α is more or less independent of time t within a certain period, it does generally change slightly after year T to α', with α' generally being smaller than α. Parameter β measures how rapidly the popularity of a book of the class diminishes from year to year. It must be smaller than unity. The smaller the parameter β is (if considerably smaller than one), the faster the mean circulation of the books of a class will drop from the previous year's mean circulation and the more rapidly the class will subside and approach the final mean circulation rate, $\alpha/(1-\beta)$ or $\alpha'/(1-\beta)$.

Analyses of the Data and Experimental Results

Chapter 5 describes in great detail the samples of this study and the methodology used. To facilitate understanding of this section, it is worth noting again that eight classes of books were specifically selected for the purpose of studying the circulation histories and verifying Morse's book-use models. These classes are Old Boston, QU, QZ, WA, WG, WM, WO, and WS. Circulation-history data of books of these eight classes were collected from the books' date-due slips, as described in "Types of Data Collection" in Chapter 5. Since there were four sample months—January, April, July, and October 1973—altogether there are thirty-two (eight times four) separate samples. With the additional manipulation and combination of analyzed data, many more than thirty-two groupings of experimental results have been generated.

Circulation distributions at the Countway Library for the three most recent years, as seen in Fig. 5.2, are similar. The circulation activities seem to stabilize with very little change in circulation volume for the corresponding months in the three years. The circulation patterns for 1968 and 1969 seem to be close to those of the last three years, although the circulation volumes during the spring and fall of the years of 1968 and 1969 were not nearly as high as those of the later years. On the other hand, the circulation patterns during the earlier years differ considerably from those of the years after 1968. We see a much more even circulation throughout the year during the early years, and the growth of circulation volume during those years is also more noticeable. Thus it is reasonable to expect that the average book-use behavior for books of the earlier years may be different from that of the later years, and separate investigation on the book-use patterns of both earlier and later years merits consideration.

It was therefore decided to group the circulation-history data into two parts, the year-pair entries from 1968 to 1972 and those from 1963 to 1968. Circulation-history data for years prior to 1963 were disregarded since there were few books with circulation records available for years before 1963. It was also felt that multicopy books may have different circulation behavior from that of single-copy books; therefore all multicopy books were separated from the rest of the sample, and their circulation-history data were analyzed separately.

After the circulation-history data of the books in the samples were collected, they were transferred to a year-pair entry form (Fig. 6.1). For example, the nine numbers entered under 1972-1973 (year $t + 1$), "1, 1, 1, 0, 0, 0, 2, 0, 1," for $m = 0$ during year t can be interpreted as follows: In the year of 1971-1972 (year t), there were nine books with no circulation ($m = 0$), and four of these also circulated zero times in 1972-1973 (year $t + 1$); another four circulated once in 1972-1973, and one circulated twice. Thus

Experimental Results and Testing of the Theoretical Models   69

t	$t+1 = 1972/73$	t	$t+1 = 1971/72$
$m=$	n		n
0	1, 1, 1, 0, 0, 0, 2, 0, 1,	0	1, 0, 1, 1, 5, 2, 0, 0,
1	2, 1, 1, 2, 2, 3, 5, 1,	1	0, 1, 0, 0, 0, 1, 1, 4,
2	2, 4, 3, 1, 1, 1, 3,	2	0, 2, 4, 2, 2, 0, 1,
3	2, 6, 3, 2, 4, 1,	3	4, 2, 3, 3,
4	7, 3,	4	1, 2, 3,
5	2, 3, 4	5	
6	5, 3,	6	3, 2,
7	5, 2, 8.	7	
8		8	8, 3,
9	7	9	

Figure 6.1 Part of a sample year-pair entry form

these nine numbers represent nine year-pair entries for the column 1972-1973. Similarly, the eight numbers under the column 1971-1972, "1, 0, 1, 1, 5, 2, 0, 0," for $m = 0$ during year t indicate that there were eight books circulated 0 times during the year 1970-1971 ($t = 1970$-1971), and of these eight books, three circulated zero times, three others once, one circulated twice, and another one circulated five times in 1971-1972 ($t + 1$).

If we combine these two year-pair entries, we can analyze and summarize the numbers in Fig. 6.1 in a much more compact form, as shown in Fig. 6.2. The presentation shown in Fig. 6.2 is identical in form to that of Table 2.1. The numbers presented in Fig. 6.2 can be plotted as shown in Fig. 6.3.

Not including the samples of multicopy books of the eight classes studied, there are altogether sixty-four samples (for each class of books studied, there are two samples for each of the four sampling periods, that is, the 1968-1973 pairs and the 1963-1968 pairs). For each of the sixty-four samples, a final table and figure were prepared, as shown in Figs. 6.2 and 6.3. For some more important and bigger classes, such as WM, straight least square fits were attempted by manual calculations. The computations, though possible, were very tedious and time-consuming.

All manually calculated and preliminary results and plots of $N(m)$ against m (as shown in Figs. 6.2 and 6.3) seem to support Morse's earlier findings and show that the simple linear formula $N(m) = \alpha + \beta m$ (Eq. 2.4) is a reasonable relationship for all classes of books and for all the year pairs studied. Of course, one should keep in mind that the sample of books studied was a biased one, because only those books that circulated during the months chosen were counted, as pointed out in Chapter 3. If α and β had been

m	$M(m)$	N_{mn}									$N(m)$
		$n=0$	1	2	3	4	5	6	7	8	
0	17	7	7	2		1					0.94
1	16	4	6	3	1	1	1				1.50
2	14	2	4	4	2	2					1.86
3	10		1	3	3	2	1				3.00
4	5		1	1	2				1		3.20
5	3			1	1	1					3.00
6	4			1	2		1				3.25
7	3			1			1			1	5.00
8	2				1					1	5.50
9	1								1		7.00

Figure 6.2 A sample of final table of circulation-history results prepared manually for each sample studied. (See Chapter 2 for explanation of m, n, $M(m)$, N_{mn}, and $N(m)$.)

Experimental Results and Testing of the Theoretical Models   71

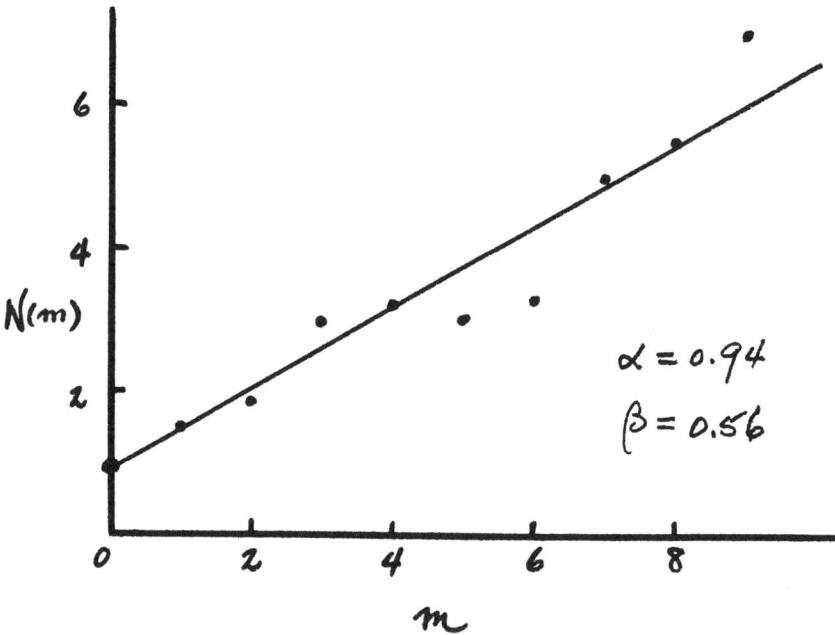

Figure 6.3 A sample figure for $N(m) = \alpha + \beta m$ prepared manually for each sample studied. (α and β can be determined by visual observation.)

calculated using only circulation from the previous year (the 1972-1973 column only in Fig. 6.1), this bias would have been serious. But one of the properties of the Markov process is that the further away in time one goes from the present, the less related is any particular book's behavior to its present behavior. For example, the distribution in circulation in 1970 of books that circulated three times in 1973 is nearly the same as the distribution in circulation in 1970 of books that circulated only once in 1973, and the equality becomes even closer as one goes back further in time. This is shown by the fact that there are a large number of books with $m = 0$ in all the columns of the year-pair entry sheets (Fig. 6.1), although no book entered the sample that had not circulated at all in 1973. Thus the past history of the books in the sample is fairly close to the past history of the average live book in the class under study. Detailed analysis indicates that the values of β, calculated by using a biased sample as described earlier, should really correspond quite well with the values of β obtained by taking a random sample of the same class from the shelves. The values of α, on the other hand, must be modified somewhat to take into account the books that did not circulate at all during the year (the live but inactive books), as was shown in Eq. 3.24.

Since there are sixty-four various samples of the eight classes of books studied, in order to compute the final results, with tables showing both experimental and theoretical results and figures plotting $N(m)$ against m, computer facilities at the MIT Information Processing Center were utilized. All data included in the manually prepared tables of the samples were punched on input cards. A weighted least-square-fit program was written in order to calculate more accurate values of α's and β's of all the samples studied. Thus the theoretical values of $N(m)$'s would also be weighted depending upon the numbers of $M(m)$'s. The decision not to use a straight least-square-fit method was made because the values of $N(m)$'s for larger m's may be statistically inaccurate. For example, in Table 6.1, there were 109 books in the sample that circulated once during the tth year and circulated on the average 1.87 (experimental $N(m)$) times in the year $t + 1$. This value of 1.87 was obtained from 109 observations, while for $m \geqslant 9$, the values of $N(m)$ were obtained by averaging the values of N_{mn}'s of no more than 4 books. It is obvious that 1.87 is statistically much more reliable than the values of $N(m)$ for $m \geqslant 9$.

As a result of the large number of samples, sixty-one tables and forty-nine figures were finally produced by computer. For each 1968-1973 year-pair sample of the eight classes, both table and figure are available for each sample month (thirty-two tables and thirty-two figures altogether). As for the 1963-1968 year-pair samples of the eight classes, data for all four sampling months for QU, QZ, WA, WG, and WO classes were combined because of the small sample size of each of the sampling months. Thus altogether five tables and five figures are available for each of the five classes. Both table and figure are presented for each sample month of the other three classes, BML, WM, and WS. In total, there are seventeen tables and seventeen figures for the 1963-1968 year-pair samples. Furthermore, for the theoretical check of Eqs. 2.4, 2.3, and 2.9,

$$N(m) = \alpha + \beta m,$$

$$T_{mn} = \frac{(\alpha + \beta m)^n}{N!} e^{-(\alpha + \beta m)},$$

and

$N_{mn} = M(m) T_{mn}$,

the 1968-1973 year-pair samples of QU, WM, and WS classes were used, and a total of twelve tables was generated.

Since all tables and figures present results that seem to substantiate the validity of the basic models tested, it was felt that there was little need to include all of them in this book. A complete set of tables and figures for the WM class, which contains the largest number of sample books of all the eight classes studied, should be sufficient for the purpose of discussion and illustration. To avoid confusion, only those tables and figures on WM books returned to Countway Library in January 1973 are presented in this chapter (Tables 6.1, 6.2, and 6.3, and Figs. 6.4 and 6.5). Those on WM books returned in the other three sample months, April, July, and October 1973, are grouped in Appendix 5.[1]

Verifying the Models

The Simple Markov Model

Tables 6.1 and 6.2, Figs. 6.4 and 6.5, Appendix 5, and the corresponding tables and figures for samples of the other seven selected classes seem to strengthen the conclusion that the simple Markov model for book circulation, represented by Eq. 2.4, is a reasonable approximation of the actual book-circulation behavior of the classes studied.

Each sample of books studied has different values of α and β. I have listed the values of α's and β's for all the samples studied in Table 6.4. All values except those of the combined samples in the columns entitled "All Pairs Combined" and "Combined" were computed with a weighted least square fit.

How rapidly the popularity of a book of the class diminishes from year to year is measured by β. It should not change with time. As discussed in Chapter 5, of the eight selected classes, all but BML are NLM-classed books acquired and cataloged after 1960, while BML are all biomedical books acquired prior to 1960. As far as the values of β's are concerned, it can be seen from Table 6.4 that there is little difference between those of the BML books and those of the books of other classes. All values of β's fall in the range suggested by Morse (1972), who indicated that parameter β must be less than unity and is usually between 0.2 and 0.8.

---

[1] For complete tables and figures presenting similar results on books of other seven selected classes, BML, QU, QZ, WA, WG, WO, and WS, see Appendix V of Chen's Ph.D. thesis (1974), 230-275.

Table 6.1 Values of $M(m)$, N_{mn}, and $N(m)$ for Different Values of m and n for WM Books Returned to Countway. 1968-1973 Pairs—January 1973 Data

m	M(m)	N_{mn}												N(m)	Theor.
		n=0	1	2	3	4	5	6	7	8	9	10	11	12		
0	91	22	26	17	13	9	2	0	1	0	0	1	0	0	1.78	1.58
1	109	22	33	22	16	6	7	2	0	1	0	0	0	0	1.87	1.95
2	116	15	32	22	22	16	3	4	1	1	0	0	0	0	2.24	2.31
3	83	8	18	19	20	11	2	3	1	1	0	0	0	0	2.45	2.68
4	73	5	7	18	15	12	10	1	2	2	1	0	0	0	3.16	3.05
5	32	2	3	4	8	6	2	1	1	2	3	0	0	0	3.91	3.41
6	22	1	2	5	1	9	1	0	2	0	0	1	0	0	3.64	3.78
7	9	0	3	2	0	1	2	0	0	1	0	0	0	0	3.22	4.14
8	14	0	3	1	0	2	2	2	2	1	0	0	0	1	4.93	4.51
9	3	0	0	0	1	0	1	1	0	0	0	0	0	0	4.67	4.88
10	3	0	0	1	0	0	1	0	0	1	0	0	0	0	5.00	5.24
11	4	0	0	1	1	0	1	0	0	1	0	0	0	0	4.50	5.61
12	0	0	0	0	0	0	0	0	0	0	0	0	0	0	0.0	5.97
13	1	0	0	0	0	0	0	0	0	0	0	0	1	0	11.00	6.34

```
                ALPHA AND BETA     1.631    0.324
WEIGHTED ALPHA AND BETA            1.581    0.366
```

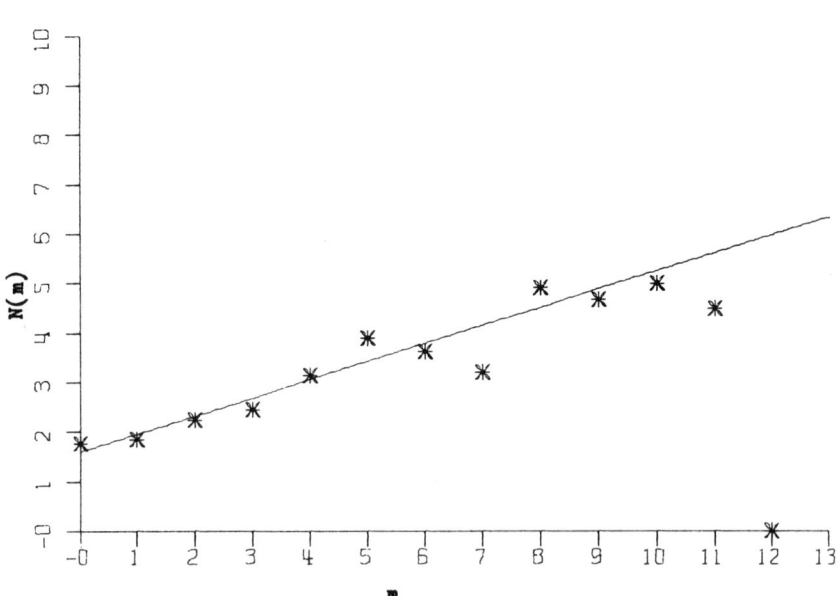

Figure 6.4 Mean circulation $N(m)$ for year $t + 1$ as a function of circulation m for previous year t—WM books. 1968-1973 pairs—January 1973 data

Table 6.2 Values of $M(m)$, N_{mn}, and $N(m)$ for Different Values of m and n for WM Books Returned to Countway. 1963-1968 Pairs—January 1973 Data

m	M(m)	N_{mn}										N(m)	Theor.
		n=0	1	2	3	4	5	6	7	8	9		
0	27	11	6	4	3	3	0	0	0	0	0	1.30	1.22
1	50	18	12	8	6	5	0	0	0	1	0	1.48	1.54
2	37	12	8	6	8	1	1	0	0	0	1	1.68	1.86
3	40	4	6	12	10	6	0	2	0	0	0	2.40	2.18
4	22	2	5	8	1	3	3	0	0	0	0	2.32	2.51
5	5	0	0	1	2	0	1	1	0	0	0	3.80	2.83
6	3	0	0	1	0	2	0	0	0	0	0	3.33	3.15
7	1	0	0	0	0	1	0	0	0	0	0	4.00	3.47
8	0	0	0	0	0	0	0	0	0	0	0	0.0	3.80
9	1	0	0	1	0	0	0	0	0	0	0	2.00	4.12
10	1	0	0	0	0	1	0	0	0	0	0	4.00	4.44

```
              ALPHA AND BETA    1.719    0.134
WEIGHTED ALPHA AND BETA         1.218    0.322
```

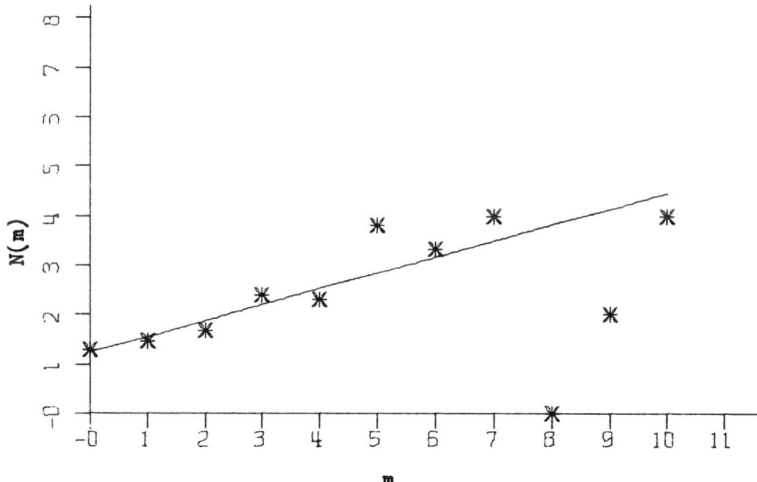

Figure 6.5 Mean circulation $N(m)$ for year $t+1$ as a function of circulation m for previous year t—WM books. 1963-1968 pairs—January 1973 data

Table 6.3 Values of $M(m)$, N_{mn}, and $N(m)$ for Different Values of m and n for WM Books with Theoretical Values of $N(m)$ and N_{mn} Obtained by Using Eqs. 2.4, 2.3, and 2.9. (Theoretical Values of N_{mn} are Printed on the Second Line.) 1968-1973—January 1973 Data

m	M(m)	N_{mn}													N(m)	Theor.
		n=0	1	2	3	4	5	6	7	8	9	10	11	12		
0	91	22	26	17	13	9	2	0	1	0	0	1	0	0	1.78	1.58
		18	29	23	12	4	1	0	0	0	0	0	0	0		
1	109	22	33	22	16	6	7	2	0	1	0	0	0	0	1.87	1.95
		19	30	29	19	9	3	1	0	0	0	0	0	0		
2	116	15	32	22	22	16	3	4	1	1	0	0	0	0	2.24	2.31
		11	26	30	23	13	6	2	0	0	0	0	0	0		
3	83	8	18	19	20	11	2	3	1	1	0	0	0	0	2.45	2.68
		9	15	20	18	12	6	2	1	0	0	0	0	0		
4	73	5	7	18	15	12	10	1	2	2	1	0	0	0	3.16	3.05
		3	10	16	16	12	7	3	1	0	0	0	0	0		
5	32	2	3	4	8	6	2	1	1	2	3	0	0	0	3.91	3.41
		1	3	6	6	5	4	2	1	0	0	0	0	0		
6	22	1	2	5	1	9	1	0	2	0	0	1	0	0	3.64	3.78
		0	1	3	4	4	3	2	1	0	0	0	0	0		
7	9	0	3	2	0	1	2	0	0	1	0	0	0	0	3.22	4.14
		0	0	1	1	1	1	1	0	0	0	0	0	0		
8	14	0	3	1	0	2	2	2	2	1	0	0	0	1	4.93	4.51
		0	0	1	2	2	2	1	1	0	0	0	0	0		
9	3	0	0	0	1	0	1	1	0	0	0	0	0	0	4.67	4.88
		0	0	0	0	0	0	0	0	0	0	0	0	0		
10	3	0	0	1	0	0	1	0	0	1	0	0	0	0	5.00	5.24
		0	0	0	0	0	0	0	0	0	0	0	0	0		
11	4	0	0	1	1	0	1	0	0	1	0	0	0	0	4.50	5.61
		0	0	0	0	0	0	0	0	0	0	0	0	0		
12	0	0	0	0	0	0	0	0	0	0	0	0	0	0	0.0	5.97
		0	0	0	0	0	0	0	0	0	0	0	0	0		
13	1	0	0	0	0	0	0	0	0	0	0	0	1	0	11.00	6.34
		0	0	0	0	0	0	0	0	0	0	0	0	0		

Table 6.4 also shows that samples of books in each class have their own values of α's. The α's for the year pairs of 1968-1973 are mostly greater than those of the 1963-1968 year pairs. This finding seems to substantiate Morse's claim that α does diminish slightly with age, though it is relatively independent of time t. Morse found that for books of the MIT Science Library, α' seemed to drop slowly to less than half of the value of α for the first five years of the life of the book when t is greater than ten (1968). This seems to be true also in the case of Countway's collection. As shown in Table 6.4, the α's for the Old Boston (BML) samples are about half of the α's for all NLM classes. Morse indicated that parameter α is usually between 0.3 and 0.7 (1972). But for Countway books, except those α's of the BML classes, all other α's are much larger than unity. The difference between the α's of the Countway books and those of the MIT Science Library books may possibly be for two reasons.

First, a large α would indicate that many books in the class don't go out of date quickly and that they continue to be useful for a long time. The β measures the immediate response just after publication, while the α measures the long-term value of a book. The collections of the MIT Science Library and the Countway Library differ from each other in both subject matter and emphasis. It is expected that the Countway collection is more applied in nature and therefore continues to be useful for a longer period of time than that of MIT.

Second, as indicated in Chapter 3, because of the stringent library book budget, the Countway book collection is far from a complete one. A large portion of books, particularly the more recent ones, is expected to continue to be useful for some time because of a much more judicious book-selection policy and the prospect of fewer new additions of books in each subject area.

Tables 6.3 and A5.3 offer the theoretical values of $N(m)$ and N_{mn}. The theoretical $N(m)$'s were obtained by using Eq. 2.4, and the N_{mn}'s were derived from Eqs 2.3 and 2.9. Except for some fluctuations when $n = 0$, there is satisfactory agreement between the experimental N_{mn}'s and the theoretical ones. Thus Eq. 2.3 seems to be adequate for the prediction of the Poisson distribution of circulation n in year $t + 1$, if the circulation in year t was m. Eq. 2.3, together with Eq. 2.9, should be adequate for this prediction particularly when the zero circulation in year $t + 1$ is discounted.

Thus we have successfully tested the basic Markov models. As

Table 6.4 Values of α's and β's of the Eight Selected Classes of Books in Countway*

Book Class	1968-1973 Pairs				
	Sample-Jan.	April	July	Oct.	Combined
BML	α = 0.550	0.585	0.697	0.591	0.592
	β = 0.432	0.375	0.391	0.322	0.376
	M = 259	294	127	305	
QU	α = 0.975	1.335	1.149	1.317	1.194
	β = 0.472	0.406	0.530	0.469	0.471
	M = 160	158	173	168	
QZ	α = 1.309	0.945	1.065	0.744	1.011
	β = 0.366	0.489	0.383	0.628	0.474
	M = 119	120	77	118	
WA	α = 1.240	1.261	1.306	0.523	1.100
	β = 0.295	0.323	0.254	0.686	0.379
	M = 191	101	76	102	
WG	α = 1.484	1.285	1.254	1.232	1.319
	β = 0.376	0.389	0.426	0.426	0.401
	M = 139	181	108	110	
WM	α = 1.581	1.507	1.510	1.685	1.565
	β = 0.366	0.383	0.434	0.381	0.389
	M = 560	625	424	422	
WO	α = 1.479	1.144	0.768	1.077	1.088
	β = 0.306	0.398	0.527	0.440	0.428
	M = 69	67	93	89	
WS	α = 1.652	1.713	1.334	1.524	1.573
	β = 0.384	0.386	0.523	0.448	0.430
	M = 189	259	173	202	

*Values of α's and β's for 1968-1973 and 1963-1968 pairs of each monthly sample of circulation history of books of the eight selected classes are the weighted α's and β's taken from Tables 6.1 and 6.2, Appendix 5, and from Appendix 5 of Chen's thesis (1974). Values of M's are also taken from these tables of the Appendixes, where $M = \Sigma M(m)$ of each sample.

was discussed in Chapter 2, Eq. 2.4 can be modified to Eq. 2.5 to predict the mean circulation of a given year. This can now be tested.

In Table 3.2, summaries of complete circulation histories of 126 WM books returned to Countway in January 1973 are presented. The mean yearly circulation $\bar{R}(t)$ was calculated for each t year after book acquisition (for t equal to 1 to 10). The values of these mean yearly circulations are again available in Table 3.2. Similar results from 146 WM books returned to Countway in April 1973, 59 WA books in January 1973, 35 WA books in April 1973, and

1963-1968					All Pairs
Jan.	April	July	Oct.	Combined	Combined
0.495	0.592	0.492	0.328	0.470	α = 0.550
0.357	0.213	0.292	0.463	0.340	β = 0.364
135	147	70	160		
—	—	—	—	1.150	α = 1.184
—	—	—	—	0.349	β = 0.442
				201	
—	—	—	—	0.644	α = 0.931
—	—	—	—	0.331	β = 0.443
				122	
—	—	—	—	1.228	α = 1.130
—	—	—	—	0.031	β = 0.296
				147	
—	—	—	—	1.259	α = 1.304
—	—	—	—	0.321	β = 0.381
				182	
1.218	1.072	1.122	1.629	1.241	α = 1.476
0.322	0.342	0.257	0.132	0.274	β = 0.357
187	270	145	174		
—	—	—	—	1.316	α = 1.137
—	—	—	—	0.337	β = 0.408
				88	
1.931	1.635	1.044	1.427	1.525	α = 1.560
0.161	0.271	0.366	0.206	0.253	β = 0.380
59	122	61	81		

53 WS books in January 1973 are also available.[2] For the convenience of comparison and illustration, these values are summarized in Table 6.5, and immediately under each experimental value, the theoretical one derived from Eq. 2.5 is also given. To simplify the computation required, instead of using different values of α's and β's for different samples of WM and WA books, combined values were used. This may produce slightly different theoretical values of $\overline{R}(t)$, but the differences are not considered significant. Table 6.5 clearly shows that when the values of α, β, and $\overline{R}(1)$ are known, Eq. 2.5 seems to be adequate in predicting the mean yearly circulation for the following years. For $t > 5$, one notices the difference between the experimental and theoretical results. This kind of deviation is not serious since the experimental data

[2] This information is available in Appendix VI of Chen's Ph.D. thesis (1974), 276-284.

were obtained from a very small number of samples. Better results can be expected from Eq. 2.8.

A few words should be said about the combined values of α's and β's used. As shown in Table 6.4, for each different sample of books, there are different values of α and β (they can be called α_1, $\alpha_2, \alpha_3, \alpha_4 \ldots$ and $\beta_1, \beta_2, \beta_3, \beta_4 \ldots$). All these values of α's are close to each other but not identical; so are the values of β's. In order to obtain more accurate values of α and β for all books of a given class (regardless of the number of samples of this class), Eq. 2.7 can be used to obtain the combined values of all α's and β's when the number of books in each sample is known (M_1, M_2, M_3, $M_4 \ldots$). For example, for the 1968-1973 year-pair samples of WM books, we have

$\alpha_1 = 1.581, \quad \alpha_2 = 1.507, \quad \alpha_3 = 1.510, \quad \alpha_4 = 1.685;$

$\beta_1 = 0.366, \quad \beta_2 = 0.383, \quad \beta_3 = 0.434, \quad \beta_4 = 0.381;$

Table 6.5 Mean Yearly Circulation $\overline{R}(t)$ of WM, WA, and WS Books at t Year after Accession*

	$t = 1$	2	3	4	5	6	7	8	9	10
WM—January 1973 Data[†]										
$\overline{R}(t)$	2.94	2.66	2.81	2.55	2.31	1.77	1.83	1.74	1.07	1.38
Theoretical	2.94	2.53	2.38	2.33	2.30	2.30	2.30	2.30	2.30	2.30
WM—April 1973 Data[‡]										
$\overline{R}(t)$	2.65	2.32	2.59	2.26	2.26	1.71	1.61	1.67	1.74	1.74
Theoretical	2.65	2.42	2.34	2.31	2.30	2.30	2.30	2.30	2.30	2.30
WA—January 1973 Data[‡]										
$\overline{R}(t)$	1.75	1.97	1.62	1.21	1.81	1.92	1.50	1.33	1.64	1.71
Theoretical	1.75	1.65	1.62	1.61	1.61	1.61	1.61	1.61	1.61	1.61
WM—April 1973 Data[‡]										
$\overline{R}(t)$	2.46	2.12	1.70	1.68	1.30	1.36	1.82	1.13	0.80	0.66
Theoretical	2.46	1.86	1.68	1.63	1.61	1.61	1.61	1.61	1.61	1.61
WS—January 1973 Data[‡]										
$\overline{R}(t)$	2.96	2.80	2.95	2.37	2.33	2.22	1.77	2.08	2.50	1.67
Theoretical	2.96	2.63	2.51	2.46	2.45	2.44	2.44	2.44	2.44	2.44

*Theoretical $\overline{R}(t)$ is derived from Eq. 2.5, that is,

$$\overline{R}(t+1) = \alpha \frac{1-\beta^t}{1-\beta} + \overline{R}(1)\beta^t,$$

and the values of α's and β's are taken from Table 6.4 (under the column "All Pairs Combined").
[†]Experimental $\overline{R}(t)$ is taken from Table 3.2.
[‡] All experimental results are taken from Appendix VI of Chen's Ph.D. thesis (1974), 276-284.

Experimental Results and Testing of the Theoretical Models 81

$M_1 = 560$, $M_2 = 625$, $M_3 = 424$, $M_4 = 422$;

then

$$\alpha = \frac{560 \times 1.581 + 625 \times 1.507 + 424 \times 1.510 + 422 \times 1.685}{560 + 625 + 424 + 422} = 1.565,$$

and

$$\beta = \frac{560 \times 0.366 + 625 \times 0.383 + 424 \times 0.434 + 422 \times 0.381}{560 + 625 + 424 + 422} = 0.389.$$

In the last section of Chapter 2, I discussed in great detail how Morse developed his simplified models for the prediction of future book circulation without using Eqs. 2.3 and 2.10 to 2.13, which require quite complex and tedious computations. Since these models are very closely related to those models presented in Chapter 3, I shall discuss and test the newly developed models, which should be used to counteract the bias in the collected data.

The Correction Models

In Chapter 3 the book-use data collected at the Countway Library were shown to be biased toward the active books, because they are based on the circulated books returned during the sample months. It was further shown that, owing to this bias, the raw experimental data should not be expected to correspond well with theoretical Eq. 3.3, $P(m) = (\overline{R})^m/(1 + \overline{R})^{m+1}$, where $P(m)$ is the fraction of books in that class circulated m times during the first year, and $\overline{R}$ is the expected mean circulation of the class during that year. Finally, Chapter 3 suggests that the number $N(j)$ of books in the class that circulated j times in the sample year can be estimated from the number $M(j)$ that were returned in the sample month and had circulated j times in the previous year immediately preceding the end of the sample month. This process involves using a correction factor, $1/[1 - (1 - \rho)^j]$, where ρ is determined by the length of the sample period. Thus the bias of the collected data can be removed by the simple equation 3.5, $N(j) = M(j)/[1 - (1 - \rho)^j]$. After the correction is made, it is expected that the distribution of $N(j)$'s is approximately goemetric, as shown in Fig. 3.2. In this section, all the experimental results related to the testing of this correction model will be presented.

From Eq. 3.5, it is clear that in order to test this model, additional data on the number of books $M(j)$ in each sample that had j circulation in the immediately preceding year are required. These data can be obtained only from the date-due slips of books in the samples; therefore, the data collection was found to be very time-consuming. The same seven NLM classes selected for the study of circulation history were chosen, and for each class, all four monthly samples were used. Thus altogether there were twenty-eight separate samples. The BML books were not included in this part of the study mainly because they are older books. They are not expected to be used actively at the Countway Library.

Among the seven classes studied, WM has the largest sample size for each of the sampling months. Altogether, 859 WM books were studied, while for the other six classes, data were obtained from 339 QU books, 240 QZ books, 244 WA books, 282 WG books, 163 WO books, and 412 WS books. For each sample of books, there were a fair number that could not be located on the library shelves (called U as described in Chapter 3) and therefore had to be excluded. For example, for the sample of WM books of the January 1973 sample month, 306 book titles were searched for needed information; 254 were located, but 52 could not be found; therefore the final size of the sample for that month was 254.

The extensive data were carefully analyzed. In this chapter, results on QZ, WM, and WS books are presented (Tables 6.6-6.8) to facilitate discussions. Results on books of the other four classes, QU, WA, WG, and WO, are presented in Appendix 6 (Tables A6.1-4). The $M(j)$'s for all four sample months were combined to $4M(j)$, from which $4N(j)$ was computed by using Eq. 3.5, with $\rho = 1/12$. The final value of $N(j)$ was obtained by dividing $4N(j)$ by 4. As mentioned earlier, the $4M(j)$ used to compute the value of $N(j)$ was corrected by taking into account those books in the sample which could not be located for data collection (U), as shown in Columns 7 and 8 of Tables 6.6 to 6.8, and Tables A6.1 to A6.4 of Appendix 6.

Equation 3.11 was used to obtain the value of parameter γ, which was then used to produce the theoretical values of $N(j)$'s by using Eq. 3.10 (see Column 11 of Tables 6.6 to 6.12 and Tables A6.1-4 for details). Finally, values of $N_\varrho(j)$'s were derived from Eq. 3.18, and the results are again available in all these tables.

It is apparent, then, that the corrected circulation distributions for all seven NLM classes are remarkably close to the theoretical geometric ones. This agreement is even more clearly visible to us in Figs. 6.6 to 6.8. Some deviations do occur when j becomes large on each semilog plot, and this could very well happen because of the smallness of the sample. In general, the corrected numbers $N(j)$

obtained from Eq. 3.5, shown by circles in the figures, correspond quite satisfactorily with the theoretical geometrical distribution marked by the straight line, while the biased numbers $M(j)$ from circulation desk data, shown by crosses in the figures, obviously are not geometrically distributed.

It is safe to conclude that the correction models have been successfully tested. Chapter 3 describes the implications of these models in terms of predictions of future circulation and estimation of yearly circulation. To avoid unnecessary redundancy, I shall offer a few illustrations and tables with only limited discussions. A summary is available in a joint paper by Morse and Chen (1975), and Chapter 3 should be referred to for a complete discussion.

Some useful equations described in Chapter 3 are grouped together in Table 6.9. An attempt was made by using these equations either to demonstrate the circulation behavior of the books of the seven classes studied in 1972-1973 or to predict their following-year circulation patterns. These detailed results are presented in Tables 6.10 and 6.11 and in Tables A6.5-6. The values of parameters α_a and β shown in these tables are taken from Table 6.4. The values of N, the total number of books in a given class, are obtained from the data of Table 5.1, in which the values of N_a, the total number of active books of a given class, and N_ℓ, the estimated live books, are both taken from Tables 6.6-6.8 and Tables A6.1-4. Thus the values of N_d, the number of dead books in a given class, can easily be computed by $N_d = N - N_\ell$.

The other values and parameters, such as α, $\gamma(t)$, $C(t)$, $\overline{R}_a(t)$, $\overline{R}_\ell(t)$, and so forth, can be derived from some of the equations listed in Table 6.9, as shown in the lefthand columns of Tables 6.10-6.11 and Tables A6.5-6. All of them show fairly high values of $C(t)$ and $\overline{R}_a(t)$. For example, for WM books, $C(0)$, the fraction of books that were active in 1972-1973, was about 0.775, which is quite high in comparison with Morse's results of the book use in the MIT Science Library. Morse found that physics books were used most actively, and the fraction of active books was 0.63. The mean circulation rate of WM active books is also high. It was found that of the estimated 2,160 WM books, 1,504 (N_a) of them were found to circulate, on the average, 2.387 times ($\overline{R}_a$) in 1972-1973. Few dead books were found, $N_d = N - N_\ell = 2,160 - 1,941 = 219$. Furthermore, all WM live books (N_ℓ) also had a fairly high mean circulation rate, about twice per year ($\overline{R}_\ell = 1.85$). Thus the total yearly circulation of WM books in Countway during the year 1972-1973 could be estimated to be about 3,600 ($\overline{R}_a N_a$ or $\overline{R}_\ell N_\ell$).

Table 6.6 Uncorrected and Corrected Circulation Distributions for QZ Books Returned in 1973

j	$M(j)$—1973				$4M(j)$
	January	April	July	October	
1	20	29	11	14	74
2	19	15	10	14	58
3	11	9	7	12	39
4	8	7	8	7	30
5	6	4	4	7	21
6	2	1	2	3	8
7	1	1	1	3	6
8		1			1
9					
10		1		1	2
11					
12	1				1
Total	68	68	43	61	240
$U^\dagger$	27	16	6	9	58

*Corrected $4M(j) = 4M(j) \times \{[\sum_j 4M(j) + \sum_j U]/\sum_j 4M(j)\}$. For example, the corrected $4M(1) = 92$, and $92 = 74 \times [(240 + 58)/240]$.
†U is the number of books for which j value is unknown.

This is a good approximation, and it agrees very well with actual circulation figures, as shown in Table 6.12.

Furthermore, the value of parameter γ can be obtained by $\gamma = 1 - (N_1/N_a)$. Once the value of γ is known, the relatively high circulation books can be identified by using Eq. 3.14, and the fraction of the total circulation accounted for by these high-circulation books can be obtained from Eq. 3.15. For WM books, it was estimated that in 1972-1973, of the 1,504 active books, about 171 books were circulated more than four times $[N(> 4) = N_a \gamma^4 = 1,504 \times (0.581)^4 = 171.4]$. These 171 books accounted for about 30 percent of the total circulation of the class, as shown by using Eq. 4.15,

$F(> 4) = [4(1 - 0.581)] \times (0.581)^4$

$= 0.305.$

Corrected $4M(j)^*$ with U	Corrected $M(j)$	$4N(j)$	$N(j)$	Geometric $N(j)$	$N_\ell(j)$
92	23	1,104	276	276	437
72	18	451	113	124	130
48	12	209	52	56	55
37	9	125	31	25	32
26	7	74	18	11	19
10	3	25	6	5	6
7	2	15	4	2	4
1		2		1	
				1	
2	1	3	1		1
1		2			
296	75	2,010	501 N_a	501	684 N_ℓ

Finally, as shown in Tables 6.10-6.11 and Tables A6.5-6, after the values of $\alpha, \beta, \gamma(t), C(t), \overline{R}_a(t), \overline{R}_\ell(t), N_a$, and N_ℓ are obtained from data taken in year t, the estimated following year $(t + 1)$ circulation behavior for the same groups of books of a given class can easily be predicted by using Eqs. 3.22 to 3.25, which are all shown in Table 6.9. The predicted circulation patterns for books of the seven classes studied are obvious from Tables 6.10-6.11 and Tables A6.5-6 without further elaboration.

Table 6.7 Uncorrected and Corrected Circulation Distributions for WM Books Returned in 1973

	$M(j)$—1973				
j	January	April	July	October	$4M(j)$
1	44	57	32	33	166
2	44	65	38	37	184
3	43	47	30	21	141
4	40	25	24	22	111
5	28	23	18	22	91
6	18	15	15	18	66
7	13	7	9	14	43
8	11	3	5	8	27
9	6	3	2	4	15
10	2	1	1	3	7
11	1	1		1	3
12	1		1		2
13	1				1
14					
15	1				1
16	1				1
Total	254	247	175	183	859
U†	52	90	38	48	228

For "*" and "†" see footnotes of Table 6.6.

Experimental Results and Testing of the Theoretical Models 87

Corrected $4M(j)$* with U	Corrected $M(j)$	$4N(j)$	$N(j)$	Geometric $N(j)$	$N_\ell(j)$
210	53	2,521	630	630	997
233	58	1,459	365	366	422
178	45	775	194	213	204
140	35	473	118	124	120
115	29	326	82	72	83
84	21	207	52	42	52
54	14	118	30	24	30
34	9	68	17	14	17
19	5	35	9	8	9
9	2	15	4	5	4
4	1	6	2	3	2
3	1	5	1	2	1
1		1		1	
				1	
1		1			
1		1			
1,086	273	6,011	1,504	1,505	1,941
			(N_a)		(N_ℓ)

Table 6.8 Uncorrected and Corrected Circulation Distributions for WS Books Returned in 1973

j	$M(j)$—1973				$4M(j)$
	January	April	July	October	
1	17	27	15	19	78
2	17	24	16	17	74
3	16	21	13	18	68
4	15	18	12	15	60
5	11	17	8	13	49
6	9	10	6	8	33
7	7	6	5	7	25
8	4	2	4	1	11
9	2	1	2	1	6
10	1	1	1	2	5
11	1	1			2
12	1				1
Total	101	128	82	101	412
U†	33	32	41	48	154

For "*" and "†" see the footnotes of Table 6.6.

Experimental Results and Testing of the Theoretical Models

Corrected $M(j)^*$ with U	Corrected $M(j)$	$4N(j)$	$N(j)$	Geometric $N(j)$	$N_\ell(j)$
107	27	1,285	321	321	508
102	26	639	160	186	185
93	23	405	101	107	107
82	21	277	69	62	71
67	17	190	47	36	48
45	11	111	28	21	28
34	9	75	19	12	19
15	4	30	7	7	7
8	2	15	4	4	4
7	2	12	3	2	3
3	1	5	1	1	1
1		2		1	
564	143	3,046	760 N_a	760	981 N_ℓ

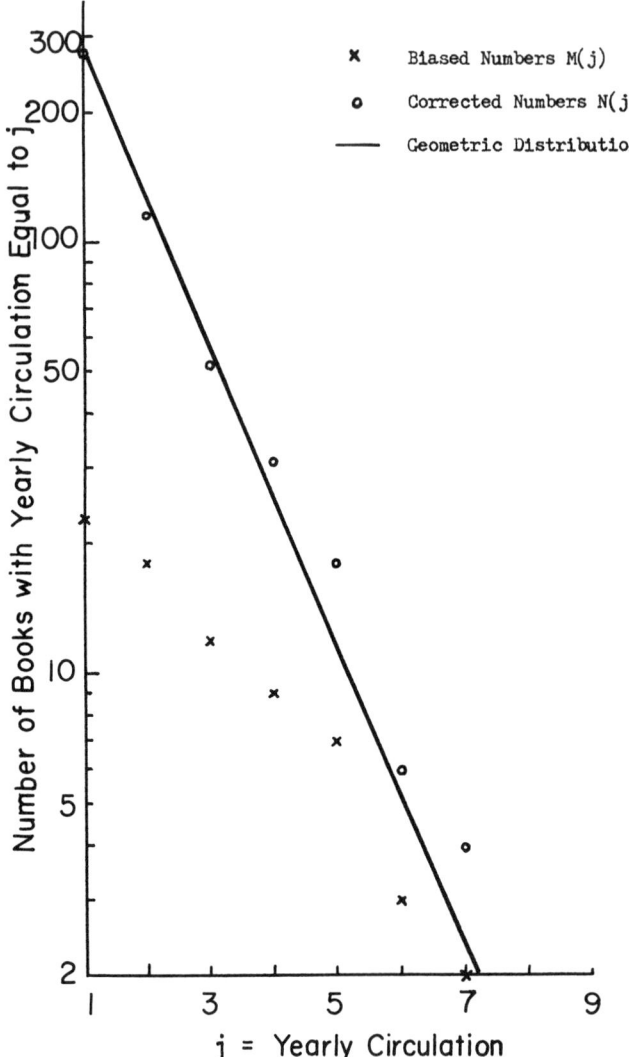

Figure 6.6 Uncorrected and corrected circulation distribution for QZ books (data taken from Table 6.6)

Experimental Results and Testing of the Theoretical Models   91

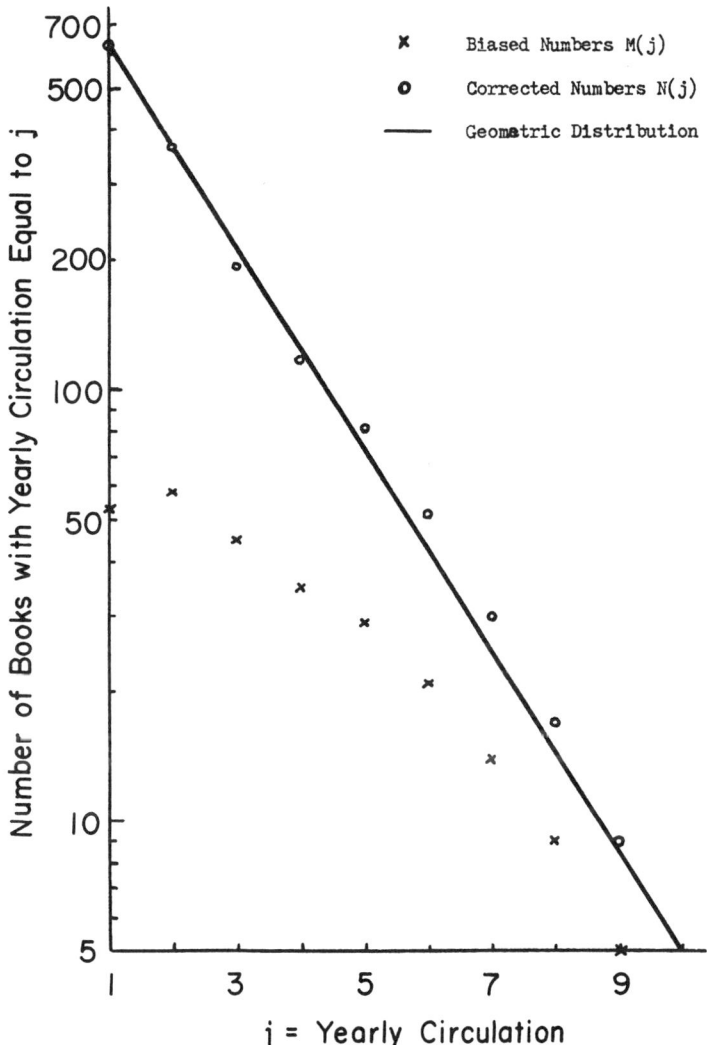

Figure 6.7 Uncorrected and corrected circulation distribution for WM books (data taken from Table 6.7)

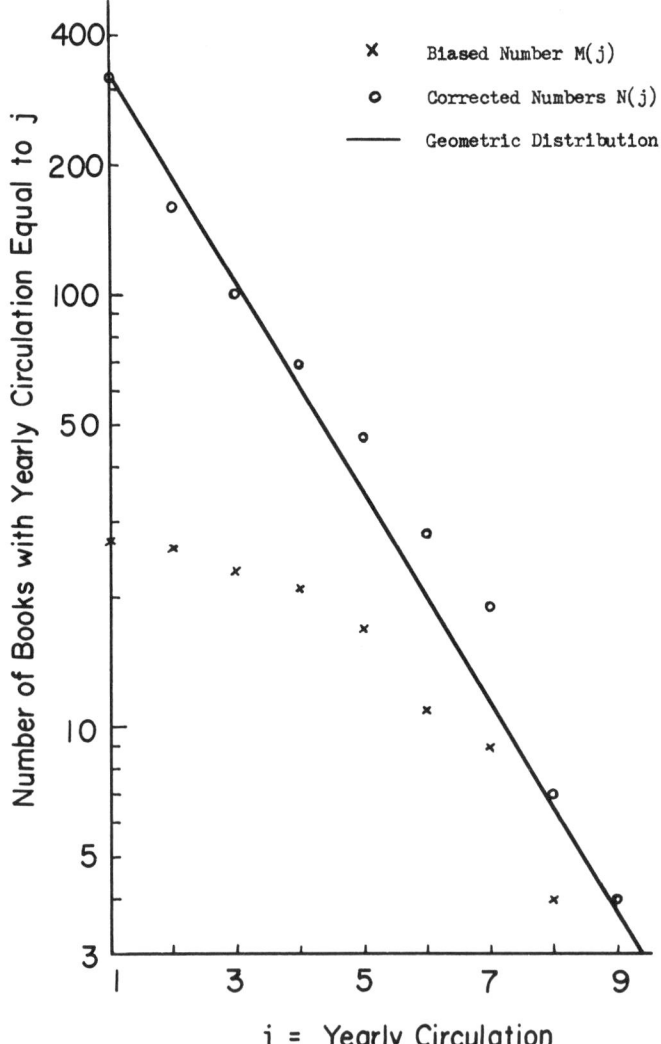

Figure 6.8 Uncorrected and corrected circulation distribution for WS books (data taken from Table 6.8)

Experimental Results and Testing of the Theoretical Models   93

Table 6.9 A Summary of Equations Used to Measure the Total Yearly Circulation and to Predict the Future Use

$N(j) = M(j)/[1 - (1-\rho)^j]$; $N_a = \sum_j N(j)$; $\gamma = 1 - (N_1/N_a)$;

$N_\ell(j) = N(j)/(1 - e^{-j})$; $N_\ell = \sum_j N_\ell(j)$; $C = N_a/N_\ell$;

$\overline{R}_a = 1/1 - \gamma$; $\overline{R}_\ell = C \times \overline{R}_a$; $\alpha_\ell = C \times \alpha_a$;

$\overline{R}_\ell(1) = \alpha_\ell + \beta \overline{R}_\ell(0)$; $C(1) = 1 - e^{-\alpha_\ell}\left[1 - \dfrac{C(0)}{1+J}\right]$

where $J = (1-\gamma)/(e^\beta - 1)$.

Table 6.10 Predicted Following-Year Circulation for the Same QZ Books Circulated in 1972-1973

QZ CLASS
$N \approx 925; N_\ell \approx 684$

$t = 0$ (1972-1973)	$t = 1$ (1973-1974)
$\alpha_a = 0.931$	
$\alpha_\ell = 0.681$	$\alpha_\ell = 0.681$
$\beta = 0.443$	$\beta = 0.443$
$\gamma(0) = 0.449$	$\gamma(1) = 0.464$
$N_a(0) \sim 501$	$N_a(1) \approx 465$
$\overline{R}_a(0) = 1.815$	$\overline{R}_a(1) = 1.867$
$C(0) = 0.732$	$C(1) = 0.680$
$\overline{R}_\ell(0) = 1.329$	$\overline{R}_\ell(1) = 1.270$
$\overline{R}_a(0)N_a(0) = \overline{R}_\ell(0)N_\ell$	$\overline{R}_a(1)N_a(1) = \overline{R}_\ell(1)N_\ell$
≈ 909	≈ 868

Table 6.11 Predicted Following-Year Circulation for the Same WM and WS Books Circulated in 1972-1973

WM Class

$N \approx 2{,}160;\ N_\ell \approx 1{,}941$

$t = 0$ (1972-1973)	$t = 1$ (1973-1974)
$\alpha_a = 1.476$	
$\alpha_\ell = 1.144$	$\alpha_\ell = 1.144$
$\beta = 0.357$	$\beta = 0.357$
$\gamma(0) = 0.581$	$\gamma(1) = 0.553$
$N_a(0) \approx 1{,}504$	$N_a(1) \approx 1{,}564$
$\overline{R}_a(0) = 2.387$	$\overline{R}_a(1) = 2.239$
$C(0) = 0.775$	$C(1) = 0.806$
$\overline{R}_\ell(0) = 1.850$	$\overline{R}_\ell(1) = 1.804$
$\overline{R}_a(0)N_a(0) = \overline{R}_\ell(0)N_\ell$	$\overline{R}_a(1)N_a(1) = \overline{R}_\ell(1)N_\ell$
$\approx 3{,}590$	$\approx 3{,}502$

Table 6.12 Comparison of the Estimated Total Yearly Circulation ($\overline{R}_a N_a$ or $\overline{R}_\ell N_\ell$) with Actual Circulation Data

Classes	QU	QZ	WA	WG	WM	WO	WS
Actual Circulation in Four Sample Months*	463	318	387	404	1,158	224	603
Estimated Yearly Circulation Based on Circulation Data†	1,389	954	1,161	1,212	3,474	672	1,809
Estimated Yearly Circulation Obtained by $\overline{R}_a N_a$ or $\overline{R}_\ell N_\ell$ ‡	1,490	909	1,100	1,185	3,590	754	1,800

*Figures taken from Table A1.1 of Appendix 1.
†Calculated by multiplying the actual circulation in four sample months by a factor of 3.
‡Figures taken from Tables 6.10-6.11 and Tables A6.5-A6.6.

Experimental Results and Testing of the Theoretical Models   95

WS Class $N \approx 1{,}050; N_\ell \approx 981$	
$t = 0$ (1972-1973)	$t = 1$ (1973-1974)
$\alpha_a = 1.560$	
$\alpha_\ell = 1.209$	$\alpha_\ell = 1.209$
$\beta = 0.380$	$\beta = 0.380$
$\gamma(0) = 0.578$	$\gamma(1) = 0.569$
$N_a(0) \approx 760$	$N_a(1) \approx 806$
$\overline{R}_a(0) = 2.368$	$\overline{R}_a(1) = 2.319$
$C(0) = 0.775$	$C(1) = 0.822$
$\overline{R}_\ell(0) = 1.835$	$\overline{R}_\ell(1) = 1.906$
$\overline{R}_a(0)N_a(0) = \overline{R}_\ell(0)N_\ell$	$\overline{R}_a(1)N_a(1) = \overline{R}_\ell(1)N_\ell$
$\approx 1{,}800$	$\approx 1{,}870$

Part Three
Interpretation of the Results

Chapter Seven

Budgetary Considerations

In this chapter a brief discussion will focus on how operations research studies in general and the Countway study in particular can provide valuable information for library administrators in making their budgetary requests and in establishing priorities for budgetary allocation. Specific references will be made to the Countway results in the later part of the chapter; therefore the discussions will emphasize book budgetary allocation since this study is of the book use at Countway.

The importance of scientific management in libraries was stressed in Chapter 1; therefore a budgetary system that is grounded in systems analysis is assumed here to be superior to other systems. Both the library literature and other professional publications offer a multitude of discussions and views on budgetary systems. The books by both Novick (1967) and Hartley (1968) are specifically recommended to librarians for their complete overall background discussions on various budgetary systems. Hartley's book stresses particularly the Planning Programming Budgetary System (PPBS), which has assumed more and more importance since the early 1960s, and its applications in the educational environment. The more recent articles by Summers (1971) and Bromberg (1972) provide excellent and brief summaries of the PPBS system and offer timely discussions on the application of this system in libraries.

Although there are numerous budgeting systems designed for a diverse audience of people in almost all kinds of organizations, at the present, the most commonly used systems in libraries are the traditional line-item budget system and the PPBS. It should be noted, though, that most budget systems in actual practice are hybrids rather than pure strains. The line-item budget, which is often called object of expenditure budget, is designed to include all of the items and services for which expenditures are to be made. It focuses on categories such as maintenance, supplies, personnel, and equipment. It is control- and input-oriented because it rests upon the assumption that if control is exercised over the input of resources, the activities of the organization can be controlled. The advantages of this system, as pointed out by Summers (1971), are that it is relatively easy to prepare, to understand, and most important, to account for. Yet because of these very advantages, it does not provide accountability for the performance and output of an organization and an opportunity to review and evaluate library effectiveness.

On the other hand, the PPBS, developed as a product of modern informational and decisional technologies, is totally different from the line-item budget. To summarize a quantity of available literature on this system, such as Hartley (1968), Novick (1967), Summers (1971), and Churchman (1968), PPBS is a methodology that requires specification of goals and stated objectives, delineates priorities among multiple alternatives, focuses on evaluation of output, and emphasizes long-range planning. The system thus involves systems analysis, program structure, multiyear planning, cost-effectiveness analysis, budgeting, and evaluation (Hartley, 1968). In order to do this, it provides for the application of a battery of new techniques, including the mathematical analytical techniques so widely used for operations research studies. These techniques could be used to quantify output and benefits—in effect, to quantify an organization's objectives and to provide a more rational decision-making basis for the efficient allocation of scarce resources among competing programs.

A library is a public system and a service organization. The traditional goals and objectives of libraries have been relatively unchallenged, and the library existence has generally been taken for granted. Few librarians, prior to the last decade, had to justify their budget by evaluating their library effectiveness, and even today most librarians still rely on the "best professional opinion" and "practices in successful libraries" for their planning and decisions. A systems approach to libraries is not a new concept. As early as 1933, Butler advocated:

"Librarianship, in particular, will become scientific only as it conforms in essentials to the habitual methods of thought in the modern temper. Every line in its intellectual synthesis must start from objective phenomena. . . . Every possible device will be utilized for the isolation of activities and their quantitative measurements."[1]

However, this kind of concept has been received by librarians with enthusiasm only since the last decade. The change of attitude on the part of librarians was prompted by the impact of a tightening economy. It has been shown that library expenses rose consistently by over 10 percent a year during the period 1949 to 1969 (Winkler, 1973). Library budgets have been either stabilized or cut in most cases. Many librarians who took for granted in the past an alloca-

---

[1] Pierce Butler, *An Introduction to Library Science* (Chicago: University of Chicago Press, 1933), 25-26.

tion of their annual budgets with percentage increases have experienced and witnessed dramatic cuts and decreases of their annual expenditures. As a matter of fact, due to the unaccountability of library output, effectiveness, and performance, many libraries are among the first of many competing programs in an organization to face budget cuts. Thus, especially in the last couple of years, budgeting and fiscal control have received much attention. More information is available in journals, such as the *ARL Management Supplement* (1973), which devote themselves to the subject of budgeting methods, and more seminars, workshops, and institutes on this topic are being offered by library schools and professional organizations.

Few libraries generally have the freedom to select unilaterally their own budget systems, because they are usually part of an organization and therefore the library's budget becomes a portion of the executive budget. However, many librarians who do have to prepare their budgets by using the PPBS system dislike this method. Many of them find it difficult to define the library objectives and goals and to quantify the library work and services because library output is not material (Etzioni, 1964).

But experience has taught us that librarians, in order to present well-grounded budgetary requests and to compete with other programs for limited resources, can no longer present arguments based on their own or their colleagues' judgment and experience. They need hard and cold facts and measurements, knowledge of the effectiveness of their collections, services, and activities, and predicted knowledge of future library use and demand. Many questions about their library, their users, and their own role in the total process of informational transfer need to be asked, and critical answers to these questions, together with quantifiable measurements, need to be obtained. This kind of evaluation, as a matter of quality control, is a continuing process (Herner, 1967).

In light of this discussion, it is hoped that this Countway study can demonstrate to librarians that there are ways to quantify and measure library effectiveness, and that a better rational basis, formed by the knowledge of present library use and careful estimates of future use rather than the librarians' own judgment and experience, can be utilized for budgetary requests and allocation. In fact, administrative decisions regarding all aspects of library planning and operation can be wisely reached with the availability of useful results such as those described in this study.

Although, as stated, this study was undertaken mainly to test further Morse's probabilistic models on book use, it has covered a

lot of ground. Many questions, such as the few examples following, related to the Countway book collection and its use behavior have been posed, and answers to them, whether complete or partial, are scattered throughout this study and can be located easily:
1. Who uses the Countway Library books?
2. How are the Countway Library books used?
3. Are the user needs satisfied?
4. Books of what subject areas are most active?
5. Are there any obsolete or potentially useless materials? If so, what is the fraction?
6. What Countway books are most frequently circulated?
7. What is the expected mean circulation of Countway books?
These valid operating data on book use can strengthen the library's position and fortify the librarian's arguments for continued support. They can also affect the librarian's ability to plan and allocate resources effectively and to assign appropriate priorities to the planning of collection building and of service programs. Similar arguments were presented recently in a report of a study of the Columbia University Libraries (Mount, 1972).

In the following part of this chapter, actual results of this Countway study will be used to illustrate their implications for budgetary considerations given by library administrators.

We shall begin with a discussion of the users of the Countway library books. Table A4.1 identifies the user groups clearly. From the table, circulation distributions among user groups are shown. These types of demographic information are obviously essential to library administrators when seeking both internal and external financial support.

We have already shown in Chapter 6 that the circulation distribution of Countway books is geometric. Another way of stating the geometric distribution is that the Countway book use obeys Bradford's law (Bradford, 1948). This will be elaborated on later. As for users of the library books, the minimal nucleus of users can be established, as shown in Tables 7.1 and 7.2 (see Goffman and Morris, 1970, for much more detailed discussions). The data presented in these two tables were taken from the user master file, which included only data from the January 1973 sample month. They both show that in that month, 1,412 Countway users returned 3,074 books. The minimal nucleus of 35 users accounted for the use of 384 books, and about half of the 3,074 books were returned by 300 of the 1,412 users. The successive zones of users returning about the same number of books formed the geometric

Budgetary Considerations 103

Table 7.1 Distribution of Countway Users in January 1973

No. of Users														
2	1	1	2	3	5	4	10	10	16	30	51	85	150	287	755

No. of Books Returned per User														
24	16	15	14	12	11	10	9	8	7	6	5	4	3	2	1

Total Number of Users	1,412
Total Number of Books Returned	3,074*

*This is the sum of (no. of users) × (no. of books returned per user). Therefore, $3{,}074 = (2 \times 24) + (1 \times 16) + (1 \times 15) + \ldots + (150 \times 3) + (287 \times 2) + (755 \times 1)$. In using this for Table 7.2, the total is divided by the number of zones to obtain the approximate size of books included in each zone.

series $1 : (1.44) : (1.44)^2 \ldots : (1.44)^7$. This minimal nucleus of users could then be identified by using Table A4.1 in Appendix 4. Areas of interest could be identified for the heavy users (in the first few zones), and acquisition policy could be established to allot an appropriate book budget for books in subjects of most interest to the library's nucleus of users (Goffman and Morris, 1970) in order to satisfy the needs of the active library-users.

Chapter 4 has already noted the Countway Library's difficult financial situation since 1969. Several economic measures have been taken by the library. These include the limitation of Countway's book and journal acquisition activities, the shortening of the Countway Library hours, and others. Although the impact of these measures on users is difficult to measure, certain indications of users' inconveniences do appear. As shown in Fig. 5.2, since 1969 the circulation activities have stabilized and are not increasing at the same rate as those of the previous years. In fact, since 1972 the circulation volume has dropped for some months in comparison with that of the corresponding month of the previous year. Since circulation is a good index of library activities, it seems safe to speculate that some of the library activities, other than the recorded book use, have also begun to drop. The Countway staff has confirmed that the number of annual registered users has been approximately the same as those of the previous year. Thus one of the contributing factors to the leveling off of book-circulation activities has to be that the library collection is becoming less adequate and effective to meet the user needs.

Table A1.7 in Appendix 1 shows the weekly circulation volume at Countway during the four sample months. The data of that table together with library attendance data could enable library administrators to plan the staffing of their service departments throughout the year. The table seems to show that the circulation volume during the day is proportional to the number of library hours. The mean volume of circulation prorated for fifteen and a half library hours per day for each day of the week is almost identical. The table further shows that the shortening of library hours on Friday seems to have some immediate impact on the users. The average number of returned books after April 22, 1973 (library closing at 5:00 P.M. instead of 11:00 P.M.), dropped to slightly more than half of the earlier volume. All this useful information should have implications for future budgetary planning.

As for the book budget allocation in a library and its book-selection policy, the results of the Countway study will serve to illustrate several important points. Ideally, a library should have a balanced collection, and books should be acquired because of their intrinsic value rather than their potential use and demand. Obviously, at this time, few libraries have this luxury. When a library's book budget is so limited, as in the case of Countway in the last few years, that its book-selection activities have to be limited to the acquisition of only course reserves, a small number of required items by its users, and a few core materials, then a much more practical and limited book-selection policy has to be established for the judicious expenditure of the scarce book budget. The collection objective is mainly, then, to obtain and to maintain an

Table 7.2 Minimal Nucleus of Countway Users

Zone*	No. of Books Returned	No. of Users	Bradford Constant
1	384	35	—
2	381	62	1.77
3	386	87	1.40
4	384	116	1.33
5	386	158	1.36
6	386	193	1.22
7	384	378	1.96
8	383	383	1.01
	3,074	1,412	1.44

*Here the number of books returned is divided into 8 zones. Thus the approximate number of books in each zone is 3,074/8 = 384. The first zone includes those books returned from the most active users, that is, the first 384 books calculated from the leftmost columns of Table 7.1.

optimum collection with the least cost but highest effectiveness to meet the ever-increasing user informational needs. This is why the models presented in Chapter 3 on analyzing the inactive and active books should be equally applicable, under a stringent financial situation, to all types of libraries despite the inherent differences between a science library collection and a humanities or social sciences library collection, as raised in Bookstein's study (1975), which comments on the Morse-Chen model.

Numerous publications can be found on the topics of determining and allocating book funds (Ramer, 1966; McGrath, 1967; Massman, 1970; Schad, 1970; Tudor, 1972). They may be different in methods and formulas used, but they all seem to agree that actual user needs are the best criterion to use in determining and allocating book funds for current acquisitions.

The user needs can best be identified from their library-use patterns. This study shows that although analyzed results on the past and present book-use behavior are as useful as those presented in the appendixes of my thesis, the real value lies in the prediction of anticipated use behavior in the future years. Knowledge of this kind of prediction can be obtained by using the operations research techniques to analyze the past book-use data as shown in Chapter 6. Few publications can be found to be exclusively devoted to the use of these analytical techniques for optimum budget allocation; however, the subject was touched on in Goyal's article (1972). In the following, we shall use the results of this study to demonstrate how operations research techniques can be used to establish a new rational basis for the control and optimization of complex library activities in accordance with the overall objectives of a large organization (Leimkuhler, 1968).

It was shown earlier that it is possible to identify the minimal nucleus of Countway Library users. The minimal nucleus of subject classes of books used by these readers can also be identified, as is seen in Table A1.1. For example, of more than fifty different NLM classes of books available in Countway, WM books accounted for 9.93 percent of the total use, and more than one-fifth of the total was accounted for by WM, WL, and WS books. Requests for books in circulation and renewals by users are both indications of more serious need for library materials. Tables A1.6 and A2.1 both seem to identify similar high-use classes as those in Table A1.1. Subject classes of books used rarely by library users can also be located with little effort.

For each class of books, more precise and useful operating data, such as the mean circulation rate of active and live books ($\overline{R}_a$ and $\overline{R}_\ell$), the fraction of active and dead books, and those for both this year and the following years can be estimated and predicted as shown in Chapter 6. Obviously, the greater part of the book budget should be allocated for subject classes that are expected to have the higher average circulations.

Furthermore, information on how fast books of a given subject area lose their popularity and how fast books will go out of date is also essential for book budget considerations. This is measured by the Markov parameters α and β, as discussed in Parts I and II. The asymptotic value of circulation of the class of books is measured by $\alpha/(1-\beta)$. For example, the expected average circulation to which WM live books will eventually subside, $\alpha_\ell/(1-\beta)$, is 1.78, and the $\alpha_\ell/(1-\beta)$ for WS books is 1.95 (values of α and β are shown in Table 6.11. These values are not far from the mean circulation of WM and WS live books for the sample year, $\overline{R}_\ell(0)$, and the following year, $\overline{R}_\ell(1)$. This means that the same group of WM and WS books will continue to be useful for some time, and even in steady state, they will still circulate about twice per year. On the other hand, for WA books, in the first place, there are a large number of potentially low use materials, $N_d = N - N_\ell = 858$ (more than 50 percent of the present WA collection). A check of the stack reveals that these are mostly government publications. But even the potentially useful books, (N_ℓ), have an $\alpha_\ell/(1-\beta)$ of 1.17, which is about half of that of WS books. Thus the results of our study suggest that a higher portion of book funds be allocated for books of classes such as WM and WS than for books of classes such as WA.

Yet book budget items should not be allocated by traditional subject or academic divisions. I (Chen, 1973) find that the nature of research interests in the last decade has become more and more interdisciplinary, requiring a reorientation in thinking in terms of the librarians' role in the total process of informational transfer. Similarly, identifications of high-use subject areas are not sufficient. The connectivity among these subject areas and those lower-use ones needs to be established (see Appendix 3) as a network of subject fields. An appropriate book budget should be allocated for a package of books in the related subject classes. This is necessary because some book titles of the lower-use classes may possibly be among the highest-use titles. Thus it is also important to obtain the minimal nucleus of book titles. Table A1.4 shows

Budgetary Considerations   107

Table 7.3 Distribution of Countway Book Circulation in 1973

Number of Books	Number of Circulations per Book
1	12
2	10
4	9
1	8
5	7
15	6
27	5
108	4
388	3
1,604	2
6,516	1
Total 8,671	11,656 (Total Circulation)*

*See footnote to Table 7.2.

the subject distribution of books circulated in Countway during the four sample months. More detailed information was obtained from the master data file of this study, and Tables 7.3 and 7.4 show that the Countway book circulation also obeys Bradford's law. The minimal nucleus of Countway books consisted of 392 book titles, which accounted for about one-eighth of the total circulation, and only 2,842 of the 8,671 titles accounted for about half of the total use. The successive zones of book titles formed the geometric series $1 : (1.23) \ldots : (1.23)^7$. Appendix 7 provides a list of the most circulated (four or more times) books in the Countway Library during the sampling months. Obviously, all these titles are included in the minimal nucleus of Zone 1. From Table 7.4, it is clear that all Countway books with two or more circulations fall in Zones 1 to 4.

Finally, a certain portion of the annual library book fund should be made available either for duplicate copies of older material or for a few useful older titles that happened to be missed at the time of publication or for both. Table A1.2 gives a circulation distribution of Countway books by publication dates, and Table 7.5 compares the results of this study with those of the earlier studies by Kilgour (1961) and Raisig et al. (1966). The Countway results seem to suggest that the Countway books have a half-life of five to six years. This agrees with Kilgour's 1961 study but differs from the 1966 study by Raisig et al. In this study, the relatively low use of books published since 1970 could be due to the sharp decrease in the library's new acquisitions since 1970. An attempt was made to prorate the estimated annual circulation in the Countway Library as if the annual book titles added to the collection were about 3,500 volumes, the same as those of the earlier years (see Column 5 of Table 7.5). In either case, those Countway books published in the last ten years accounted for about 70 percent of the total circulation. About one-third of the total was accounted for by those books which are about six to ten years old. This is rather expected because of the high values of $[\alpha/(1-\beta)]$'s as described earlier. Since library resources are limited, decisions to acquire additional copies of either older or newer materials should not be made hastily. Librarians should find lists such as that of Appendix 7 helpful in identifying high-circulation titles. Further information on how to make a decision for acquiring a duplicate copy of a book title will be given in the following chapter.

As stated earlier, because of the tight economy, there is a growing demand for a budgeting system that requires increased measures of accountability of activities and performances. A study such as this one can be very useful to library administrators in their processes of decision-making and budget-planning. It has been shown that book-use data, when analyzed with operations research techniques, can provide a measure of user needs and satisfaction and, to some degree, the availability of a sought item, the comprehensiveness of a collection (Kraft and Hill, 1973), and the

Table 7.4 Minimal Nucleus of Countway Books

Zone*	Number of Circulations	Number of Books	Bradford Constant
1	1,455	392	—
2	1,457	649	1.66
3	1,458	729	1.12
4	1,457	1,072	1.47
5	1,457	1,457	1.36
6	1,457	1,457	1.00
7	1,457	1,457	1.00
8	1,458	1,458	1.00
	11,656	8,671	Average 1.23

*See footnote to Table 7.2.

Budgetary Considerations

Table 7.5 Comparison of the Countway Circulation Distribution Data by Date of Publication with Two Earlier Studies

Chen's Countway Study (1973)					Kilgour's (1961)		Raisig et al. (1966)		
Date	No. of Cir.	% of Total Cir.	No. of Cir.	% of Total Cir.	Date	%	Date	%	
1973	365	(Partial)*			1960		1964 (Partial)		
1972	1,561	6.7	3,120†	11.6	1959	38.0	1963	17.9	
1971	1,467	6.3	2,450†	9.1	1958		1962	16.1	
1970	1,608	6.9 ⎫ 35.9	2,410†	9.0 ⎫ 43.5	1957		1961	9.4 ⎫ 57.8	
1969	1,898	8.2		7.1	1956		1960	9.7	
1968	1,812	7.8		6.7	1955	24.0	1959	4.7	
1967	1,803	7.8		6.7	1954		1958	6.1	
1966	1,729	7.5		6.4	1953		1957	3.9	
1965	1,606	6.9 ⎫ 33.3		6.0 ⎫ 28.7	1952		1956	4.2 ⎫ 21.4	
1964	1,413	6.1		5.3	1951	15.0	1955	3.1	
1963	1,158	5.0		4.3	1950		1954	4.1	
		69.2		72.2	1949	77.0		79.2	

*The Countway data shown in this table are taken from Table A1.2. Only incomplete data on the use of 1973 books are available.
†Prorated by using Table 4.5 as if the annual book titles for the years 1970 to 1972 were approximately 3,500, the same as those of the earlier years.

operational efficiency (Burns, 1971). These measurements can then be used by library administrators to make better and wiser decisions on allocating the limited library resources to build a book collection with "maximum economies" and "minimum sacrifices in quality" (Carnegie Commission, 1972).

Chapter Eight
Book Selection and Duplication Policy

It should be pointed out that library budgetary considerations, book-selection and weeding policies, and decisions on multicopy acquisitions are interrelated. Thus many arguments presented in Chapter 7 as well as in Chapters 9 and 10 are pertinent here. In Chapter 7, which focuses on the allocation of a library book budget, much has already been said about the selection of single copies of new library materials. Therefore, to avoid repetition, this chapter will emphasize the selection policy on duplicate copies, particularly in an academic environment.

Book Selection Policy

Many useful publications (Carter and Bonk, 1969; Danton, 1963; Gaver, 1969; Spiller, 1971; Broadus, 1973) can be used to provide background reading on the developments, processes, policies, and procedures of academic book selection. Therefore discussions in these areas will be brief. In this chapter we shall not discuss tools and methodologies used for book selection, such as the use of core lists (Stearns and Radcliff, 1970), book reviews (Chen, 1974), and citation studies (Broadus, 1973), nor shall we concern ourselves with the mechanics of the selection programs, such as blanket order and approval order plans (Danton, 1967; Morrison, 1968; Dobbyn, 1972; Meyer, 1970; Rouse, 1970).

Library "book selection" is actually a rather new phenomenon. In the last century and well into the 1900s, book selection in university libraries was monopolized by members of the faculty. Librarians were considered more as "keepers of the books," assuming a passive role in collection building and development. However, the concept was introduced as far back as 1897, when Alfred C. Potter, the Order Librarian for the Harvard College Library, advocated that a librarian should be "alive to his responsibilities" in book selection (1897). It was not until the late 1960s, however, that emphasis was placed on librarian-oriented book selection (Kosa, 1972; Lane, 1968). The studies of Haro (1967) and Lyle (1970) found that librarians were becoming increasingly involved in this activity. This development, though advocated mostly by librarians (Brenni, 1967; Schad, 1969), has been also supported by faculty members (Burdick, 1964). The factors contributing to this trend are many, such as the growth of higher education, the changing behavior of faculty teaching and research, and the growth of subject literature. It should be kept in mind that, although faculty members are playing a less important role in book selection, most librarians seem to agree that faculty cooperation is essential and valuable for collection development (Carter and Bonk, 1969; Goldhor, 1963, Jenks, 1972). One of the most important reasons is that they provide librarians with helpful input on the research trends and interests of their potential users, and help to keep librarians abreast of the new developments in each subject area.

Many have stated that "the collection is the raison d'être of a library" (Kraft, 1967). Librarians should make every effort to select materials and provide a collection that can best fulfill both the current and future needs of their users. In order to achieve this, selection should be a careful and ongoing activity. It should not be based on intuition and chance but should be a planned selection (Ettlinger, 1968). However, it is unfortunate that while most librarians realize the importance of book selection, there has been little agreement on methods and procedures, as found by Haro (1967). Few libraries have selection policies, and book selection has been haphazard in most libraries.

A library needs to define its goals and objectives clearly. Collection objectives should be outlined and evaluated constantly. Librarians should first decide whether they need a comprehensive research collection or an efficient working one. At this time, in most financially pressed libraries, "comprehensiveness" has given way to "selectivity" (Kraft, 1967). Most libraries are found to have very limited resources—staff, space, funds, and time (Burns, 1971). On the other hand, the volume of available literature is growing at a steady rate (Rider, 1944; de Solla Price, 1965; Danton, 1963). The Committee on Scientific and Technical Communication of the National Academy of Sciences (SATCOM) reported in 1969 that the most obvious problem faced by libraries today is that of the "sheer size" of literature (SATCOM, 1969). The rising price of books and journals will in turn contribute to the continued escalation of expenses (Winkler, 1973); the Council of Library Resources reported in 1972 that book expenditures rose by 11.4 percent annually. The cost involved in the processing, organizing, and maintenance of a collection will also continue to rise. The CLR's report indicated that outlays for wages and salaries increased at a rate of 9.7 percent a year; therefore a rising relative cost per unit of service is an unavoidable consequence. Furthermore, the space used to house the book collection is not only costly but also scarce. Most libraries are overcrowded. To fill up the prime shelf space with potentially low-use, superfluous, and irrelevant materials increases user frustration and wastes library staff time and effort to maintain the collection. Thus many librarians are forced to be selective in building their collections. They have explored other avenues to obtain less-needed information, such as interlibrary loan and the cooperative acquisition at the Ohio College Library Center (Kilgour, 1973).

Particularly in view of the limited library budget, libraries should employ "user needs" as criteria for book selection, as stated in Chapter 7. This has also been stressed by many administrators and educators (Brenni, 1967; Goyal, 1972). Even in 1957, R. L. Ackoff advocated the need for a decision model to identify "what information is required and hence what information is relevant." The SATCOM report stated that the first guiding principle is that "the scientific and technical communication activities must be as responsive as possible to the needs, desires, and innovative ideas of the scientific and technical groups that they serve" (1969). Although a book collection developed in relation to library use may tend to be unbalanced, it is considered to be more important to use the limited book fund judiciously to acquire a basic collection that can effectively meet a high percentage of the user needs (Trueswell, 1969). Thus the user frustration and dissatisfaction can be kept at a minimum.

Table 5.1 shows that the estimated size of the Countway book collection is approximately 150,000 volumes, of which about one-third are of NLM books and two-thirds BML older books. Since the total number of book titles is unknown, Table 4.5 is the best possible approximation. It was estimated that during the period of 1960-1973, the Countway Library added about 37,000 NLM book titles, or 45,000 volumes. Table A1.4 shows that the estimated number of books circulated in the sample year is 23,166 titles, of which 21,604 are NLM books. Thus approximately 60 percent of the Countway NLM books were actually used. This fraction of total NLM active books is quite high. But if we combined all the NLM and BML books, then only about 20 percent of the total collection would be active. This figure is quite close to Trueswell's findings (1965) that approximately 25 percent of the current holdings of a technical library should satisfy over 99 percent of the current circulation requirements. F. F. Leimkuhler also indicated that 15 to 20 percent of the collection has the greatest likelihood of yielding the target information (1968). The reason for this high percentage of active NLM books could possibly be the effective separation of high- and low-use materials and the highly critical and selective acquisition of a small number of books in the last few years.

My study, like many other use studies (Jain, 1966; Synder, 1965), found that, among Harvard community members, students certainly use the library much more frequently than faculty, researchers, and staff. This suggests that librarians, in setting up selection policies and planning for future collections, should be concerned with both the current and long-range teaching directions and emphasis (Richter, 1970). They should also cooperate with faculty on curriculum development. Furthermore, recent radical changes in the educational climate of this country, which encourage opportunities for students' independent study and research, should add another critical dimension to the librarians' role in book selection. Librarians ought to be up to date on current issues and problems and social concerns.

Table A4.1 also indicates that among the three schools served by Countway, members of the Medical School are by far the most active book users, while those of the Dental School are the most inactive ones. Further research seems to be necessary to find out whether this pattern persists, and if so, why?

We have discussed in Chapter 7 how heavy-use subject classes could easily be identified. Interesting interpretations can be made when we compare these data (Table A1.1, etc.) with the connectivity data shown in Appendix 3. For example, WM (Psychiatry) has been identified as the most active class in Countway. Table A3.1 shows that WM books were borrowed most frequently by the same users, together with books of the following classes: in descending order, WL (nervous system), W (medical profession), BF (psychology), WS (Pediatrics), and WA (public health). All these classes are among those of the ten most highly circulated classes, as indicated in Table A1.1. A further check of the list of most frequently circulated books at Countway (Appendix 7) reveals that these classes also generate a rather large number of high-circulation books. A real interest in information related to general health care and society, community and public health, medical-care practices, problems and programs, and so forth, is clearly shown. This is a good reflection of the medical era we are in. Daniel H. Funkenstein (1973), in his excellent summary on the medical developments since Flexner, stated that since 1970, the new medical era, called "the community era," has begun. It is the result of many forces: concern for community, demands by students, delivery of patient care, demands by the community, government-financed health-care medical programs, and changing emphasis from research to health care. Thus we find among today's medical students high interest in human behavior and in working with people, inspiration for practice in the community, and increased concern for the emotional, social, and family aspects of care. In view of this discussion, it seems necessary that librarians provide greater book-budget allocations for materials to meet these types of interests.

This does not mean that clinical and research-oriented materials are not demanded. Materials in classes such as WL (nervous system), WG (cardiovascular system), WE (musculoskeletal system), QU (biochemistry), QZ (pathology), and QW (immunology) are used quite actively, as shown in Tables A1.1 and A1.4. These areas seem to correlate quite well with those research areas where strong federal support has been provided. It was reported recently ("New Federal Budget...," 1974) that in 1974 the area of medical research receiving the highest federal support is cancer, other areas being, in descending order, cardiovascular disease, environmental mental health, infectious diseases, and so on.

Furthermore, there is a trend toward more specialized and interdisciplinary research and study (Chen, 1973). Levit (1974) concludes in his recent study of samples of 1960 and 1964 graduates of medical schools in the United States that the motivation for graduate education and specialty training is overwhelming. This interest seems to be reflected in the kind of books selected by Countway users. A careful observation of the list of the 163 most active books in 1973 (Appendix 7) reveals that except for a few titles on general medical care, practice, and community medicine, all the other most demanded books are generally more specialized materials.

Thus we can conclude that, in addition to the useful data obtained with modern mathematical and analytical techniques, librarians need to be flexible and to adapt rapidly to changes in user needs and requirements, in close touch with modern trends in research and professional practices, and concerned with current issues and problems. Only in this way can they develop selectively and critically an optimum collection tailored to their users' needs and requirements. The sample principle should apply well to other types of libraries.

Duplication Policy

One of the questions frequently confronting all librarians is: How many copies of a high-demand book should be acquired? There are many answers to this question, but none of them seems to be satisfactory. In most cases, librarians have dealt with this problem intuitively, with a personal approach (Franklin, 1966). Some suggest the acquisition of paperbacks of the same books as an economical method to meet patron demand (Moreland, 1968), some rely on faculty members' recommendations, while others try to make decisions based on the number of circulation reserves or requests accumulated.

But "a decision based on intuition is seldom right, and it usually happens that more copies of a book are ordered than are required" (Goyal, 1972). While faculty members' input is extremely helpful, their estimates of student's requirements tend to be exaggerated. Reserve requests placed on a book in circulation are indications of current demand, but they offer no prediction of future needs. In other words, some books may attract a great deal of reader interest shortly after publication but may lose popularity soon after that. To make decisions based on current demand would thus create an overordering of books.

Underutilized duplicate acquisition is a waste of limited library resources. It requires both money and staff time to acquire, organize, process, and maintain, occupies the scarce and valuable prime library space, and, finally, creates inconvenience to library users by crowding the library shelves with low-use materials. At a time when libraries are facing a great financial crisis, in terms of cost-benefit, overordering is a mistake no library can afford to make.

The real difficulty in formulating duplicate policy involves determining user needs, both current and future, balancing the financial and spatial considerations with potential use, and ensuring that the expenditure involved will satisfy more user demand than another new acquisition.

Several studies (Goyal, 1972; Trueswell, 1965; Buckland and Hindle, 1969; Buckland and Woodburn, 1968; Buckland, 1972; Grant, 1974; and Buckland, 1975) have demonstrated that operations research and other analytical techniques can be applied to help librarians find the answers. Among them, shortening of the loan period could be one alternative method of increasing the availability of books in libraries (Buckland and Hindle, 1969). Both Trueswell (1965) and Grant (1971) suggest the identification of a small percentage of most frequently used materials for possible acquisition of duplicates. To do this, many factors need to be considered, such as age, popularity, current and future user demand, and circulation interference. For example, this study identifies 163 book titles (0.44 percent of the total NLM books in

Countway), which are listed in Appendix 7, as the most frequently circulated books in Countway. Many of them (51.5 percent approximately) are books more than five years old. Are they still going to be useful for some time? If so, how often will they be used? Many such questions need to be answered before actual duplications should be ordered. We shall use Countway data to answer these questions.

A complete literature search on the analytical approach to the book-duplication problem has revealed that Morse has provided by far the most detailed and authoritative treatment. He proposes the Markov model together with the queuing model for circulation interference to solve this problem (1968, 1972). These models measure both user satisfied and unsatisfied demands, offer guides for decisions on book duplication, measure the effect of reducing the loan period and duplicating some books, and predict future demand. Most of these models can be used to analyze the Countway data, except those which involve the use of λ, demand rate, since in this study, data were not collected to determine the demand rate of various classes of books.

In the following discussion Morse's models will be utilized to provide illustrations of how decisions on multicopy acquisition of a book title can be made with the help of some useful operating data.

In Chapter 3 it was mentioned that the fraction of a year a given class of books is off the shelf is measured by $\overline{R}\mu$. This is also the fracion of time that prospective borrowers would not find it on the shelf if there were no duplicate copy available. The mean fraction of a year that the class of books is off the shelf during one circulation is μ, and in the case of Countway, Appendix 2 shows clearly that the mean loan period is approximately one month; therefore $\mu = 1/12$. As defined earlier, $\overline{R}$ is the mean circulation rate. According to Morse, the circulation factor, $\overline{R}\mu$, begins to be important when it is about $1/3$ and is quite serious by the time it becomes $1/2$ (Morse, 1968). For example, Goodman and Gilman's *Pharmacological Basis of Therapeutics* is listed in Appendix 7. During the four sample months, it circulated eleven times. If the Goodman and Gilman book circulated twenty times during a year, and the average loan period was about two weeks, then $R\mu$ for a single copy of this book would be $20/25 = 0.8$, which means that the circulation interference is very serious. In order to increase the availability of this book to users, it may be decided to purchase an additional copy; thus $R\mu$ would be decreased because of the

Book Selection and Duplication Policy   117

smaller value of R per single copy. Shortening the loan period from two weeks to a specially controlled one-week circulation may also be proposed. In this case, $\mu = 1/52$, and $R\mu = 20/52 = 0.38$. Although the circulation interference is then not as serious as before, the users in this case are actually paying a penalty for not being able to use the book as long and as conveniently as before. The librarians are also required to spend more time and effort to control the circulation of this book. These factors should be weighed against the actual purchase of a duplicate copy.

In order to decide whether it is "worth" having an additional copy of a book, we must be able to predict the circulation of the present single copy next year and for subsequent years. Morse estimated that if a book circulated $R(1)$ during its first year, then its total single-copy circulation during the next ten years in the library was expected to be approximately

$$R_{10} = \frac{10\alpha + \beta R(1)}{1 - \beta} - \frac{\alpha \beta}{(1 - \beta)^2}, \qquad (8.1)$$

where α and β are Markov parameters for the class of books to which the book belongs. The increase in circulation over and above R_{10}, which is produced by having a duplicate copy present from year 2 to 10 is R_i. This increase can be computed by using the following formula:

$$R_i = \mu \left\{ \left(\frac{\alpha}{1-\beta}\right)^2 \left(10 - \frac{1+\beta}{1-\beta}\right) + \left[\frac{\alpha}{1-\beta} + \beta R(1)\right]^2 \left(\frac{1}{1-\beta^2}\right) \right\} \cdot (8.2)$$

To illustrate these formulas (Morse, 1972), Goldman's *Principles of Clinical Electrocardiography* is used as an example, since it is a WG book for which the values of α and β are available.

During the four sample months in 1973, Goldman's book circulated nine times, as shown in Appendix 7. The values of α and β can be obtained from Table 6.4. Supposedly, the first yearly circulation $R(1)$ for Goldman's book is 25, and μ is $1/12$; then, by using Eqs. 8.1 and 8.2, we obtain $R_{10} = 35.2$ and $R_i = 16.0$. This means that an additional copy of Goldman would add about 1.6 additional circulations each year in the following ten years. In other words, a single copy of Goldman's book would have a mean yearly circulation of 3.5 times in the following ten years, while two copies would have about 5. Table A6.6 indicates that the mean circulation for active WG books for the next year, $\overline{R}_a(1)$, is predicted to be 2.054, and the mean circulation for live WG books,

$\overline{R}_\ell(1)$, is 1.565. Thus an additional copy of Goldman's book, though published in 1967, is still as good an investment as an average live WG book.

I have thus demonstrated how book-use data can be analyzed by using probabilistic techniques to help librarians in making judicious decisions on book duplication.

Chapter Nine

Weeding Policy

Today, all libraries are facing the problem of a publication explosion, as has been stated in Chapter 8. It was estimated that the number of books published in the world in 1960 alone was about 240,000 (Cooper, 1968). In the fields of science and technology, the world's journal literature increased roughly sixteen times between 1930 and 1970, doubling in annual output every decade (Knox, 1973), and the number of monographs and handbooks in 1970 was four to five times the number in 1930 (Benjamin, 1968). Libraries are therefore depending upon active weeding programs to combat the serious space problem due to the increased size of library holdings in order to make their collections more relevant and more easily accessible to their users.

To placate librarians who are fastidious about terminology, a brief discussion of various terms used may be helpful. Many librarians consider "weeding" an appropriate word to explain that the old and little-used material should be eliminated in the same manner as weeds in a flower garden (Martin, 1971). Some agree with Katz (1969) and prefer "negative selection" or "reverse selection." Other librarians recommend "retention policy" or "retirement program." Finally, *Library Literature* simply uses the most direct expression: "Discarding of books, periodicals, etc." For the convenience of our discussions in this chapter, "weeding" will be used most frequently, since material may be weeded either for total withdrawal from the collection or for remote storage.

There are various issues and concerns involved in weeding. While such topics are interesting, some are of little relevance to this book. I shall attempt to show which of the following topics are relevant to this study:
1. Whether a library should weed. The stereotyped librarian considers himself or herself the conservator and preserver of published items and considers the book a sacred object never to be destroyed (Allen, 1968; Neufeld, 1968); others disagree, believing that only the most important and most useful items should remain in a library collection (Meier, 1963; Morse, 1968; Shores, 1935; Trueswell, 1965). In this study, it is assumed that weeding is not only a necessary but also a healthy process. It is as important as book selection. It should be a continuous and systematic activity (Carter and Bonk, 1969).
2. Barriers to weeding. Some discussions can be found in library literature on why weeding has not been regularly carried out in libraries, such as fear of criticism (Castagna, 1967), fear of making the mistake of weeding a valuable item (Martin, 1971). In this

study, since weeding is taken for granted as a required library operation, my concern is concentrated on how to help librarians to make as few mistakes as possible in the weeding process.
3. Cost of weeding. Realizing that the cost of weeding differs from one study to another because of the inconclusive factors involved in each study, it is considered in this study that the cost of weeding is not as high as the cost of retention and preservation (Martin, 1971).
4. Weeding criteria. Although there are many weeding criteria used by librarians, such as the elimination of duplicates, superseded editions, and so on (Ash, 1963; Martin, 1971; McGaw, 1956), this study concerns itself only with the use of the past use records.
5. Disposal of materials. This study does not concern itself with the weeded materials, whether by discarding them or by creating both on-campus and off-campus storage facilities (Cooper, 1968; Totten, 1971). It also does not discuss the problem and techniques of remote storage (Cassata, 1971; Cox, 1964; Ellsworth, 1969; Leimkuhler, 1971; Lister, 1967; Raffel, 1965).

How should one formulate a judicious weeding policy? I shall attempt to answer the question in this chapter.

In Appendix 3 browsing and search theory are discussed. In order to maximize the chance of finding a particular wanted book, the number of books in a searched area should not be too large. In fact, when open-shelf subject sections come to contain more than about 5,000 volumes, they begin to be inefficient for browsing (Morse, 1972). In order to increase the users' success rate in finding what they want, to decrease the users' frustration, search time, and effort, and to facilitate the library staff's maintenance effort, the low-use books can be removed from the open shelves and placed in a less accessible place. This will increase convenience and ease of use, which were found by both Wood's (1971) study and Chen's (1974) survey on physicists' information needs to be more important to users than the potential value of the library materials.

For example, in the Countway Library all NLM books acquired and cataloged after 1960 are separated from all BML books acquired prior to 1960. Currently, this is a good arrangement and is convenient to the Countway users. As discussed in Chapter 8, this study finds that 60 percent of NLM books are active ones, while only about 2 percent of the BML books are circulated. Table A1.1 shows that 95.1 percent (11,082 of the total 11,656 circulations) of the total use was accounted for by NLM books. Essentially, the

Countway book collection is divided into two sections that can be called the low-use BML books (about 100,000 volumes) and the high-use NLM books (approximately 50,000 volumes). This division increases the efficiency and use of the recent books.

As noted in Chapter 4, the Harvard Medical Library and the Boston Medical Library merged in 1960. Thus it seems clear that the original intent of separating the NLM and BML books could very well be due more to the difference in classification characteristics than to the usefulness of materials to the users. To divide a collection in 1960 by a cutoff acquisition date of 1960 is just like separating the present Countway collection by a cutoff date of 1975. It can be seen that with the longer half-life of five to six years as discussed in Chapter 8, there were two equally active book collections using two different classification schemes which existed in the Countway Library during the first half of the 1960s, although the NLM collection was very small in size then. For a number of years after the division of acquisitions in 1960, Countway users had to look for needed materials in two separate locations. The inconvenience to users can be clearly imagined. However, as time went on, the NLM collection grew bigger in size and was also updated with new additions yearly, while the BML collection became more and more dated. Thus, at this time, more than a decade after the division was made in 1960, the separation of the high- and low-use books in the Countway Library becomes naturally desirable and effective.

There are several criteria that could be used to weed a library collection, such as gross characteristics, acquisition date, publication date, and circulation-use history. The first two criteria mentioned are the ones used at Countway, though originally the separation of the collection was not meant for weeding purposes. It has been indicated that at the time of division (1960) and during the following five to ten years, to weed materials of a certain gross characteristic from the prime collection was not convenient for the users. It was an artificial separation. Raffel and Shishko (1969) and Fussler and Simon (1961) found that weeding by acquisition date is a more expensive process than that by publication date, and they are all in favor of using "publication date" as a criterion for weeding. In this study, Tables A1.1 and 7.5 indicate quite clearly that to use the publication date to separate a library's high-use and low-use material can be satisfactory only if the cutoff date of publication used was set far enough from the current year. In other words, Countway books published prior to 1960 were found to account for less than 20 percent of the total use. But if the cutoff date was 1965, then almost half of the use would be of books published prior to 1965. Then the separation of library books would be quite unsatisfactory and inefficient for users. Furthermore, Table A7.1 shows that although on the average BML books are by far less active than the NLM books (this is also indicated by the smaller value of α as discussed in Chapter 6), there are books published prior to 1950 that were found to circulate more than four times during the four sample months, as shown in Appendix 7. Thus the book-use data shown in this study support the theory (Fussler and Simon, 1961; Trueswell, 1965; Raffel and Shishko, 1969; Seymour, 1972) that circulation history is generally a far better weeding criterion than publication date in determining whether or not books are meeting the user needs. Circulation data, when properly analyzed by probabilistic technique, will take into account a combination of related factors, such as age, judgment, and circulation history, and predict future use (Leimkuhler and Cooper, 1971). Morse, in his discussions and recommendations on book retirement and weeding, also advocated that to retire the oldest portion of the books that have not circulated in the past year is a more viable action than to retire the oldest portion without considering whether these books have circulated or not. The former action not only reduces the number of inconvenienced borrowers but also considerably reduces, for the first few years, the number of books that might have to be resurrected (Morse, 1968 and 1972). This point will be elaborated on later by actually using the Countway data.

Trueswell (1965) stated that a weeding decision based on recorded circulation data when properly analyzed can improve library service to the user by increasing the probability of the user finding what he or she wants. He suggested that the "last circulation date" be used to separate a research library's holdings into a low-use storage area and a high-use holding area. The latter could be used to satisfy a predefined, say 99 percent, proportion of user requirements. In other words, the "last circulation date" located on a date-due slip of a book is predictive not only of future use but also of a "core collection" (Trueswell, 1969). For example, 99 percent of the current circulation sample was made up of books that had circulated at least once during the previous X-year (or month) period. Then the library can remove all books that have not circulated during the previous X-year period. After doing this, it is expected that no more than one percent of the users would be disappointed in not finding the books they required.

The discussions in Chapters 7 and 8 make it clear that this study can easily identify a minimum nucleus of Countway books that can satisfy a predefined proportion of user requirements. The list in Appendix 7 is essentially a general "core collection" based on user demand (reserve books are not included in this study). The Countway study extends further than what was proposed by Trueswell. It can provide much more predictive measurements of user needs.

For example, if the Countway's NLM book stacks were overcrowded and about 15 percent of the NLM collection had to be removed every two years, either the oldest 15 percent of the NLM book collection could be removed every two years or the oldest of the noncirculating books could be retired, up to 15 percent of the NLM collection. In Chapter 8, the total number of NLM books in the Countway Library has been estimated to be approximately 37,000 titles; therefore 15 percent would be about 5,500 titles. Table 4.5 shows that there were about 2,517 books added to Countway in 1963-1964. It seems reasonable to estimate the number of Countway NLM books published in 1960 and 1961 as 2,700 titles per year. Thus altogether these 5,400 books would be candidates for retirement if the first alternative mentioned above were taken. Since the values of α and β are not available in Table 6.4, those of BML books will be used for the purpose of illustration. Thus on the average, each retired book would have circulated $\alpha/(1-\beta)$ times a year if it had stayed in the regular NLM collection. Here, $\alpha/(1-\beta) = 0.550/(1-0.364) = 0.865$ (this result indicates that the 1960 and 1961 books are still fairly active). This corresponds to a total of $5,400 \times 0.865 \times 2 \simeq 9,342$ borrowings for the two years, that is, about 9,342 "inconveniences" during the two years. Supposedly these 5,400 retired books are the oldest books that have not circulated in the past year; Morse suggests that by choosing the noncirculating ones among the oldest books to retire, the circulation of the retired books has been reduced by the factor $[(\beta/t) \times (1-\beta^t)/(1-\beta)]$. Therefore the total number of circulations for the two years would be reduced from 9,342 to 7,023. Whether this reduction of user inconvenience would be worth the additional effort of selecting the noncirculated books would have to be weighed against the amount of this additional effort.

Of course, from the library operational point of view, to weed all books by publication date is a much easier and economical process than to weed those older but noncirculated books. Librarians have to ask themselves a difficult question: Can we justify spending this extra staff time and effort? Besides the kind of analytical answers mentioned, librarians ought to consider first the possible outcomes of unjudicious weeding. If books were weeded by date of publication only, the probability of having weeded few heavy-use and a number of potentially useful books is great, and a number of more recent but useless books will continue to stay with other useful books and thus increase inconvenience to library users. Of the few-high use books weeded, either new copies would have to be purchased because of total discards, or they would have to be called back from the remote storage for the requesters. If the number of useful books discarded is large, a rather heavy interlibrary-loan activity will also result. At the same time, library shelves will have more and more potentially useless books crowding the scarce and expensive prime library shelves.

Not only have library expenditures skyrocketed since 1949, but the costs of acquiring, maintaining, and weeding library materials are also rising rapidly. Costs of weeding vary considerably from one report to another. Raffel and Shishko (1969) estimate weeding cost at $0.20 to $0.40 per volume for weeding by publication date. L. Ash estimates $0.80 to $1.00 per volume for weeding by circulation criteria (1964). The more up-to-date ARL report (1966, 1972) estimates a weeding cost of $3.03 per volume for a 10 percent reduction of the collection and a $24.00 per volume cost for a one percent reduction. Meaningful comparison of these figures cannot be made because of the different methodologies involved in these studies. Nevertheless, they do give us some indications of the cost of the weeding operation.

As for the cost of preservation, the 1966 ARL report estimates that each volume of books cost approximately $7.25 to preserve. The present figure should be much higher than that. Prime library shelf space is very expensive. Even in 1967, it was estimated that conventional housing in Chicago was about $1.25 per square foot per year, exclusive of costs of shelving (Simon, 1967).

Finally, the cost of acquisition and processing is usually much higher than the costs of weeding and preservation. As an example, my study of biomedical book reviewings (Chen, 1974) reveals that an average biomedical book in 1970 cost $16.65 per volume, which is in close agreement with figures given in *Bowker's Annual* (1973), of $16.19. The processing cost of a book, from the beginning of acquisition to the time the book is ready for use, can easily be estimated to be between $15.00 and $20.00 per item (see sources listed in Dougherty and Leonard, 1970; Dougherty and Maier, 1971). The costs of other activities, such as interlibrary loan, and operations such as retrieving materials from remote storage can also be great when staff salary and overhead are considered.

Thus it seems obvious to us that injudicious and ineffective weeding that does not consider the actual user needs could cost a great deal of already limited library resources. Furthermore, while the cost for which a library is responsible can be determined without too much difficulty, dollar value cannot be easily assigned to account for the user frustration, waiting, and inconvenience. The penalty that library users have to pay because of librarians' ineffective weeding policy should have a profound effect on the evaluation of the weeding decision (Lister, 1967). It is not difficult, then, for librarians to argue for a slightly more time-consuming but a much more careful and critical weeding policy.

The Countway study further shows that if useful circulation data have been kept, more useful information on library use can be obtained, and more precise predictions can be made on the future use of library books. The high-use and low-use classes of books can be identified (Appendix 1). Furthermore, Tables 6.10, 6.11, A6.5, and A6.6 demonstrate clearly how useful results, such as the fractions of active, live, and dead books of a given class, can be estimated for the year and can be predicted for the next and the following years, by using the probabilistic models presented in Part I. Once the size of the collection in the class is known, then the corresponding total numbers of active (N_a), live (N_ℓ), and dead ($N_d = N - N_\ell$) books can also be calculated (see Tables 6.6 to 6.8, and A6.1 to A6.4). Thus for each class of books the most likely number of books that can be weeded is known, and this number varies greatly from one class to the other. This means that an individualized weeding decision can be made on each class of books. For example, Tables 6.10, 6.11, A6.5 and A6.6 suggest the following percentages of dead books in each of the seven NLM classes studied: QU—24.2 percent; QZ—26.1 percent; WA—50.5 percent; WG—56.7 percent; WM—10.1 percent; WO—56.2 percent; and WS—6.5 percent. To determine the high percentage of potentially useless titles, WA books were checked in the stacks. They were found to be mostly government publications. These results suggest that more books can be weeded out from book classes such as WA, WG, and WO than from those of WM and WS. In fact, it probably would not be cost-beneficial to weed WM and WS books, since the risk of weeding a useful book is high and the time and effort needed to identify the small number of dead books are proportionately much greater than would be spent on classes with a larger number of dead books.

Thus we have illustrated that circulation data, when properly analyzed with operations research techniques, can help librarians in their weeding decision process. A weeding policy formulated with the help of these useful data on book-use behavior and prediction of future use is, in effect, one established with the user's indirect involvement and participation in the decision-making.

Chapter Ten

Further Illustrations

In this chapter, I shall attempt to elaborate further the usefulness of the operational quantities that can be generated from this study and that have not been utilized fully in earlier discussions.

Loan Period

This subject was touched upon briefly when the duplication policy was discussed in Chapter 8. It merits further attention.

Every library has a loan policy. Loan periods can range anywhere from one hour to a year or longer. The library loan decision directly affects the availability of library material to its users. "Availability," as stated by Buckland and Hindle (1969, 1972), is "a rather complex concept and considerations of economy and of the convenience to the user lead to a tangle of conflicting objectives." There is a strong conflict between the convenience to an individual user who has a given book and the convenience to other users who may wish to borrow the circulated book. Thus many factors should be considered in establishing an effective loan policy so that it can best balance the convenience to current borrowers and prospective users against considerations for an economical administrative cost. Yet it has usually been formulated by librarians based on their intuition, tradition, and experience.

Data on the loan period can be analyzed, as shown in Appendix 2, to obtain the mean loan period, μ, of a given class of books. In Morse's queuing models, μ is a very important factor. It measures how effectively the library facilities and services are being used. Discussions of the usefulness of this quantity can be found in Chapters 5 and 8 and Appendix 2. In this chapter, additional interpretations of the Countway data will be offered.

Tables A2.2 and A2.3 seem to suggest that the Countway two-week loan policy is not working. Although some users return library books around the due dates (as shown by the peaks near thirteen days in Figs. A2.1 and A2.2), the average mean loan period is a month. Only 15 percent of the borrowed books are renewed, as indicated by Table A2.1 (when compared with the data shown in Table A1.1). This suggests that the Countway users generally ignore the loan policy of the library, as indicated by the random manner in which they return books (Figs. A2.1 and A2.2).

Knowing the value of μ, we can easily calculate the fraction of a year a given class of books is off the shelf, $\overline{R}\mu$, when the mean rate of circulation, $\overline{R}$, is known. For example, $\overline{R}_a$ for WM books is estimated to be 2.387 (Table 6.11); therefore, for all WM active

books that circulated at least once, the fraction off the shelf is
$2.387 \times 1/12 \approx 0.20$. This fraction should be equivalent to the
fraction of books in circulation, J/N (where J is the number of circulation cards in file and N is the total number of books in the
class).

Although the fraction of WM books off the shelf is not large, it
does not mean that user demand and need are generally met. Several studies (Meier, 1963; Roy, 1963; Trueswell, 1964) have shown
that there is approximately a fifty-fifty chance of the user not
finding the book he wants in the stacks. The reason for this high
probability is mainly difficulty in finding higher-circulation books.
Table 6.7 shows that of the 1,504 WM books expected to circulate
at least once this sample year (N_a), 509 (33.8 percent) are expected
to circulate three or more times. Of these 509 books, 315 would circulate four or more times, with a mean circulation of 5.38. For
WM books with more than one circulation, Table A2.2 indicates a
shorter mean loan period of about twenty-two days; thus $\mu = 1/15$,
approximately. The fraction of these high-circulation WM books
which are off shelf is, then, $5.38/15 = 0.36$, and the circulation interference becomes significant.

In view of Countway's tight financial situation, the acquisition
of duplicate copies of high-demand books has been very limited.
The need for better user understanding and cooperation in returning library books promptly is certainly imperative. If books
can be returned faster by reducing the actual mean loan period
from one month to two weeks, then, with a $\mu = 1/26$, $\bar{R}\mu$ would be
reduced from 0.36 to 0.21 even for the 315 high-circulation WM
books. This is a striking improvement.

One of the principal methods of enforcing loan policies has been
the charging of fines. Many librarians feel that fines are necessary
to ensure compliance with regulations. Yet the relationship between fines and borrower behavior is still to be investigated, and
the value of this assumption is still uncertain (Buckland and
Hindle, 1969). Fines could be used for the frequent and consistently irresponsible offenders. More extensive public relations
work, to keep readers informed of these quantitatively analyzed
results and to make them more aware of the problems that both
the users and the library are facing, should be helpful. In order
for the library to provide an effective service, library users need
to have a sense of responsibility toward the material, the library,
and the other library users. Tables A2.2 to A2.3 show that there
are still a fair number of users who keep books for more than 100

days. In the month of January alone, 116 books were returned after having been detained by their borrowers for over 100 days, and 84 of them were held for an average of 226 days, with one book out to a user for as long as 531 days. This kind of irresponsible behavior should not be allowed to continue.

Nonuse of the Library

While I have stressed the use of the Countway Library books in this book, it should be pointed out that the nonuse of the same collection should offer an equally fruitful and important area for research. Appendix 4 identifies the active user groups of the Countway Library. Concurrently, the inactive ones can be found easily. In order to improve library effectiveness, library administrators need to explore further the reasons for inactive or zero use of the library by a certain homogeneous group of potential users.

Browsing and Linear Arrangement of Library Books

Browsing is considered by scientific researchers to be an important method of finding the information desired as found in my recent survey of the physicists' information needs (Chen, 1974). In order to enable Countway users to be effective in their browsing efforts, the search area must be as small as possible (Appendix 3). As indicated in Chapter 9, weeding potentially useless items for discards and separating the less used materials from the active books are essential operations. These operations increase the users' opportunities of finding useful material in their searching process. Chapter 9 has stated that at this time the division of the Countway Library books into the BML and NLM collections is an effective way of separating the total collection into the higher-use and lower-use volumes. Yet not all NLM book classes are equally active. Tables 6.10 to 6.12 and Tables A6.5 to A6.6 suggest to us that classes such as WA have a rather large number of books that have very little potential use. In order to improve the browser's chances of success, these dead books should be removed.

Linear arrangement of library materials should also be of concern to librarians. Information on "connectivity of interests" among books of various classes is difficult to obtain manually, as is discussed in Appendix 3. Nevertheless, the sample results, though limited, together with discussions as presented in both Appendix 3 and Chapter 8, should be sufficient to demonstrate the possible effects on users if this kind of consideration is not properly given in book arrangement and selection. For instance, if Countway's NLM books had to be separated because of space limitations, it would be very inconvenient to library users if the collection were divided as A-WL and WM-Z and housed on two separate floors. Appendix 3 shows that there is a very high "connectivity of interest" among books of the two classes. Since WL and WM books are frequently checked out by the same user at the same time, separate locations for these books would undoubtedly increase user inconvenience.

Chapter Eleven
Conclusions

It has been shown in this book that although a library is a complex system engaged in providing information to its users, many of its operations can be described quantitatively, by means of probability distributions, and its achievements can be expressed in terms of various measures of effectiveness.

The primary objectives of this book-use study, as outlined in the Preface and elaborated on in Chapter 5, have been achieved in the following ways:

First, Morse's Markovian book-use models, which were backed by a limited amount of data collected at the MIT Science Library, have been tested fully in this study by using the up-to-date and comprehensive book-use data gathered at one of the nation's largest medical libraries. The theoretical predictive models are now solidly backed by a broad data base collected in an entirely different library environment frequented by a totally different type of users. It has been shown that the use pattern of books of a given class can be predicted by using the past-circulation-history data.

Second, because new kinds of data are now available, this study has been able to demonstrate how additional probabilistic models can be developed to correct the biased circulation data. These models can be used to predict future use and thus to help the library administrator see more clearly the probable consequences of alternative policies in terms of library budgetary planning, book selection, weeding, and so forth.

Third, I hope that I have filled some gaps between operations researchers and librarians. Part III of this book interprets the results of this study and discusses their implications for librarians. It has been shown that mathematical models, once fully developed and tested, are easy tools to use in a library for measuring library effectiveness. They can be used as aids to the library decision-makers. Results can be obtained by simply plugging the right values of parameters into the formula already developed. Librarians do not have to be concerned about the modification and improvement of models, which are a systems analyst's responsibility.

In order to provide maximum services to users of a library and to develop an optimum collection with the least cost, librarians must have a thorough understanding of its operations as well as an awareness of the current and future user needs and requirements. With this knowledge and the application of the analytic techniques, it is possible to predict, not merely guess, what it is a library is seeking and ought to accomplish.

Although this study touches on many topics, it is mainly a book-use study intended primarily for the testing of the Markov book-use models and their extensions. There are, however, many additional research areas that deserve to be explored further. In the following, I shall list the obvious ones that are related to a use study:

1. The application of Markov prediction models
a. How applicable are these models to humanities and social sciences libraries?
b. How different are the values of α, β, γ of books on humanities and social sciences subjects from those of scientific and medical books?
c. Can other new models be developed for humanities and social sciences libraries?

2. The Countway book use study
a. What about a similar study but on a smaller scale being carried out after a certain time span?
b. Do the same use patterns persist?
c. If not, why?

3. Book use
a. To what extent does book circulation measure the value of a library book?
b. What about the use of reserve books?
c. What about the use of new books?
d. What about the in-library book use?
e. Are the models developed in this study applicable to these cases?
f. What about requests for high-circulation books? How effective is a request satisfying the user? How rarely is it used? What kind of queuing model best represents what actually is going on?
g. What about the loan period of books?

4. Journal use
a. How are journals used? If no circulation is allowed, do users generally request Xerox copies?
b. What is the core journal collection? Are these journals also most often cited? Can probabilistic models be developed to describe and predict journal use?
c. What is the relationship between frequency of use and date of publication? Language of materials?

5. Use of other types of materials
a. What about the use of government documents?
b. What about the use of technical reports?
c. What about the use of micromaterials?

d. What about the use of audiovisual materials? Media?
e. Can we predict the future use of these materials?
6. Users
a. Who uses these types of informational materials? How are they used?
b. What are the general library-use patterns of students, faculty members, researchers, and staff? What about the other users?
7. Library nonusers
a. Who are the nonusers?
b. Why don't they use the library?
8. Use of library facilities
a. What are the purposes of library visits? What facilities are used most by visitors? Why?
b. Does library attendance reflect the volume of library use and library activities? What library services are considered to be most essential to the users?
c. What should be the criteria for library effectiveness?

Appendix One
Detailed Book Circulation Statistics

The Countway Library has statistics on the total number of books circulated each month, but there have been no detailed book-use statistics by class breakdown. In this study, book-use data were recorded by class on a daily basis. Thus a compilation of detailed statistics by class was possible. Table A1.1 is a summary of four-month circulation data collected for this study. In this table, heavy-use classes were identified.

Within each month's circulation, an attempt was made to determine the number of books returned two or more times. The results were further prepared by date of publication (Table A1.2) and subject class (Table A1.4). A summary of these can also be found in Table A1.3. It was found that about 6.5 percent of the books returned during each sample month were used two or more times.

A further attempt was made to determine the number of books that circulated during the two sample months of January and April 1973. Results are shown in Table A1.5. It was found that approximately 18 percent of the books returned to Countway circulated in both January and April.

Statistical data on requests were taken from the requesters' information, which was either imprinted or written on the back of the circulation charge cards. This is likely to be only incomplete data. Nevertheless, Table A1.6 does show some interesting results. Requests and reserves are all indicators for high-use materials; therefore the results should be useful to librarians in making decisions on ordering duplicate copies, and so forth.

Finally, since the book-circulation record was made on a daily basis for the four sample months, it was possible to tabulate the circulation-return activity by date of the week. The results are presented in Table A1.7. It is interesting to note that if the mean circulation volumes for each day of the week are prorated for the same number of library hours each day, fifteen and a half hours, then we see a fairly close circulation volume. The shortening of library hours on Fridays after April 22, 1973, seemed to have some effect on the library circulation activity, as shown in Table A1.7.

Table A1.1 Circulation Frequency Distribution by Subjects (during the Four Sample Months at Countway)

Book Class	No. of Books Circulated					% of Total Cirs.
	Jan.	April	July	Oct.	Total	
BML	145	202	88	139	574	4.92
B	82	95	49	63	289	2.48
D-G	17	22	9	13	61	0.52
H*	146	126	79	130	481	4.13
J-P	24	24	7	14	69	0.59
Q-QA	23	18	7	34	82	0.70
QC	22	10	2	13	47	0.40
QD	41	57	34	58	190	1.63
QH*	123	115	80	69	387	3.32
QJ-QP	54	44	25	39	162	1.39
QS	58	51	39	65	213	1.83
QT	55	50	41	55	201	1.72
QU*	123	115	111	114	463	3.97
QV	93	89	70	53	305	2.62
QW	78	81	53	68	280	2.40
QX-QY	46	15	33	27	121	1.04
QZ	104	90	52	72	318	2.73
S	20	10	26	6	62	0.53
T-V	11	7	10	18	46	0.39
W*	152	149	66	86	453	3.89
WA*	129	113	64	81	387	3.32
WB	87	79	73	58	297	2.55
WC	25	32	24	31	112	0.96
WD	30	44	26	42	142	1.22
WE*	83	116	67	83	349	2.99

Appendix One 137

Table A1.1 (Continued)

Book Class	No. of Books Circulated					% of Total Cirs.
	Jan.	April	July	Oct.	Total	
WF	51	44	38	59	192	1.65
WG*	93	149	79	83	404	3.47
WH	45	51	46	64	206	1.77
WI	32	33	32	31	128	1.10
WJ	25	47	16	27	115	0.99
WK	69	74	42	58	243	2.08
WL*	237	200	170	171	778	6.68
WM*	323	365	222	248	1,158	9.94
WN	55	55	36	20	166	1.42
WO	60	56	60	48	224	1.92
WP	39	44	34	36	153	1.31
WQ	39	40	18	53	150	1.29
WR	18	21	13	14	66	0.57
WS*	141	171	131	160	603	5.17
WT	26	39	19	19	103	0.88
WU	38	42	32	31	143	1.23
WV	24	38	7	29	98	0.84
WW	50	38	24	53	165	1.42
WX	22	39	31	43	135	1.16
WY	8	22	7	10	47	0.40
WZ	31	33	12	35	111	0.95
Z	28	20	20	18	86	0.74
ZW	23	22	19	27	91	0.78
Total	3,248	3,397	2,243	2,768	11,656	100.00
Aesc.†	384	380	351	343		

*The ten NLM classes of books with highest circulation volumes during the four sample months.
†Books for the Aesculapian Room are intended mainly for recreational reading; therefore their circulations are not included in the grand total.

Table A1.2 Countway Circulation Frequency Distribution by Book Publication Dates

Date of Publication	No. of Books Circulated during the 4 Sample Months			No. of Books Estimated to Circulate in 1973			Total Estimate of Circulated Books
	No. of Circulations			No. of Circulations			
	1	2-3	4-12	1	2-3	4-12	
1973	105	29		315	50		356 (720)†
1972	409	177	25	1,227	304	30	1,561(3,120)†
1971	376	192	8	1,128	330	9	1,467(2,450)†
1970	422	189	14	1,266	325	17	1,608(2,410)†
1969	517	191	15	1,551	329	18	1,898
1968	493	182	17	1,479	313	20	1,812
1967	489	184	17	1,467	316	20	1,803
1966	487	146	14	1,461	251	17	1,729
1965	452	135	15	1,356	232	18	1,606
1964	392	131	10	1,176	225	12	1,413
1963	322	107	7	966	184	8	1,158
1962	295	71	7	885	122	8	1,015
1961	280	62	7	840	107	8	955
1960	272	44	2	816	76	2	894
1955-59	576	96	3	1,728	165	4	1,897
1950-54	252	29	1	756	50	1	807
1940-49	115	20	1	345	34	1	380
1930-39	75	1		225	2		227
1900-29	132	3		396	5		401
Pre-1900	55	3		165	5		170
Total No. of Books	6,516	1,992	163	19,548	3,425	193	23,166
Total No. of Cirs.	6,516	4,372	768	19,548	7,720	909	28,177

*Correct the biased data by using the correction factor $1/[1 - (1 - \rho)^j]$, as described in Chapter 3. Here $\rho = 1/3$, and j is the number of circulation(s). Therefore the correction factor for one-circulation books is 3; for 2- and 3-circulation books, about 1.72; and for 4- to 12-circulation books, about 1.18.
†Prorated by using Table 4.5 as if the new titles for the years 1970 to 1973 were approximately 3,500 titles, the same as those of the earlier years. The data for 1973 are incomplete.

Table A1.3 Number of Books Circulated j Times in Countway during the Sample Months

Sample Month in 1973	Number of Books Circulated j Times							Total	
	$j = 1$	2	3	4	5	6	7	No. of Books	No. of Cirs.
January	2,849	171	15	3				3,038	3,248
		6.22% of 3,038							
April	2,998	161	16	4		1	1	3,181	3,397
		5.75% of 3,181							
July	1,953	131	5	2	1			2,090	2,243
		6.65% of 2,090							
October	2,549	105	3					2,657	2,768
		4.06% of 2,657							
								Grand Total 10,966	11,656

Table A1.4 Subject Distribution of Books Circulated in Countway

Book Class	No. of Books Circulated during the 4 Sample Months			No. of Books Estimated to Circulate in 1973*			Total Estimate of Circulated Books
	No. of Circulations			No. of Circulations			
	1	2-3	4-12	1	2-3	4-12	
BML	505	27		1,515	46		1,561
B	172	54	1	516	93	1	610
D-G	43	6		129	10		139
H†	315	78	2	945	134	2	1,081
J-P	48	11		144	19		163
Q-QA	65	8		195	14		209
QC	39	4		117	7		124
QD	127	27	1	381	46	1	428
QH†	203	81	3	609	139	4	752
QJ-QP	109	26		327	45		372
QS	107	46	2	321	79	2	402
QT	99	38	3	297	65	4	366
QU†	230	84	12	690	144	14	848
QV	168	49	5	504	84	6	594
QW	119	59	7	357	102	8	467
QX-QY	85	13	2	255	22	2	279
QZ	155	69	6	465	119	7	591
S	35	12		105	21		126
T-V	41	3		123	5		128
W†	209	89	9	627	153	11	791
WA†	250	45	7	750	77	8	835
WB	155	56	3	465	96	4	565
WC	70	13	2	210	22	2	234
WD	66	29	3	198	50	4	252
WE†	175	69	3	525	119	4	648
WF	85	30	7	255	52	8	315
WG†	191	69	10	573	119	12	704

Table A1.4 (Continued)

Book Class	No. of Books Circulated during the 4 Sample Months			No. of Books Estimated to Circulate in 1973*			Total Estimate of Circulated Books
	No. of Circulations			No. of Circulations			
	1	2-3	4-12	1	2-3	4-12	
WH	109	33	5	327	57	6	390
WI	77	20	2	231	34	2	267
WJ	58	25	1	174	43	1	218
WK	103	46	6	309	79	7	395
WL†	361	158	16	1,083	272	19	1,374
WM†	602	222	16	1,806	382	19	2,207
WN	107	27		321	46		367
WO	122	41	4	366	71	5	442
WP	81	30	2	243	52	2	297
WQ	77	30	2	231	52	2	285
WR	43	11		129	19		148
WS†	267	115	18	801	198	22	1,021
WT	63	16	1	189	28	1	218
WU	94	22		282	38		320
WV	45	22	1	135	38	1	174
WW	90	28		270	48		318
WX	90	20		270	34		304
WY	31	6		93	10		103
WZ	96	8		288	14		302
Z	57	9		171	15		186
ZQ-ZW	77	8	1	231	14	1	246
Total Book Titles	6,516	1,992	163	19,548	3,426	192	23,166

*See footnote for Table A1.2.
†The ten NLM classes of books with highest-circulation volumes during the four sample months.

Table A1.5 Number of Countway Books Circulated in both January and April 1973 (Selected NLM Classes)

Class	No. of Books Circulated in Jan. and April 1973	No. of Cirs. in Jan. Only	No. of Cirs. in April Only
QU	26	123	115
QZ	15	104	90
WA	13	129	113
WG	21	93	149
WM	72	323	365
WO	11	60	56
WS	29	141	171
Total	187	973	1,059

Appendix One   143

Table A1.6 Request Distribution by Subjects (during the Four Sample Months)

Book Class	No. of Requests					Book Class	No. of Requests				
	Jan.	April	July	Oct.	Total		Jan.	April	July	Oct.	Total
BML		4			4	WF		1		1	2
A-G	2	5	1	2	10	WG	2	7	3	3	15
H	2	12	2	9	25	WH			2	4	6
J-P	1	1			2	WJ		1	2	3	6
Q-QC		1	1	1	3	WK	1	3	2		6
QD	2		1	1	4	WL	9	11	4	3	27
QH	3	5	3	2	13	WM	8	20	10	10	48
QL-QR	4	3	1	3	11	WN		5	2	1	8
QS		1		2	3	WO	2	4	2	2	10
QT	3	2	3		8	WP	1	2	2	1	6
QU	5	4	11	3	23	WQ	2		1	1	4
QV	3	3	1		7	WR				1	1
QW	2	1	1	3	7	WS	7	7	4	9	27
QX-QY	2		1		3	WT		1		2	3
QZ		1			1	WU		2		1	3
S-V			1		1	WV	2			1	3
W	4	9	2	4	19	WW	2				2
WA	2	2		5	9	WX	1	3		3	7
WB	1	3	7	1	12	WY			1		1
WC	1				1	Z	1		1		2
WD			2	2	ZW	1	1	1	1	4
WE	2	4	1	2	9	Total	78	128	74	88	368

Table A1.7 Circulation Distribution by Day of the Week

Time Period 1973	Sun.	Mon.	Tues.	Wed.	Thurs.	Fri.	Sat.
1/1-1/6		*	239	218	182	181	55
1/7-1/13	69	107	117	146	80	110	43
1/14-1/20	78	166	149	129	128	107	52
1/21-1/27	77	144	149	119	125	109	63
1/28-1/31	64	158	132	136			
4/1-4/7	70	171	136	120	132	127	43
4/8-4/14	69	159	137	97	138	113	50
4/15-4/21	63	87	155	160	163	153	54
4/22-4/28	62	166	126	183	101	75	62
4/29-4/30	80	145					
7/1-7/7	122	119	107	*	105	74	39
7/8-7/14	48	112	64	95	56	53	100
7/15-7/21	33	104	75	87	70	81	15
7/22-7/28	43	83	67	96	†	76	†
7/29-7/31	†	†	†				
10/1-10/6		95	122	91	110	61	67
10/7-10/13	82	61	86	108	95	97	62
10/14-10/20	80	82	101	131	88	97	43
10/21-10/27	51	69	126	125	98	49	95
10/28-10/31	75	108	115	98			
Mean Circulation	69	119	122	126	111	129 (before April 22, 1973)	56
						74 (after April 22, 1973)	
No. of Lib. Hrs.	9½	15½	15½	15½	15½	15½ (to April 22, 1973)	8
						9 (after April 22, 1973)	
Mean Cir. Prorated for 15½ Hrs.	112	119	122	126	111	120	108

*Library closed.
†Day-circulation not available.

Appendix Two

Mean Loan Period

For each book returned to the Countway Library, information on the loan period of that book was obtained. There are two methods that could be used:
1. Each renewal of circulation is considered a new circulation; therefore the loan period is computed by counting the number of days from the last renewal date to the date of return. In other words, a book that was renewed on January 23, 1973, and returned on January 28, 1973, is considered to have a five-day loan period even though it was originally checked out in November 25, 1972, or renewed several times in between by the user.
2. Renewals are disregarded. The loan period of a book is interpreted as the total number of days a book was out to a user and not available for other users of the library. Therefore the book described above would have a loan period of sixty-four days.

Theoretically, the mean loan period should be calculated by using the second method. A mean loan period computed by using this method would be longer than one computed by using the first one. The degree of difference depends heavily on how often and how conscientiously the users renewed their library books after the due dates.

An attempt was made to gather information on renewals made by library users during the four sample months. The total data base was used. The complete summary of the renewal information is available in Table A2.1. It has been found that about 15 percent of the book titles returned had been renewed at least once.

In order to estimate the difference among the mean loan periods derived by the methods just discussed, it was decided that the first method would be used to calculate the loan periods of all books returned in the months of January and April 1973, while the second method would be used for those of the July and October returns.

Among all the books used by the Countway users, W classes are the most popular ones since they are the subject classes in medical sciences. Therefore results on loan-period distribution for W books are presented in Table A2.2.[1] The summary results for all classes are also available in Table A2.3. All these data were plotted on semilog paper, and they all come out consistently. (See Figs. A2.1 and A2.2.) The straight-line distribution of books returned suggests that the users returned books in a random manner. The peak at about thirteen days of loan is expected since the library has a loan period set for two weeks.

[1] See Appendix II of my Ph.D. thesis for more results on loan-period distributions for books of B to U, BML, and Z classes.

Tables A2.2 and A2.3 seem to show that in the month of April there were fewer long-overdue books (over 115 days) and the mean loan period was much shorter than those of the other months. A certain change in circulation policy was suggested. A check with the circulation librarian confirmed that a strongly worded letter was sent to urge all users to return long-overdue books earlier.

Appendix Two   147

Table A2.1 Renewal Distribution by Subjects (during the Four Sample Months)

Book Class	No. of Renewals					Book Class	No. of Renewals				
	Jan.	April	July	Oct.	Total		Jan.	April	July	Oct.	Total
BML	24	39	9	14	86	WG	10	14	7	10	41
A-G	22	20	6	9	57	WH	5	6	1	2	14
H	22	17	9	15	63	WI	2	4	4	1	11
J-P	9	3		3	15	WJ	3	8		1	12
Q-QC	8	7	1	6	22	WK	10	21	7	4	42
QD	4	9	3	6	22	WL	49	30	22	15	116
QH	18	11	9	6	44	WM	47	72	46	36	201
QK			1		1	WN	9	8	2	5	24
QL-QR	10			5	15	WO	8	10	9	5	32
QS	7	9	6	7	29	WP	9	5	3	3	20
QT	3	11	5		19	WQ	7	5	4	4	20
QU	15	10	13	7	45	WR	1	6	1	4	12
QV	9	18	14	3	44	WS	28	22	20	19	89
QW	7	10	2	2	21	WT	6	5	3	2	16
QX-QY	8	1	4	3	16	WU	6	7	5	6	24
QZ	18	16	5	3	42	WV	7	7	1	2	17
S-V	4	1	10		15	WW	7	3	2	10	22
W	24	25	9	7	65	WX	5	13	3	1	22
WA	22	9	6	13	50	WY	2	5	2		9
WB	10	8	13	9	40	WZ	5	10		1	16
WC	5	7	4	6	22	Z	4	4			8
WD	2	9		2	13	ZW	3	4	3	1	11
WE	12	18	12	10	52						
WF	3	3	7	16	29	Total	499	530	293	284	1,606

Table A2.2 Loan-Period Distribution of Books of W Classes in Countway (during the Four Sample Months)

No. of Days on Loan	1-Circulation Books			
	Jan.*	April*	July†	Oct.†
0-5	134	147	103	117
6-10	174	185	87	138
11-15	398	408	228	370
16-20	172	297	143	181
21-25	117	173	123	176
26-30	106	127	119	159
31-35	70	87	61	71
36-40	87	65	57	33
41-45	61	48	38	50
46-50	53	59	48	21
51-55	50	41	24	27
56-60	39	28	18	18
61-65	34	29	18	22
66-70	32	27	13	20
71-75	7	14	8	13
76-80	20	13	14	10
81-85	4	10	17	14
86-90	5	12	12	4
91-95	15	11	2	8
96-100	6	3	9	12
101-105	7	10	4	5
106-110	5	8	9	4
111-115	4	7	10	
Over 115	58 (116-531 days)	52 (118-262 days)	40 (120-256 days)	61 (118-384 days)
Mean Loan (Days)	33.46	28.73	32.51	30.97

Table A2.2 (Continued)

No. of Days on Loan	2-Circulation Books			
	Jan.*	April*	July†	Oct.†
0-5	26	41	19	21
6-10	24	33	17	15
11-15	66	49	32	43
16-20	28	22	23	12
21-25	16	22	17	7
26-30	9	10	7	8
31-35	11	9	12	4
36-40	7	8	8	5
41-45	7	10	4	3
46-50	5	3	6	2
51-55	4	4	5	
56-60	4		3	
61-65	6	3	4	1
66-70	5	1	6	1
71-75	3		2	2
76-80	3	2		
81-85	2		1	
86-90	1	1		
91-95				
96-100	2	2	3	
101-105				1
106-110		1	1	
111-115			1	
Over 115	3 (132-248 days)	5 (123-180 days)	2 (145 days)	5 (123-253 days)
Mean Loan (Days)	25.94	22.62	28.31	24.19

*Method 1: Renewals are considered new circulations.
†Method 2: Loan period is considered the total number of days a book was out to a user (renewal is disregarded).

Appendix Two   150

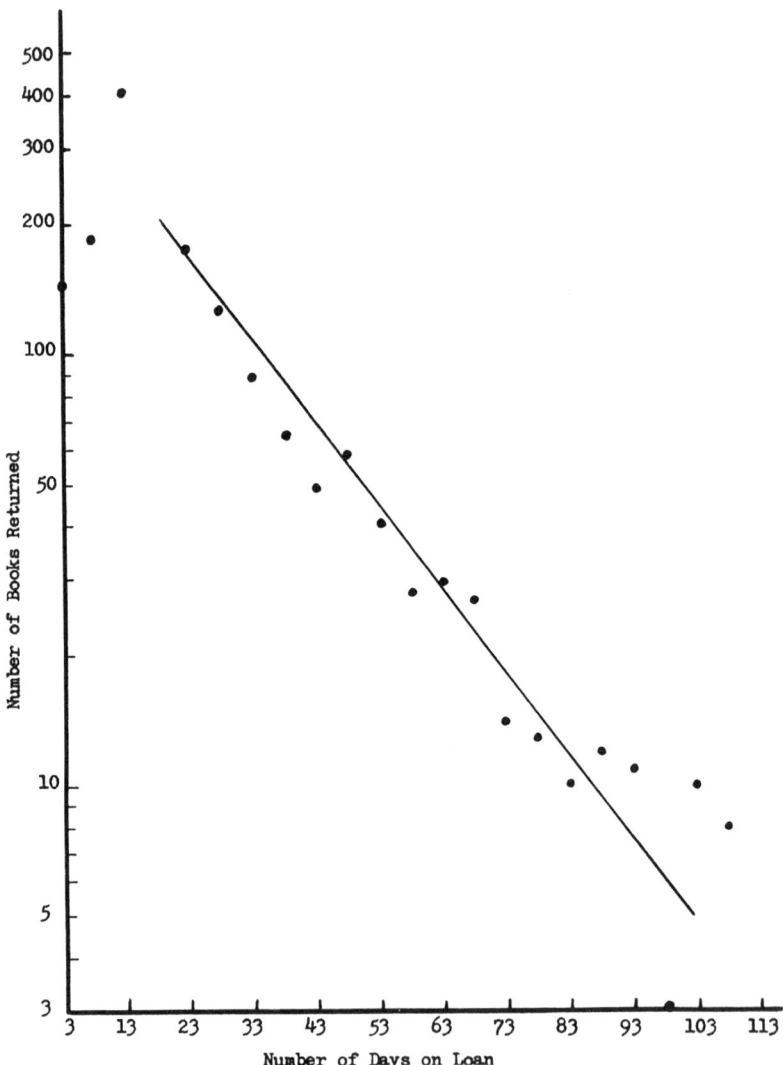

Figure A2.1 Loan-period distribution of W book classes—April 1973 data

Table A2.3 Loan-Period Distribution of All Countway Books Returned during the Four Sample Months

No. of Days on Loan	1-Circulation Books				2-Circulation Books			
	Jan.*	April*	July†	Oct.†	Jan.*	April*	July†	Oct.†
0-5	229	246	198	220	39	59	32	31
6-10	300	303	155	251	36	44	26	25
11-15	663	679	347	634	91	74	52	64
16-20	298	442	254	292	40	36	33	22
21-25	222	295	194	271	26	27	25	13
26-30	193	206	174	223	16	19	12	15
31-35	143	147	95	136	15	11	20	7
36-40	154	116	81	64	15	10	9	6
41-45	105	81	60	70	8	10	9	3
46-50	84	94	73	48	8	6	7	3
51-55	77	72	35	42	6	4	8	2
56-60	64	50	35	33	8	3	3	1
61-65	55	37	29	32	9	3	5	2
66-70	48	36	20	28	6	1	6	3
71-75	17	16	19	15	4		2	2
76-80	40	22	20	14	3	4		
81-85	5	20	20	24	2		1	
86-90	12	16	16	8	2	1		
91-95	22	15	10	11			1	
96-100	10	3	10	15	3	2	3	1
101-105	11	14	15	9	1	1		1
106-110	7	12	10	9		2	2	1
111-115	12	9	12	5			2	1
Over 115 (Mean Loan Days)	80 (226)	67 (152)	71 (173)	95 (182)	4 (235)	5 (150)	4 (145)	7 (170)
Mean Loan (Days)	31.93	27.20	32.53	29.84	26.74	21.49	25.84	24.87

*See footnotes of Table A2.2.
†See footnotes of Table A2.2.

Appendix Two   152

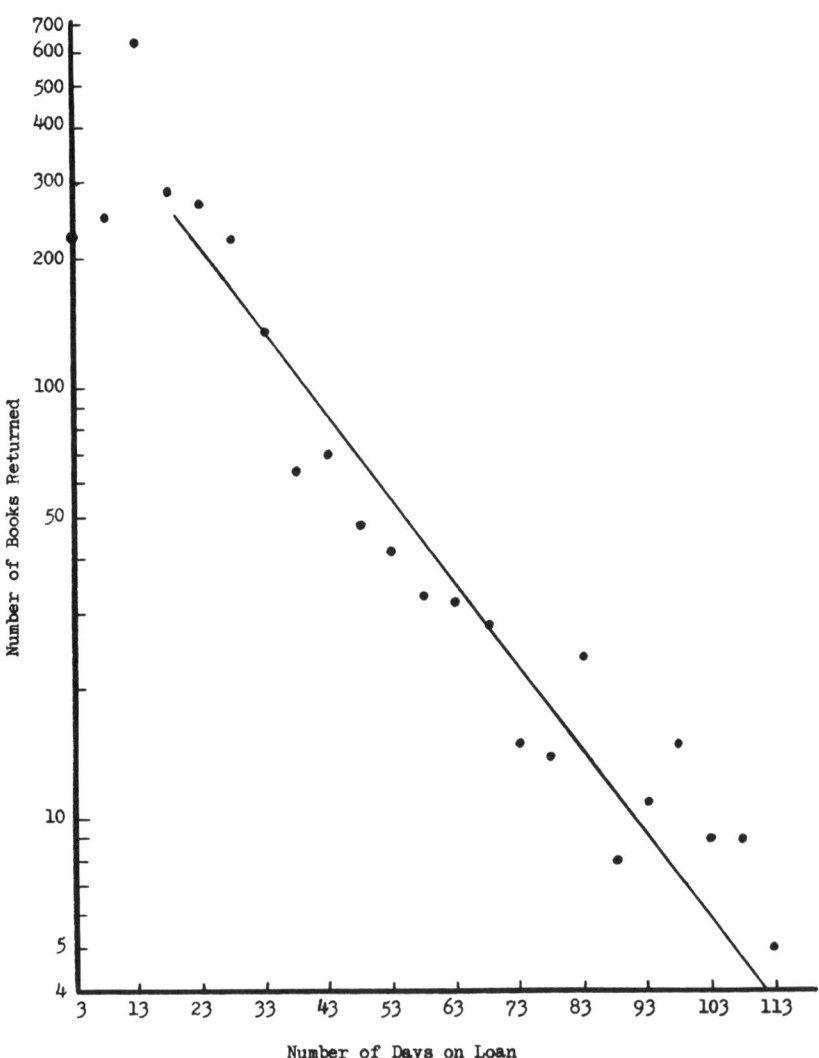

Figure A2.2 Loan-period distribution of all Countway books returned in October 1973

Appendix Three
Browsing, Search Models, and the Linear Arranging of Library Books

Browsing, as a method of finding the information desired, is commonly employed by library users. Morse found at the MIT Libraries that browsing is at least as popular as the use of the library card catalog (1968). It has generally been used more frequently by researchers and faculty members. Raisig et al. investigated in 1966 how biomedical investigators use library books at the Yale Medical Library. Of the 484 researchers responding, 104 (or 21.5 percent) indicated that browsing was their method of learning about the books that they borrowed. The Johns Hopkins University's operations research and systems engineering study on its research libraries (1963) reported that 46.8 percent of the library patrons of its science and engineering library group browsed through library shelves while also engaging in other activities in the library, and similar percentages were reported for other user groups. Most recently, my library school students and I conducted a questionnaire survey on the information needs of the academic physicists and chemists (all faculty members) of six large universities in the Greater Boston area, including Harvard University and MIT (1974). The survey results show that browsing was a very popular method among scientists, used for locating needed information.

It is obvious, then, that in planning library facilities and arranging library information items, librarians should keep the browsers in mind. Morse's publications (1972, 1970) should be referred to for detailed discussions on browsing and search theory. Since this topic is beyond the scope of this study, only a brief discussion will be given here in light of some useful data collected by this investigator.

Morse's search model on browsing modified the models used for air or submarine searches (Koopman, 1957). For library book browsing, a browser scans N number of books on a set of shelves in the library. The chance that he will spot a particular book of his interest, placed at random among the N books, is

$$P_s = 1 - e^{-\rho T/N} \tag{A3.1}$$

where ρ is called the browsing rate, and T is the time spent in browsing.

Therefore, to maximize the chance of finding a particular book, the number N should not be large, so that the search coverage $(\rho T/N)$ for a given search time is not small. If books of different interest areas are placed in noticeable sections, and the number of books in each section is relatively small, then the search coverage in a given time is large, and therefore a browser's chance of success is also large. In the case of the Countway Library, separating the 100,000 volumes older than twelve years from the other 50,000 more recent volumes is an effective way of decreasing the potential search area and thus increasing the chance of success for the browsers.

As for the location of library materials, a shelf arrangement by call numbers (subject) is considered to be much superior to either the author or the title arrangement. This is due to the fact that library users do not look for books randomly. They usually want specific information when they go to a library. I found that 160 of 179 physics faculty members who responded to my questionnaire on the reason(s) for library use listed "specific information" as one (1974). It should be pointed out that when circulation of library materials is considered a *random* process, this is not to say that library users borrowed library materials randomly, in the sense that they did not know what to borrow but just randomly picked any available library material. It is a random process to librarians. Librarians, unless prewarned, generally do not know when a library user will come to the library or what he will borrow.

Library books of related subjects are usually checked out by users at the same time. Thus it is necessary to arrange books of closely connected interests as near to each other as possible in order to minimize user inconvenience. Information on "connectivity of interest" among subject books such as those presented in Table A3.1 should help librarians to identify these closely related areas. These data were obtained from the user file based on the January 1973 circulation records. Once charge cards are arranged alphabetically by users' last names, it is possible to know the number of times books of both classes i and j are borrowed during a specific period by the same borrower. Then the degree of "connectedness" between the two classes i and j, N_{ij}, can be measured, as described in Morse's article on optimal linear ordering of information items (1972). The data presented in Table A3.1, though limited, are sufficient to demonstrate the "connectivity of interest" among the classes of Countway books.

Table A3.1 Connectivity of Interest among Subject Books as Measured by the Frequency of Pair Circulations to the Same User (Based on January 1973 Data)*

W Books		WB Books		WM Books		WS Books	
Pair with	No. of Times	Pair with	No. of Times	Pair with	No. of Times	Pair with	No. of Times
E	1	E	1	BF	5	BF	4
H	1	HN	1	QD	2	HM	1
HA	1	QD	1	QS	1	HV	1
HM	1	QH	1	QU	3	LB	1
QL	1	QT	3	QV	3	QL	1
QS	1	QU	2	QW	1	QS	1
QW	2	QV	1	QZ	2	QU	2
WA	7	QW	3	W	6	QV	1
WB	5	QY	1	WA	4	QY	1
WF	1	QZ	1	WB	3	QZ	1
WL	1	W	5	WD	1	W	1
WM	6	WA	4	WG	1	WA	1
WS	1	WE	2	WH	1	WB	2
WT	2	WG	1	WI	1	WE	3
WU	1	WH	1	WL	10	WF	2
WW	2	WL	3	WO	1	WG	1
WX	3	WM	3	WP	2	WH	1
WZ	1	WN	1	WR	1	WL	4
		WS	2	WS	5	WM	5
		WW	1	WV	2	WO	1
		WZ	1	Z	1	WQ	1
				ZW	2	WW	1
						WY	1

*Library of Congress classes for books from class B to classes Q, and NLM classes for all W books.

Appendix Four

Users of the Countway Library

The user information should be extremely easy to obtain if the circulation operations are computerized. However, to obtain data on Countway users is not an easy task. Thus, for the purpose of illustration, only circulation records of the January 1973 sample month will be used. There were 3,248 records, and they were arranged by the users' last names.

As shown in Fig. 4.1, a user checks out a book either by using a student identification card, if a student, or by using the Countway Library borrower card. The students were identified by their school codes, such as 60 for the Medical School, on their ID imprints, while other borrowers were identified by the borrowers' codification symbols shown on their cards. The names of faculty members, researchers, and staff of the Harvard University and of Harvard graduate and undergraduate students were checked against the 1971-1972 and 1972-1973 *Harvard University Directory of Officers and Students* for both school affiliation and status.

Summarized results of the collected user data are presented in Table A4.1. They are self-explanatory. On the average, the January 1973 data reveal that each library user returned 2.3 books. A perusal of some of the large number of books returned by the same users seems to substantiate the assumption that Countway users return books rather casually, without caring about the due dates. One user returned eleven books in January 1973, and the loan periods for these books ranged from eight to eighty-nine days.

Table A4.1 Circulation Distribution among User Groups of the Countway Library*—January 1973 Data

No. of Cirs.	School of Medicine				
Total No. of Books Borrowed by Same User	F	R	St.	S	Total
1	58	67	81	30	236
2	18	14	38	7	77
3-4	8	15	22	7	52
5-6	6	3	4	1	14
7-10			7	1	8
11-20			2		2
Total No. of Users	90	99	154	46	389
Total No. of Cirs.	154	170	350	83	757

No. of Cirs.	Other Harvard Students					
Total No. of Books Borrowed by Same User	G	HC	Rad.	Other	Other Harvard Staff	Total
1	29	22	5	9	7	72
2	4	11	3	14	1	33
3-4	10	21	6	5	4	46
5-6	5	10	2	1	2	20
7-10	2	3	2		3	10
11-20	2	1	2			5
Over 20			1			1
Total No. of Users	52	68	21	29	17	187
Total No. of Cirs.	160	254	111	62	61	648

*Abbreviations used in this table:
F Faculty
R Research Fellows
S Staff
St. Students
G Graduate Students
HC Harvard College
Rad. Radcliffe
MGH Mass. Gen. Hosp.
CHMC Children's Hosp. Medical Center

Table A4.1 (Continued)

School of Public Health					School of Dental Medicine				
F	R	St.	S	Total	F	R	St.	S	Total
2	13	29	15	59	4	1	7	4	16
4	3	12	5	24	3	2	4		9
3	5	16	2	26				1	1
2	2	2	2	8	1				1
		2	1	3					
11	23	61	25	120	8	3	11	5	27
31	45	137	60	273	16	7	19	8	50

MDs and Staff of Teaching and Other Hospitals					BML MMS Users	ILL	Other
MGH	CHMC	PBBH	Other	Total			
19	41	22	50	132	178	58	4
4	16	17	31	68	62	13	1
9	12	14	9	44	48	15	3
2	3	3	8	16	20	1	1
	4	1	4	9	10		
		1		1	2	1	1
						1	
34	76	58	102	270	320	89	10
72	162	154	226	614	693	179	34

Grand Total No. of Users: 1,412
Grand Total No. of Circulations: 3,248

PBBH	Peter Bent Brigham Hospital	MMS	Mass. Medical Society
BML	Boston Medical Library	ILL	Interlibrary Loan

Appendix Five

Additional Analyzed Circulation-History Results for Checking Markov Models

These tables and figures, together with Tables 6.1 and 6.3 and Figs. 6.4 to 6.5, represent the complete results on WM books returned to Countway in the four sample months. They are used mainly to test the Markov book-use models as discussed in Chapter 6.

Appendix Five   162

Table A5.1a Values of $M(m)$, N_{mn}, and $N(m)$ for Different Values of m and n for WM Books Returned to Countway.
1968-1973 Pairs—April 1973 Data

m	M(m)	N_{mn}											N(m)	Theor.
		n=0	1	2	3	4	5	6	7	8	9	10		
0	103	23	36	23	11	6	3	1	0	0	0	0	1.55	1.51
1	127	28	36	31	19	6	5	1	0	0	1	0	1.72	1.89
2	126	17	38	23	16	15	3	4	2	0	2	1	2.25	2.27
3	92	9	11	27	16	13	9	4	2	1	0	0	2.78	2.65
4	77	6	10	15	17	13	9	3	2	1	1	0	3.08	3.04
5	51	1	7	11	7	9	8	1	3	0	3	1	3.73	3.42
6	17	1	2	2	1	8	0	3	0	0	0	0	3.47	3.80
7	14	0	0	2	0	5	3	1	1	1	0	1	5.00	4.18
8	8	0	0	3	1	1	2	1	0	0	0	0	3.63	4.57
9	8	1	0	1	1	2	1	1	1	0	0	0	3.88	4.95
10	2	0	0	0	0	1	0	1	0	0	0	0	5.00	5.33

```
           ALPHA AND BETA         1.698      0.316
   WEIGHTED ALPHA AND BETA        1.507      0.383
```

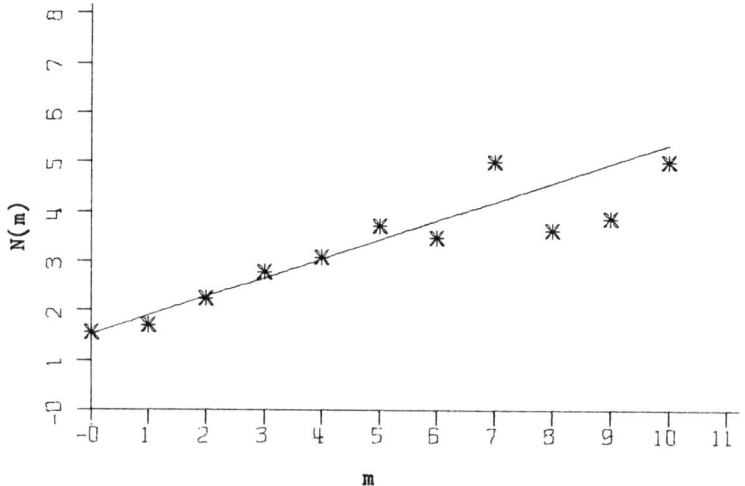

Figure A5.1a Mean circulation $N(m)$ for year $t + 1$ as a function of circulation m for previous year t—WM books.
1968-1973 pairs—April 1973 data

Appendix Five 163

Table A5.1b Values of $M(m)$, N_{mn}, and $N(m)$ for Different Values of m and n for WM Books Returned to Countway.
1968-1973 Pairs—July 1973 Data

m	M(m)	N_{mn}											N(m)	Theor.
		n=0	1	2	3	4	5	6	7	8	9	10		
0	88	30	27	16	8	3	3	1	0	0	0	0	1.32	1.51
1	82	16	22	14	17	4	4	4	0	1	0	0	2.06	1.94
2	87	17	16	20	15	9	6	2	1	1	0	0	2.23	2.38
3	66	5	7	18	13	9	7	1	4	1	1	0	3.09	2.81
4	44	3	6	8	6	5	8	2	3	2	1	0	3.59	3.25
5	23	0	3	3	6	6	2	1	1	0	1	0	3.61	3.68
6	12	0	2	2	1	3	1	2	1	0	0	0	3.75	4.12
7	11	0	2	2	1	1	0	1	0	2	1	1	4.91	4.55
8	7	0	0	2	2	0	1	1	1	0	0	0	4.00	4.98
9	3	1	0	0	0	0	1	0	1	0	0	0	4.00	5.42
10	1	0	0	0	0	0	0	1	0	0	0	0	6.00	5.85

```
              ALPHA AND BETA          1.675      0.366
WEIGHTED      ALPHA AND BETA          1.510      0.434
```

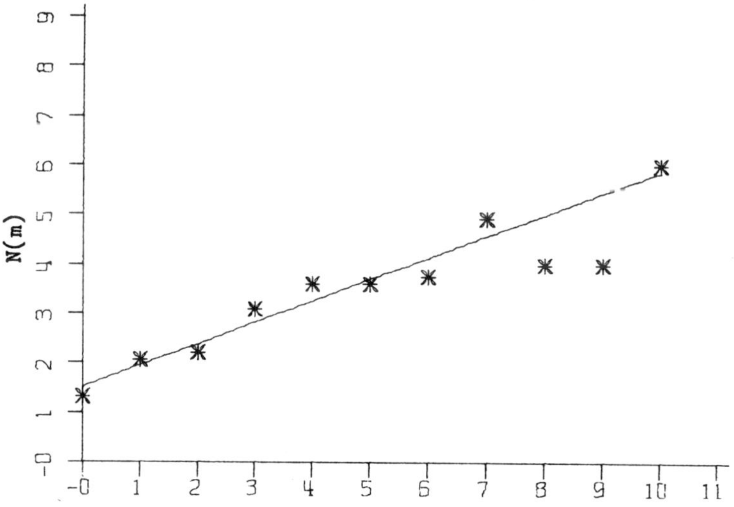

Figure A5.1b Mean circulation $N(m)$ for year $t+1$ as a function of circulation m for previous year t—WM books.
1968-1973 pairs—July 1973 data

Table A5.1c Values of $M(m)$, N_{mn}, and $N(m)$ for Different Values of m and n for WM Books Returned to Countway.
1968-1973 Pairs—October 1973 Data

m	M(m)	N_{mn}													N(m)	Theor.
		n=0	1	2	3	4	5	6	7	8	9	10	11	12		
0	69	25	19	9	6	4	3	1	1	1	0	0	0	0	1.55	1.69
1	94	15	24	14	13	19	6	0	1	0	1	1	0	0	2.37	2.07
2	71	14	15	18	5	8	5	4	2	0	0	0	0	0	2.27	2.45
3	64	3	16	11	14	6	5	3	5	1	0	0	0	0	2.97	2.83
4	36	5	4	7	8	2	6	2	1	1	0	0	0	0	2.97	3.21
5	30	1	4	10	5	1	3	3	2	1	0	0	0	0	3.27	3.59
6	21	2	4	1	4	2	1	1	5	1	0	0	0	0	3.81	3.97
7	19	0	1	3	4	3	3	3	1	1	0	0	0	0	4.16	4.36
8	8	0	0	2	1	2	0	0	1	0	1	0	0	1	5.38	4.74
9	5	0	1	0	1	0	0	0	2	1	0	0	0	0	5.20	5.12
10	2	0	0	0	0	1	1	0	0	0	0	0	0	0	4.50	5.50
11	1	0	0	0	0	0	0	0	0	0	1	0	0	0	9.00	5.88
12	2	0	0	0	0	0	1	0	0	0	0	0	1	0	8.00	6.26

```
          ALPHA AND BETA      1.194    0.512
WEIGHTED ALPHA AND BETA       1.685    0.381
```

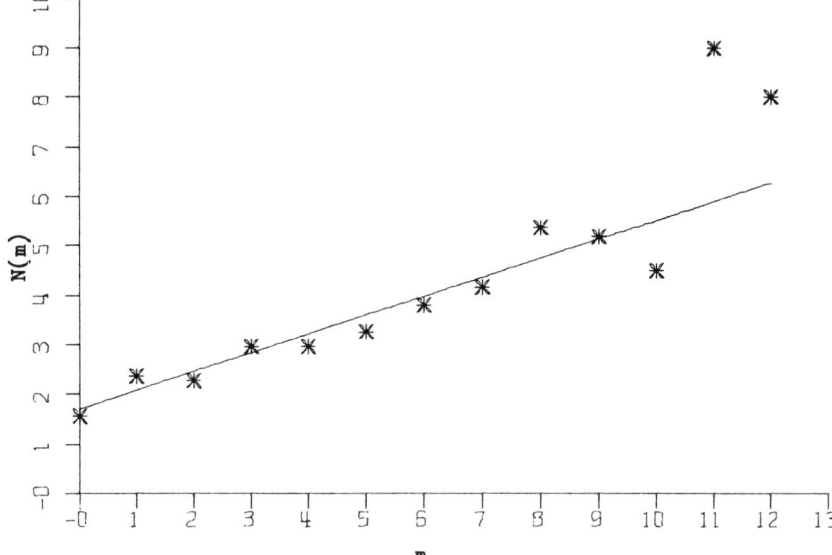

Figure A5.1c Mean circulation $N(m)$ for year $t+1$ as a function of circulation m for previous year t—WM books.
1968-1973 pairs—October 1973 data

Table A5.2a Values of $M(m)$, N_{mn}, and $N(m)$ for Different Values of m and n for WM Books Returned to Countway.
1963-1968 Pairs—April 1973 Data

m	M(m)	N_{mn}									N(m)	Theor.
		n=0	1	2	3	4	5	6	7	8		
0	47	15	16	6	5	4	0	0	1	0	1.40	1.07
1	72	25	22	11	9	5	0	0	0	0	1.26	1.41
2	50	11	19	9	4	5	2	0	0	0	1.58	1.76
3	43	9	14	11	5	2	2	0	0	0	1.60	2.10
4	31	3	4	5	6	4	4	2	2	1	3.29	2.44
5	14	2	1	1	2	4	3	1	0	0	3.29	2.78
6	9	0	4	1	2	1	1	0	0	0	2.33	3.12
7	3	1	1	0	0	0	0	1	0	0	2.33	3.47
8	1	0	0	0	0	0	0	1	0	0	6.00	3.81

```
         ALPHA AND BETA        0.914   0.413
WEIGHTED ALPHA AND BETA        1.072   0.342
```

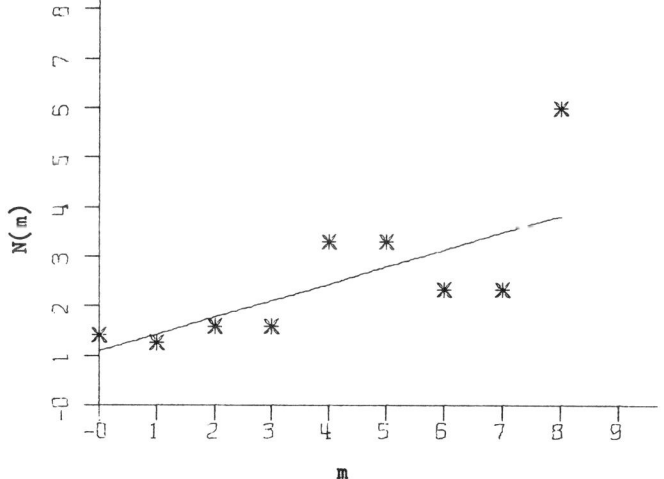

Figure A5.2a Mean circulation $N(m)$ for year $t+1$ as a function of circulation m for previous year t—WM books.
1963-1968 pairs—April 1973 data

Table A5.2b Values of $M(m)$, N_{mn}, and $N(m)$ for Different Values of m and n for WM Books Returned to Countway.
1963-1968 Pairs—July 1973 Data

m	M(m)	N_{mn}							N(m)	Theor.
		n=0	1	2	3	4	5	6		
0	26	9	8	2	5	2	0	0	1.35	1.12
1	36	18	6	5	3	4	0	0	1.14	1.38
2	38	14	5	7	8	3	0	1	1.61	1.64
3	21	2	6	3	2	2	1	0	1.95	1.89
4	15	2	4	2	2	1	2	2	2.67	2.15
5	5	1	1	3	0	0	0	0	1.40	2.41
6	3	0	0	2	1	0	0	0	2.33	2.67
7	1	0	0	0	0	1	0	0	4.00	2.92
		ALPHA AND BETA							1.028	0.293
	WEIGHTED ALPHA AND BETA								1.122	0.257

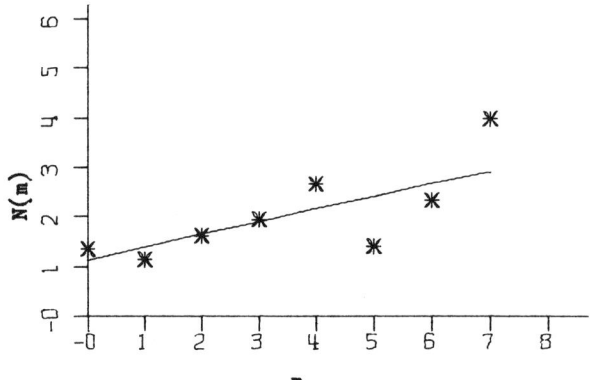

Figure A5.2b Mean circulation $N(m)$ for year $t + 1$ as a function of circulation m for previous year t—WM books.
1963-1968 pairs—July 1973 data

Appendix Five 167

Table A5.2c Values of $M(m)$, N_{mn}, and $N(m)$ for Different Values of m and n for WM Books Returned to Countway.
1963-1968 Pairs—October 1973 Data

m	M(m)	N_{mn}								N(m)	Theor.
		n=0	1	2	3	4	5	6	7		
0	22	5	4	5	3	4	0	1	0	2.05	1.63
1	42	10	13	7	8	1	2	1	0	1.69	1.76
2	45	8	19	9	5	2	1	1	0	1.58	1.89
3	31	5	6	8	8	2	2	0	0	2.06	2.02
4	19	1	5	4	5	0	2	1	1	2.68	2.16
5	9	1	3	3	0	2	0	0	0	1.89	2.29
6	5	2	0	0	3	0	0	0	0	1.80	2.42
7	1	0	0	0	0	0	0	1	0	6.00	2.55

ALPHA AND BETA 1.228 0.355
WEIGHTED ALPHA AND BETA 1.629 0.132

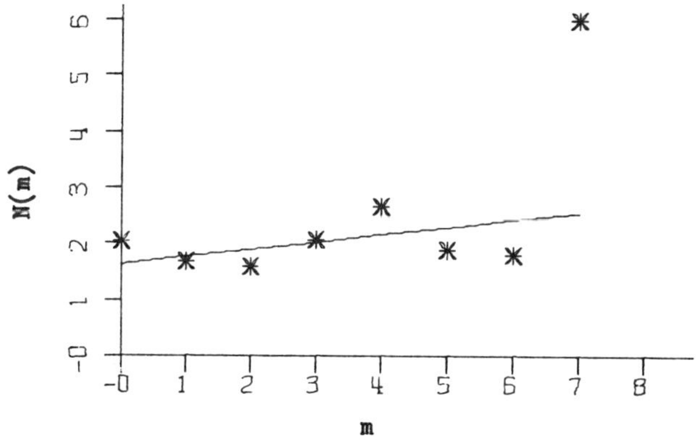

Figure A5.2c Mean circulation $N(m)$ for year $t+1$ as a function of circulation m for previous year t—WM books.
1963-1968 pairs—October 1973 data

Appendix Five   168

Table A5.3a Values of $M(m)$, N_{mn}, and $N(m)$ for Different Values of m and n for WM Books with Theoretical Values of $N(m)$ and N_{mn} Obtained by Using Eqs. 2.3, 2.4, and 2.9. (Theoretical Values of N_{mn} Are Printed on the Second Line.)
1968-1973 Pairs—April 1973 Data

m	M(m)	N_{mn}											N(m)	Theor.
		n=0	1	2	3	4	5	6	7	8	9	10		
0	103	23	36	23	11	6	3	1	0	0	0	0	1.55	1.51
		22	34	25	13	4	1	0	0	0	0	0		
1	127	28	36	31	19	6	5	1	0	0	1	0	1.72	1.89
		19	36	34	21	10	3	1	0	0	0	0		
2	126	17	38	28	16	15	3	4	2	0	2	1	2.25	2.27
		12	29	33	25	14	6	2	0	0	0	0		
3	92	9	11	27	16	13	9	4	2	1	0	0	2.78	2.65
		6	17	22	20	13	7	3	1	0	0	0		
4	77	6	10	15	17	13	9	3	2	1	1	0	3.08	3.04
		3	11	17	17	13	7	4	1	0	0	0		
5	51	1	7	11	7	9	8	1	3	0	3	1	3.73	3.42
		1	5	9	11	9	6	3	1	0	0	0		
6	17	1	2	2	1	8	0	3	0	0	0	0	3.47	3.80
		0	1	2	3	3	2	1	0	0	0	0		
7	14	0	0	2	0	5	3	1	1	1	0	1	5.00	4.18
		0	0	1	2	2	2	1	0	0	6	0		
8	8	0	0	3	1	1	2	1	0	0	0	0	3.63	4.57
		0	0	0	1	1	1	1	0	0	0	0		
9	8	1	0	1	1	2	1	1	1	0	0	0	3.88	4.95
		0	0	0	1	1	1	1	0	0	0	0		
10	2	0	0	0	0	1	0	1	0	0	0	0	5.00	5.33
		0	0	0	0	0	0	0	0	0	0	0		

Appendix Five   169

Table A5.3b Values of $M(m)$, N_{mn}, and $N(m)$ for Different Values of m and n for WM Books with Theoretical Values of $N(m)$ and N_{mn} Obtained by Using Eqs. 2.3, 2.4, and 2.9. (Theoretical Values of N_{mn} Are Printed on the Second Line.)
1968-1973 Pairs—July 1973 Data

m	M(m)	N_{mn}											N(m)	Theor.
		n=0	1	2	3	4	5	6	7	8	9	10		
0	88	30	27	16	8	3	3	1	0	0	0	0	1.32	1.51
		19	29	22	11	4	1	0	0	0	0	0		
1	82	16	22	14	17	4	4	4	0	1	0	0	2.06	1.94
		11	22	22	14	6	2	0	0	0	0	0		
2	87	17	16	20	15	9	6	2	1	1	0	0	2.23	2.38
		8	19	22	18	10	5	2	0	0	0	0		
3	66	5	7	18	13	9	7	1	4	1	1	0	3.09	2.81
		3	11	15	14	10	5	2	1	0	0	0		
4	44	3	6	8	6	5	8	2	3	2	1	0	3.59	3.25
		1	5	9	9	7	5	2	1	0	0	0		
5	23	0	3	3	6	6	2	1	1	0	1	0	3.61	3.68
		0	2	3	4	4	3	2	1	0	0	0		
6	12	0	2	2	1	3	1	2	1	0	0	0	3.75	4.12
		0	0	1	2	2	1	1	0	0	0	0		
7	11	0	2	2	1	1	0	1	0	2	1	1	4.91	4.55
		0	0	1	1	2	1	1	0	0	0	0		
8	7	0	0	2	2	0	1	1	1	0	0	0	4.00	4.98
		0	0	0	0	1	1	1	0	0	0	0		
9	3	1	0	0	0	0	1	0	1	0	0	0	4.00	5.42
		0	0	0	0	0	0	0	0	0	0	0		
10	1	0	0	0	0	0	0	1	0	0	0	0	6.00	5.85
		0	0	0	0	0	0	0	0	0	0	0		

Table A5.3c Values of $M(m)$, N_{mn}, and $N(m)$ for Different Values of m and n for WM Books with Theoretical Values of $N(m)$ and N_{mn} Obtained by Using Eqs. 2.3, 2.4, and 2.9. (Theoretical Values of N_{mn} Are Printed on the Second Line.)
1968-1973 Pairs—October 1973 Data

m	M(m)	N_{mn}													N(m)	Theor.
		n=0	1	2	3	4	5	6	7	8	9	10	11	12		
0	69	25	19	9	6	4	3	1	1	1	0	0	0	0	1.55	1.69
		12	21	18	10	4	1	0	0	0	0	0	0			
1	94	15	24	14	13	19	6	0	1	0	1	1	0	0	2.37	2.07
		11	24	25	17	9	3	1	0	0	0	0	0			
2	71	14	15	18	5	8	5	4	2	0	0	0	0	0	2.27	2.45
		6	15	18	15	9	4	1	0	0	0	0	0			
3	64	3	16	11	14	6	5	3	5	1	0	0	0	0	2.97	2.83
		3	10	15	14	10	5	2	1	0	0	0	0			
4	36	5	4	7	8	2	6	2	1	1	0	0	0	0	2.97	3.21
		1	4	7	8	6	4	2	1	0	0	0	0			
5	30	1	4	10	5	1	3	3	2	1	0	0	0	0	3.27	3.59
		0	2	5	6	5	4	2	1	0	0	0	0			
6	21	2	4	1	4	2	1	1	5	1	0	0	0	0	3.81	3.97
		0	1	3	4	4	3	2	1	0	0	0	0			
7	19	0	1	3	4	3	3	3	1	1	0	0	0	0	4.16	4.36
		0	1	2	3	3	3	2	1	0	0	0	0			
8	8	0	0	2	1	2	0	0	1	0	1	0	0	1	5.38	4.74
		0	0	0	1	1	1	1	0	0	0	0	0			
9	5	0	1	0	1	0	0	0	2	1	0	0	0	0	5.20	5.12
		0	0	0	0	0	0	0	0	0	0	0	0			
10	2	0	0	0	0	1	1	0	0	0	0	0	0	0	4.50	5.50
		0	0	0	0	0	0	0	0	0	0	0	0			
11	1	0	0	0	0	0	0	0	0	0	1	0	0	0	9.00	5.88
		0	0	0	0	0	0	0	0	0	0	0	0			
12	2	0	0	0	0	0	1	0	0	0	0	1	0	0	8.00	6.26
		0	0	0	0	0	0	0	0	0	0	0	0			

Appendix Six

Additional Results for Checking the Extended Theoretical Models Discussed in Chapter Three

The tables included in this appendix should be used together with Tables 6.6 to 6.11. In Chapter 6, analyzed results of QZ, WM, and WS books returned to Countway Library during four sample months are presented, while in this appendix, results of QU, WA, WG, and WO books are given. They are specifically used to test the models presented in Chapter 3.

Table A6.1 Uncorrected and Corrected Circulation Distributions for QU Books Returned in 1973

j	$M(j)$—1973				$4M(j)$
	Jan.	April	July	Oct.	
1	14	18	20	8	60
2	20	19	18	11	68
3	22	17	11	19	69
4	13	12	13	11	49
5	5	8	7	15	35
6	5	6	7	6	24
7	3	1	1	7	12
8	5	1	3	2	11
9	2	1	1	1	5
10	1		2	1	4
11					
12				1	1
13				1	1
Total	90	83	83	83	339
U†	24	24	23	24	95

*Corrected $4M(j) = 4M(j) \times \{[\sum_j 4M(j) + \sum_j U]/\sum 4M(j)\}$. For example, the corrected $4M(1)$ is 77, and $77 = 60 \times [(339 + 95)/339]$.
†U is the number of books for which j value is unknown.

Appendix Six

Corrected $4M(j)^*$ with U	Corrected $M(j)$	$4N(j)$	$N(j)$	Geometric $N(j)$	$N_\ell(j)$
77	19	924	231	231	366
87	22	545	136	140	158
88	22	383	96	85	101
63	16	213	53	52	54
45	11	128	32	31	32
31	8	76	19	19	19
15	4	33	8	11	8
14	4	28	7	7	7
6	2	11	3	4	3
5	1	9	2	3	2
				2	
1		2		1	
1		2		1	
433	109	2,354	587 N_a	587	750 N_ℓ

Table A6.2 Uncorrected and Corrected Circulation Distributions for WA Books Returned in 1973

j	$M(j)$—1973				$4M(j)$
	Jan.	April	July	Oct.	
1	25	27	6	20	78
2	23	17	14	9	63
3	12	10	6	6	34
4	8	8	5	2	23
5	7	2	6	5	20
6	6	3	1	2	12
7	2	1	2	1	6
8	1		1		2
9	1	1		2	4
10				1	1
11					
12	1				1
Total	86	69	41	48	244
U†	34	36	21	26	117

*See the footnotes of Table A6.1.
†See the footnotes of Table A6.1.

Corrected $M(j)^*$ with U	Corrected $M(j)$	$4N(j)$	$N(j)$	Geometric $N(j)$	$N_\ell(j)$
115	29	1,381	345	345	546
93	23	582	146	152	168
50	13	218	54	67	57
34	9	115	29	29	29
30	8	85	21	13	21
18	5	44	11	6	11
9	2	20	5	3	5
3		6	2	1	2
6	1	11	3	1	3
1		2			
1		2			
360	90	2,466	616 N_a	616	842 N_ℓ

Table A6.3 Uncorrected and Corrected Circulation Distributions for WG Books Returned in 1973

j	$M(j)$—1973				$4M(j)$
	Jan.	April	July	Oct.	
1	13	29	15	14	71
2	14	28	13	16	71
3	10	17	7	6	40
4	11	9	6	8	34
5	6	8	5	6	25
6	4	5	3	6	18
7	3	2	1	3	9
8	2	1	1	1	5
9	1	1		2	4
10		2		1	3
11		1			1
12				1	1
Total	64	103	51	64	282
U†	23	30	22	15	90

*See the footnotes of Table A6.1.
†See the footnotes of Table A6.1.

Corrected $M(j)^*$ with U	Corrected $M(j)$	$4N(j)$	$N(j)$	Geometric $N(j)$	$N_\varrho(j)$
94	24	1,128	282	282	446
94	24	589	147	144	170
53	13	231	58	74	61
45	11	152	38	38	39
33	8	94	23	19	24
24	6	59	15	10	15
12	3	26	7	5	7
7	2	14	4	3	4
5	1	9	2	1	2
4	1	7	2	1	2
1		2			
1		2			
373	93	2,313	578 N_a	577	770 N_ϱ

Table A6.4 Uncorrected and Corrected Circulation Distributions for WO Books Returned in 1973

j	$M(j)$—1973				$4M(j)$
	Jan.	April	July	Oct.	
1	5	10	12	11	38
2	7	11	11	7	36
3	8	11	12	6	37
4	4	4	6	7	21
5	2	4	4	3	13
6	2	1	2	4	9
7	1	1		3	5
8					
9		1		1	2
10	1			1	2
Total	30	43	47	43	163
$U^\dagger$	26	10	10	3	49

*See the footnotes of Table A6.1.
†See the footnotes of Table A6.1.

Appendix Six   179

Corrected $4M(j)^*$ with U	Corrected $M(j)$	$4N(j)$	$N(j)$	Geometric $N(j)$	$N_{\ell}(j)$
49	12	588	147	147	233
47	12	294	74	82	85
48	12	209	52	46	55
27	7	91	23	26	23
17	4	48	24	14	24
12	3	30	7	8	7
7	2	15	4	5	4
				3	
3	1	6	1	1	1
3	1	5	1	1	1
213	54	1,286	333 N_a	333	433 N_ℓ

Table A6.5 Predicted Following-Year Circulation for the Same QU and WA Books Circulated in 1972-1973

QU Class
$N \approx 990; N_\ell \approx 750$

$t = 0$ (1972-1973)	$t = 1$ (1973-1974)
$\alpha_a = 1.184$	
$\alpha_\ell = 0.927$	$\alpha_\ell = 0.927$
$\beta = 0.442$	$\beta = 0.442$
$\gamma(0) = 0.606$	$\gamma(1) = 0.564$
$N_a(0) \approx 587$	$N_a(1) \approx 590$
$\overline{R}_a(0) = 2.538$	$\overline{R}_a(1) = 2.296$
$C(0) = 0.783$	$C(1) = 0.786$
$\overline{R}_\ell(0) = 1.986$	$\overline{R}_\ell(1) = 1.805$
$\overline{R}_a(0)N_a(0) = \overline{R}_\ell(0)N_\ell$	$\overline{R}_a(1)N_a(1) = \overline{R}_\ell(1)N_\ell$
$\approx 1{,}490$	$\approx 1{,}354$

Table A6.6 Predicted Following-Year Circulation for the Same WG and WO Books Circulated in 1972-1973

WG Class
$N \approx 1{,}780; N_\ell \approx 770$

$t = 0$ (1972-1973)	$t = 1$ (1973-1974)
$\alpha_a = 1.304$	
$\alpha_\ell = 0.979$	$\alpha_\ell = 0.979$
$\beta = 0.381$	$\beta = 0.381$
$\gamma(0) = 0.512$	$\gamma(1) = 0.513$
$N_a(0) \approx 578$	$N_a(1) \approx 587$
$\overline{R}_a(0) = 2.050$	$\overline{R}_a(1) = 2.054$
$C(0) = 0.751$	$C(1) = 0.762$
$\overline{R}_\ell(0) = 1.539$	$\overline{R}_\ell(1) = 1.565$
$\overline{R}_a(0)N_a(0) = \overline{R}_\ell(0)N_\ell$	$\overline{R}_a(1)N_a(1) = \overline{R}_\ell(1)N_\ell$
$\approx 1{,}185$	$\approx 1{,}205$

Table A6.5 (Continued)

WA Class
$N \approx 1{,}700; N_\ell \approx 842$

$t = 0$ (1972-1973)	$t = 1$ (1973-1974)
$\alpha_a = 1.130$	
$\alpha_\ell = 0.827$	$\alpha_\ell = 0.827$
$\beta = 0.296$	$\beta = 0.296$
$\gamma(0) = 0.440$	$\gamma(1) = 0.436$
$N_a(0) \approx 616$	$N_a(1) \approx 577$
$\overline{R}_a(0) = 1.786$	$\overline{R}_a(1) = 1.773$
$C(0) = 0.732$	$C(1) = 0.685$
$\overline{R}_\ell(0) = 1.307$	$\overline{R}_\ell(1) = 1.214$
$\overline{R}_a(0)N_a(0) = \overline{R}_\ell(0)N_\ell$	$\overline{R}_a(1)N_a(1) = \overline{R}_\ell(1)N_\ell$
$\approx 1{,}100$	$\approx 1{,}023$

Table A6.6 (Continued)

WO Class
$N \approx 990; N_\ell \approx 433$

$t = 0$ (1972-1973)	$t = 1$ (1973-1974)
$\alpha_a = 1.137$	
$\alpha_\ell = 0.874$	$\alpha_\ell = 0.874$
$\beta = 0.408$	$\beta = 0.408$
$\gamma(0) = 0.559$	$\gamma(1) = 0.524$
$N_a(0) \approx 333$	$N_a(1) \approx 326$
$\overline{R}_a(0) = 2.265$	$\overline{R}_a(1) = 2.102$
$C(0) = 0.769$	$C(1) = 0.754$
$\overline{R}_\ell(0) = 1.742$	$\overline{R}_\ell(1) = 1.585$
$\overline{R}_a(0)N_a(0) = \overline{R}_\ell(0)N_\ell$	$\overline{R}_a(1)N_a(1) = \overline{R}_\ell(1)N_\ell$
≈ 754	≈ 686

Table A7.2 Subject Distribution of the 163 High-Circulation Books

Subject (NLM Class)	No. of Books	Subject (NLM Class)	No. of Books
WS Pediatrics	18	QT Human Physiology	3
WL Nervous System	16	QS Human Anatomy	2
WM Psychiatry	16	WC Infectious Diseases	2
QU Biochemistry	12	WI Gastrointestinal System	2
WG Cardiovascular System	10	WP Gynecology	2
W Medical Profession	9	WQ Obstetrics	2
QW Bacteriology and Immunology	7	BF Psychology	1
WA Public Health	7	HA Statistics	1
WF Respiratory System	7	HQ Family; Marriage; Woman	1
QZ Pathology	6	QD Chemistry	1
WK Endocrine System	6	QX Parasitology	1
QV Pharmacology	5	QY Clinical Pathology	1
WH Hemic and Lymphatic System	5	WJ Urogenital System	1
WO Surgery	4	WT Geriatrics; Chronic Diseases	1
QH Biology	3	WV Otorhinolaryngology	1
WB Practice of Medicine	3	ZW Bibliographies of Medicine	1
WD Noninfectious Diseases	3	Total	163
WE Musculoskeletal System	3		

A List of the Most Frequently Circulated Books in Countway

12 Circulations

1. Tepperman, J. *Metabolic and Endocrine Physiology*. Chicago: Yearbook Medical, 1962 and 1968. (WK)

10 Circulations

1. Goodman, L. S., and Gilman, A., eds. *The Pharmacological Basis of Therapeutics*. 3d ed. New York: Macmillan, 1965. (QV)

2. Shands, A. R., and Raney, R. B. *Handbook of Orthopaedic Surgery*. St. Louis: Mosby, 1967. (WE)

9 Circulations

1. Goldman, M. J. *Principles of Clinical Electrocardiography*. 6th ed. Los Altos, Calif.: Lange, 1967. (WG)

2. Harrison, T. R., ed. *Principles of Internal Medicine*. 5th ed. New York: McGraw-Hill, 1966. (WB)

3. Klarman, H. E. *The Economics of Health*. New York: Columbia University Press, 1965. (W)

4. Nelson, W. E., ed. *Textbook of Pediatrics*. 8th ed. Philadelphia: Saunders, 1964. (WS)

8 Circulations

1. McDonald, George A., et al. *Atlas of Haematology*. 2d. ed. Edinburgh: Livingstone, 1968. (WH)

7 Circulations

1. DiMascio, A., and Shader, R. F., eds. *Clinical Handbook of Psychopharmacology*. New York: Science House, 1970. (QV)

2. Ganong, W. F., and Martini, L., eds. *Frontiers in Neuroendocrinology*. New York: Oxford University Press, 1969. (WK)

3. Jakoby, W. B., ed. *Enzyme Purification and Related Techniques*. Methods of Enzymology, edited by S. P. Colowick and N. O. Kaplan, vol. 22. New York: Academic Press, 1971. (QU)

4. Markowitz, M., and Gordis, L. *Rheumatic Fever*. 2d ed. Major Problems in Clinical Pediatrics, vol. 2. Philadelphia: Saunders, 1972. (WS)

5. West, John B. *Ventilation: Blood Flow and Gas Exchange*. Oxford: Blackwell, 1965. (WF)

6 Circulations

1. Brewer, George J., ed. *Red Cell Metabolism and Function: Proceedings of the First International Conference on Red Cell Metabolism and Functions.* Advances in Experimental Medicine and Biology, vol. 6. New York: Plenum, 1970. (W)

2. Caro, C. G., ed. *Advances in Respiratory Physiology.* Baltimore: Williams & Wilkins, 1966. (WF)

3. Erikson, E. H. *Childhood and Society.* New York: Norton, 1950. (WS)

4. Estabrook, R. W., and Pullman, M. E. *Oxidation and Phosphorylation.* Methods in Enzymology, edited by S. P. Colowick and N. O. Kaplan, vol. 10. New York: Academic Press, 1967. (QU)

5. Ginzberg, E., and Ostow, M. *Men, Money, and Medicine.* New York: Columbia University Press, 1969. (WA)

6. Grant, J. C. B. *An Atlas of Anatomy.* 5th. ed. Baltimore: Williams & Wilkins, 1962. (QS)

7. Harris, J. W. *The Red Cell: Production, Metabolism, Destruction: Normal and Abnormal.* Cambridge, Mass.: Harvard University Press, 1963. (WH)

8. Haurowitz, F. *Immunochemistry and the Biosynthesis of Antibodies.* New York: Interscience, 1968. (QW)

9. Luriia, A. R. *The Role of Speech in the Regulation of Normal and Abnormal Behavior*, edited by J. Tizard. New York: Liveright, 1961. (WS)

10. Norman, J. C., ed. *Cardiac Surgery.* New York: Appleton-Century-Crofts, 1967. (WG)

11. Novak, Emil, and Novak, E. R. *Textbook of Gynecology*, edited by Edmund R. Novak et al. 7th ed. Baltimore: Williams & Wilkins, 1965. (WP)

12. Pitts, R. F. *Physiology of the Kidney and Body Fluids.* Chicago: Yearbook Medical, 1963. (WJ)

13. Stanbury, John B., et al., eds. *The Metabolic Basis of Inherited Disease.* New York: McGraw-Hill, 1966. (WD)

14. Truex, R. C., and Carpenter, M. B. *Human Neuroanatomy.* 6th ed. Baltimore: Williams & Wilkins, 1964. (WL)

15. Weibel, E. R. *Morphometry of the Human Lung.* New York: Academic Press, 1963. (WF)

5 Circulations

1. Bartalos, M., ed. *Genetics in Medical Practice.* Philadelphia: Lippincott, 1968. (QZ)

2. Ciba Foundation. *Symposium on Physiology, Emotion and Psychosomatic Illness, London.* New York: Associated Scientific Publisher, 1972. (WM)

3. Colowick, S. P., and Kaplan, N. O. *Preparation and Assay of Enzymes.* Methods in Enzymology, vol. 1. New York: Academic Press, 1955. (QU)

4. Dahlstrom, W. G., et al. *An MMPI Handbook*, vol. 1: *Clinical Interpretation.* Rev. ed. Minneapolis: University of Minnesota Press, 1972. (WM)

5. Dubin, D. *Rapid Interpretation of EKG's.* Tampa, Florida: Cover Publishing Co., 1970. (WG)

6. Eastman, N. J., and Hellman, L. M., eds. *Williams Obstetrics.* New York: Appleton-Century-Crofts, 1966. (WQ)

7. Felson, B. *Fundamentals of Chest Roentgenology.* Philadelphia: Saunders, 1960. (WF)

8. Flatt, A. E. *The Care of the Rheumatoid Hand.* St. Louis: Mosby, 1968 and 1972. (WE)

9. Hume, M., et al. *Venous Thrombosis and Pulmonary Embolism.* Cambridge, Mass.: Harvard University Press, 1970. (WG)

10. James, J. A. *Renal Disease in Childhood.* 2d. ed. St. Louis: Mosby, 1972. (WS)

11. Krugman, S., and Ward, R. *Infectious Diseases of Children.* St. Louis: Mosby, 1968. (WC)

12. Kugel, R., and Wolfensberger, W., eds. *Changing Patterns in Residential Services for the Mentally Retarded.* Washington D.C.: Government Printing Office, 1969. (WM)

13. Kupfer, D. J., comp. *Lithium and Psychiatry Journal Articles.* Flushing, N.Y.: Medical Examination Publishing Co., 1971.' (QV)

14. Lees, F. *The Diagnosis and Treatment of Diseases Affecting the Nervous System.* New York: American Elsevier, 1970. (WL)

15. Lesse, S., ed. *An Evaluation of the Results of the Psychotherapies.* Springfield, Ill.: C. C. Thomas, 1968. (WM)

16. Lidz, Theodore, et al. *Schizophrenia and the Family.* New York: International Universities Press, 1967. (WM)

17. MacAlpine, D., et al. *Multiple Sclerosis: A Reappraisal.* Baltimore: Williams & Wilkins, 1966. (WL)

18. Masters, W. H., and Johnson, V. E. *Human Sexual Response.* Boston: Little, Brown, 1966. (HQ)

19. Moore, F. D., et al. *Post-Traumatic Pulmanary Insufficiency.* Philadelphia: Saunders, 1969. (WF)

20. Oski, F., and Naiman, J. R. *Hematologic Problems in the Newborn.* Major Problems in Clinical Pediatrics, vol. 4. Philadelphia: Saunders, 1972. (WS)

21. Ruch, T. C., et al. *Neurophysiology.* Philadelphia: Saunders, 1961. (WL)

22. Schubert, M., and Hamerman, D. *A Primer on Connective Tissue Biochemistry.* Philadelphia: Lea & Febiger, 1968. (QS)

23. Somers, A. R., and Somers, H. M. *Doctors, Patients, and Health Insurance.* Washington D.C.: Brookings, 1961. (W)

24. Stanier, R. Y., et al. *The Microbial World.* Englewood Cliffs, N. J.: Prentice-Hall, 1963. (QW)

25. Symposium on System Analysis Applied to Health, Washington, D.C., 1971. *System Analysis Applied to Health.* Pan American Sanitary Bureau Scientific Publication, no. 239. Washington, D.C.: Pan American Sanitary Bureau, 1972. (WA)

26. Upjohn Company. *Diabetes.* Kalamazoo, Mich.: Upjohn Co., 1967. (WK)

27. Watson, J. D. *Molecular Biology of the Gene.* New York: W. A. Benjamin, 1965. (QH)

4 Circulations

1. Adair, J., and Deuschle, K. *The People's Health.* New York: Appleton, 1970. (WA)

2. Adams, C. W., ed. *Neurohistochemistry.* Amsterdam: Elsevier, 1965. (WL)

3. Bahn, A. K. *Basic Medical Statistics.* New York: Grune & Stratton, 1972. (HA)

4. Bailey, H. *Demonstrations of Physical Signs in Clinical Surgery.* Baltimore: Williams & Wilkins, 1960. (WO)

5. Baker, B. R. *Design of Active-Site-Directed Irreversible Enzyme Inhibitors.* New York: Wiley, 1967. (QU)

6. Balin, H., and Glasser, S., eds. *Reproductive Biology.* Amsterdam: Excerpta Medica, 1972. (WQ)

7. Ballhausen, C. J., and Gray, H. B. *Molecular Orbital Theory.* New York: W. A. Benjamin, 1964. (QD)

8. Becker, H. S. *Boys in White: Student Culture in Medical School.* Chicago: University of Chicago Press, 1961. (W)

9. Beecher, H. K. *Research and the Individual: Human Studies.* Boston: Little, Brown, 1970. (W)

10. Beeson, R. and McDermott, W., eds. *Textbook of Medicine.* 12th ed. Philadelphia: Saunders, 1967. (WB)

11. Behrman, S. J., and Kistner, R. W., eds. *Progress in Infertility.* Boston: Little, Brown, 1968. (WP)

12. Belding, D. L. *Textbook of Parasitology.* 3d ed. New York: Appleton, 1965. (QX)

13. Berne, E. *Principles of Group Treatment.* New York: Oxford University Press, 1966. (WM)

14. Berne, R. M., and Levy, M. N. *Cardiovascular Physiology.* St. Louis: Mosby, 1967. (WG)

15. Birch, H., ed. *Brain Damage in Children: The Biological and Social Aspects.* Baltimore: Williams & Wilkins, 1964. (WS)

16. Blesser, W. B. *A Systems Approach to Biomedicine.* New York: McGraw-Hill, 1969. (QT)

17. Bourne, G. H. *The Structure and Function of Nervous Tissue.* New York: Academic Press, 1968. (WL)

18. Brain, W. R. *Clinical Neurology.* London: Oxford University Press, 1964. (WL)

19. ———. *Diseases of the Nervous System.* London: Oxford University Press, 1962. (WL)

20. Brodsky, I., and Benham, S., eds. *Cancer Chemotherapy II: Twenty-Second Hahnemann Symposium.* New York: Grune & Stratton, 1972. (QZ)

21. Browne, K., and Freeling, P. *The Doctor-Patient Relationship.* Edinburgh: Livingstone, 1967. (W)

22. Bryant, J. H. *Health and the Developing World.* Ithaca, N.Y.: Cornell University Press, 1969. (WA)

23. Burnet, M. F. *Cellular Immunology.* Cambridge, England: Cambridge University Press, 1969. (QW)

24. Cailliet, R. *Low Back Pain Syndrome.* 2d ed. Philadelphia: Davis, 1968. (WE)

25. Castellanos, A., Jr., and Lemberg, L. *Electrophysiology of Pacing and Cardioversion.* New York: Appleton, 1969. (WG)

26. Chalfant, J. C., and Schefflin, M. A., eds. *Central Processing Dysfunctions in Children.* National Institute for Neurological Diseases and Stroke Monograph, no. 9. Bethesda, Md.: U.S. Department of Health, Education, and Welfare, 1969. (WS)

27. Chapman, A. H. *Textbook of Clinical Psychiatry.* Philadelphia: Lippincott, 1967. (WM)

28. Clayton, R. B., ed. *Steroids and Terpenoids.* Methods in Enzymology, edited by S. P. Colowick and N. O. Kaplan, vol. 15. New York: Academic Press, 1969. (QU)

29. Comroe: J. H., et al. *The Lung: Clinical Physiology and Pulmonary Function Tests.* 2d ed. Chicago: Yearbook Medical, 1962. (WF)

30. Curran, Robert C. *Color Atlas of Histopathology.* New York: Oxford University Press, 1966. (QZ)

31. Dalessio, D. J., ed. *Headache.* 3d ed. New York: Oxford University Press, 1972. (WL)

32. Damm, H. C. *Practical Manual for Clinical Laboratory Procedures.* Cleveland: Chemical Rubber Co., 1965. (QY)

33. Davson, H. *Physiology of the Cerebrospinal Fluids.* London: Churchill, 1967. (WL)

34. Deutsch, H. *Selected Problems of Adolescence, with Special Emphasis on Group Formation.* New York: International Universities Press, 1967. (WS)

35. Florey, H. C. *General Pathology.* Philadelphia: Saunders, 1962. (QZ)

36. Fritz, I., ed. *Insulin Action.* Proceedings of Symposium on Insulin Action, Toronto, 1971. New York: Academic Press, 1971. (WK)

37. Fry, J., and Farndale, W. A. J., eds. *International Medical Care.* Wallington, Pa.: Washington Square East, 1972. (WA)

38. Fudenberg, H. H., et al. *Basic Immunogenetics.* New York: Oxford University Press, 1972. (QW)

39. Gilroy, J., and Meyer, J. J. *Medical Neurology.* New York: Macmillan, 1969. (WL)

40. Glasser, A. J., and Zimmerman, I. L. *Clinical Interpretation of the Wechsler Intelligence Scale for Children.* New York: Grune & Stratton, 1967. (BF)

41. Grant, R. P. *Clinical Electrocardiography.* New York: McGraw-Hill, 1957. (WG)

42. Greenfield, H. I. *Allied Health Manpower: Trends and Prospects.* New York: Columbia University Press, 1969. (W)

43. Grossman, L., and Moldave, K., eds. *Nucleic Acids.* Methods in Enzymology, edited by S. P. Colowick and N. O. Kaplan, vol. 12B. New York: Academic Press, 1968. (QU)

44. Hartmann, H. *Essays on Ego Psychology: Selected Problems in Psychoanalytic Theory.* New York: International Universities Press, 1964. (WM)

45. Hausman, L. *Illustrations of the Nervous System: Atlas III.* Springfield, Ill.: C. C. Thomas, 1961. (WL)

46. Hay, E. D. *Regeneration.* New York: Rinehart, 1966. (QH)

47. Heald, F. P., and Hung, W., eds. *Adolescent Endocrinology.* New York: Appleton, 1970. (WS)

48. Henriksen, S. D. *Immunology.* Baltimore: Williams & Wilkins, 1970. (QW)

49. Horney, K. *Our Inner Conflicts.* New York: Norton, 1945. (WM)

50. Humphrey, J. H., and White, R. G. *Immunology for Students of Medicine.* Philadelphia: Davis, 1963. (QW)

51. Hurst, J. W., and Logue, R. B., eds. *The Heart.* New York: Blakiston, 1966. (WG)

52. *International Conference on Nosocomial Inflections, 1970.*

Proceedings. Sponsored by Center for Disease Control. Chicago: American Hospital Association, 1971. (WC)

53. Kaplan, H. S. *Hodgkin's Disease.* Cambridge, Mass.: Harvard University Press, 1972. (WH)

54. Kessler, J. W. *Psychopathology of Childhood.* Englewood Cliffs, N.J.: Prentice-Hall, 1966. (WS)

55. Kissane, J. M., and Smith, M. G. *Pathology of Infancy and Childhood.* St. Louis: Mosby, 1967. (WS)

56. Kopin, Erwin J., ed. *Neurotransmitters.* Baltimore: Williams & Wilkins, 1972. (WL)

57. Kovar, L. C. *Faces of the Adolescent Girl.* Englewood Cliffs, N.J.: Prentice-Hall, 1968. (WS)

58. Krieg, W. J. *Functional Neuroanatomy.* 3d rev. ed. Evanston, Ill.: Brain Books, 1966. (WL)

59. Levey, S., and Loombe, M. P., eds. *Health Care Administration.* Philadelphia: Lippincott, 1972. (WA)

60. Lichtenberg, P., and Norton, D. C. *Cognitive and Mental Development in the First Five Years of Life.* Chevy Chase, Md.: National Institute of Mental Health, 1970. (WS)

61. Lillie, R. D., ed. *Biological Stains: A Handbook on the Nature and Uses of the Dyes Employed in the Biological Laboratory.* 8th ed. Baltimore: Williams & Wilkins, 1969. (QH)

62. Luce, G. G. *Body Time: Physiological Rhythms and Social Stress.* New York: Pantheon, 1971. (QT)

63. McCormick, D. B., and Wright, L. D. *Vitamins and Coenzymes.* Methods in Enzymology, edited by S. P. Colowick and N. O. Kaplan, vol. 18C. New York: Academic Press, 1971. (QU)

64. McDonald, G. A., et al. *Atlas of Haematology.* Baltimore: Williams & Wilkins, 1965. (WH)

65. MacFarlane, D. A., and Thomas, L. P. *Textbook of Surgery.* 3d. ed. Baltimore: Williams & Wilkins, 1972. (WO)

66. McKusick, W. A. *Heritable Disorders of Connective Tissue.* 4th ed. St. Louis: Mosby, 1972. (WD)

67. Martini, L., and Ganong, W. F., eds. *Neuroendocrinology,* vol. 1. New York: Academic Press, 1966. (WK)

68. Massachusetts. Division of Maternal and Child Health. *Maternal and Child Health Services in Boston.* Boston: Department of Public Health, 1962. (WA)

69. Milhorat, A. T., ed. *Exploratory Concepts in Muscular Dystrophy and Related Disorders: Proceedings of the International Congress Convened by Muscular Dystrophy Association of America at Arden House, Harriman, New York, October 22-27, 1966.* Excerpta Medica International Congress Series, no. 147. Amsterdam: Excerpta Medica Foundation, 1967. (ZW)

70. Neel, J. V., et al; eds. *Genetics and the Epidemiology of Chronic Diseases.* Washington, D.C.: United States Public Health Services, 1963. (WT)

71. Nelson, G. J., ed. *Blood Lipids and Lipoproteins.* New York: Wiley, 1972. (QU)

72. Odgers, R. S., and Wenberg, B. F., eds. *Introduction to Health Professions.* St. Louis: Mosby, 1972. (W)

73. Paul, G. L. *Insight vs. Desensitization in Psychotherapy.* Stanford, Calif.: Stanford University Press, 1966. (WM)

74. Perloff, J. K. *The Clinical Recognition of Congenital Heart Disease.* Philadelphia: Saunders, 1970. (WG)

75. Polezhaev, L. V. *Loss and Restoration of Regenerative Capacity in Tissues and Organs of Animals.* Cambridge, Mass.: Harvard University Press, 1972. (QZ)

76. Porter, R., ed. *The Role of Learning in Psychotherapy.* Ciba Foundation Symposium. London: Churchill, 1968. (WM)

77. Porter, R., and Birch, J., eds. *Identification of Asthma.* Ciba Foundation Study Group, no. 38. Edinburgh: Livingstone, 1971. (WF)

78. Porter, R., and O'Conner, M., eds. *Cystic Fibrosis.* Boston: Little, Brown, 1968. (WI)

79. Prechtl, H., and Beintema, D. *The Neurological Examination of the Full Term Newborn Infant.* London: Spastics Society of Medical Education and Information, 1964. (WL)

80. Rapaport, F. T., and Dausset, J. *Human Transplantation.* New York: Grune & Stratton, 1968. (WO)

81. de Reuck, A. V. S., and Cameron, M. P., eds. *Symposium on*

Lysosomes, London, 1963. Ciba Foundation Symposium. Boston: Little, Brown, 1963. (QU)

82. Robson, J. R., et al. *Malnutrition, Its Causation and Control: With Special Reference to Protein Calorie Malnutrition,* vol. 1. New York: Gordon & Breach, 1972. (WD)

83. Ruch, T. C., et al. *Neurophysiology.* 2d ed. Philadelphia: Saunders, 1965. (WL)

84. Rushmer, R. F. *Cardiovascular Dynamics.* Philadelphia: Saunders, 1961. (WG)

85. Sawyer, C. H., and Gorski, R. A., eds. *Steroid Hormones and Brain Function.* Los Angeles: University of California Press, 1971. (WB)

86. Schiff, L., ed. *Diseases of the Liver.* 3d ed. Philadelphia: Lippincott, 1969. (WI)

87. Scrimshaw, N. B., et al., eds. *Interactions of Nutrition and Infection.* Monograph Series, no. 57. Geneva: World Health Organization, 1968. (QZ)

88. Slavson, S. R. *A Textbook in Analytic Group Psychotherapy.* New York: International Universities Press, 1964. (WM)

89. Smith, D. W., and Marshall, R. E. *Introduction to Clinical Pediatrics.* Philadelphia: Saunders, 1972. (WS)

90. Spitz, R. *The First Year of Life.* New York: International Universities Press, 1965. (WS)

91. Steiner, M. M. *Clinical Approach to Endocrine Problems in Children.* St. Louis: Mosby, 1970. (WS)

92. Stendler, C. *Readings in Child Behavior and Development.* New York: Harcourt, Brace & World, 1964. (WS)

93. Sullivan, H. S. *Schizophrenia as a Human Process.* New York: Norton, 1962. (WM)

94. Sutherland, V. C. *Synopsis of Pharmacology.* Philadelphia: Saunders, 1970. (QV)

95. Timasheff, S. N., and Fasman, G. D., eds. *Subunits in Biological Systems.* Part A. New York: Dekker, 1971. (QU)

96. Torrey, E. F. *Ethical Issues in Medicine: The Role of the Physician in Today's Society.* Boston: Little, Brown, 1968. (W)

97. Tuttle, W. W., and Schottelius, B. A. *Textbook of Physiology.* St. Louis: Mosby, 1965. (QT)

98. Umbreit, W. W., et al. *Manometric Techniques.* Minneapolis: Burgess, 1972. (QU)

99. U.S. Food and Drug Administration. Advisory Committee on Obstetrics and Gynecology. *Second Report on Oral Contraceptives.* Washington D.C.: FDA, 1969. (QV)

100. Varley, H. *Practical Clinical Biochemistry.* New York: Wiley, 1967. (QU)

101. Weiner, I. B. *Psychodiagnosis in Schizophrenia.* New York: Wiley, 1966. (WM)

102. Williams, R. H. *Textbook of Endocrinology.* 3d ed. Philadelphia: Saunders, 1962. (WK)

103. Wilner, D. M., and Kassebaum, G., ed. *Narcotics.* New York: McGraw-Hill, 1965. (WM)

104. Wing, L. *Autistic Children.* New York: Brunner-Mazel, 1972. (WM)

105. Wintrobe, M. M. *Clinical Hematology.* 5th ed. Philadelphia: Lea & Febiger, 1961. (WH)

106. Wolstenholme, G. E. W., and Knight, J., eds. *Complement.* Boston: Little, Brown, 1964. (QW)

107. ———. *Taste and Smell in Vertebrates.* London: Churchill, 1969. (WV)

108. Wylie, W. D., and Churchill-Davidson, H. C. *A Practice of Anaesthesia.* London: Lloyd-Luke, 1972. (WO)

Glossary of Symbols

Symbol	Definition	First Reference
C	Fraction of active (N_a) to live (N_l) books	Eq. 3.19, Table 6.6
$C(t)$	Fraction of active (N_a) to total books (N) in tth year	Eq. 2.15
e	= 2.718, base of natural logarithms	Eq. 2.1
$F(\geq m)$	Fraction having m or more	Eq. 3.15
j, m, n	Number of circulations (integers)	Eqs. 2.1, 3.1 Table 2.1
M	Total number of examples in the sample	Table 2.1
$M(a)$	Number of books of a given sample returned during a sample period	Eq. 3.5
$M(j)$	Number of $M(a)$ books circulated j times during the year preceding the end of the sample period	Eq. 3.5
$M(m)$	Number of examples with m circulations in year t	Table 2.1
N	Total number of books in a sample collection	Eq. 2.14
N_a	Number of active (or circulated) books	Eqs. 2.14, 3.6
N_d	Number of dead (potentially little used) books	Eq. 3.16
N_{ij}	The degree of "connectedness" between two classes of books	Table A3.1
N_l	Number of live (potentially useful) books, $N_l > N_a$	Eq. 3.16, Table 6.9
N_{mn}	Number of examples that have m circulations in year t and n circulations in year $t+1$	Table 2.1
N_0	Number of inactive (or noncirculated) books	Eq. 2.14

Glossary of Symbols

Symbol	Definition	First Reference
$N(j)$	The expected number of books with j circulations during the year	Eq. 3.5, Table 6.9
$N(>m)$	Number of books circulated more than m	Eq. 3.14
$N(m)$	Mean circulation during year $t+1$ given that the sample has m circulations in year t	Table 2.1
$n!$	$= 1 \cdot 2 \cdot 3 \cdots (n-1) \times n$	Eq. 2.1
$P(\geqslant m)$	Probability of m or greater circulations	Eq. 2.11
P_n	Probability of n occurring	Eq. 2.1
$P(n\|m)$	Conditional probability of n, given the occurrence of m	
$P_0(t)$	Fraction of inactive books during their tth year	Eq. 2.15
$\overline{R}$	Mean circulation rate	Eq. 2.5
$\overline{R}_a$	Mean circulation of the active books	Eq. 3.12, Table 6.9
$\overline{R}_a N_a$	Total circulation for a given period	Eq. 3.21
$\overline{R}_\ell$	Mean circulation of live books	Eq. 3.20, Table 6.6
T_{mn}	Transition probability in Markov process	Eq. 2.3
t	Time interval	Eq. 2.2
U	Number of books for which the value of j is unknown	Eq. 3.7, Table 6.6
α, β	Markov circulation parameters	Eqs. 2.3, 2.4, 2.7
γ	Parameter in the geometric distribution of circulation	Eq. 2.11
ρ	Fraction of a time period; also used as a browsing rate	Table 3.3, Eq. A3.1
μ	Mean fractional loan period	Eq. 3.26

Bibliography

Ackoff, R. L., and Sasieni, M. W. *Fundamentals of Operations Research*. New York: Wiley, 1968.

Allen, A. "[Letter]." *RQ*, 6 (Winter 1968), 91.

Ash, L. "Opening the Chambered Nautilus." *Library Journal*, 89 (May 15, 1964), 2040-2043.

——. *Yale's Selective Book Retirement Program*. Hamden, Conn.: Shoe String Press, 1963.

Association of Research Libraries. *Newsletter. ARL Management Supplement*, no. 62 (April 1973).

Atkin, Pauline. *A Bibliography of Use Surveys 1950-70*. London: The Library Association, 1971.

Batchelor, James H. *Operations Research: An Annotated Bibliography*, vol. 2. St. Louis, Mo.: St. Louis University Press, 1962.

Bellomy, F. L. "The Systems Approach Solves Library Problems." *ALA Bulletin*, 62 (October 1968), 1121-1125.

Benjamin, C. G. *Scientific Research*, 3 (September 16, 1968), 32.

Bharucha-Reid, A. T. *Elements of the Theory of Markov Process and Their Applications*. New York: McGraw-Hill, 1960.

Bookstein, Abraham. "On Morse-Chen Book-Use Model." *Library Quarterly*, 45 (April 1975), 195-198.

Booz, Allen, and Hamilton, Inc. *Organization and Staffing of the Libraries of Columbia University: A Case Study*. Westport, Conn.: Redgrave Information Resources Corp., 1973.

——. *Problems in University Library Management*. Washington, D.C.: Association of Research Libraries, 1970.

Bowker Annual of Library and Book Trade Information. 18th ed. New York: R. R. Bowker, 1973.

Bradford, S. C. *Documentation*. London: Lockwood, 1948.

Brenni, Vito J. "Book Selection and the University." *Catholic Library World*, 38 (March 1967), 425-429.

Broadus, Robert N. *Selecting Materials for Libraries*. New York: H. W. Wilson, 1973.

Bromberg, Erik. "Simplified PPBS for the Librarians." *Protean*, 2 (Spring 1972), 9-15.

Buckland, Michael K. *Book Availability and the Library Use*. New York: Pergamon, 1975.

——. "An Operations Research Study of a Variable Loan and Duplication Policy at the University of Lancaster." *Library Quarterly*, 42 (January 1972), 97-106.

Buckland, Michael K., and Hindle, A. "Loan Policies, Duplication and Availability." In *Planning Library Services: Proceedings of a Research Seminar Held at the University of Lancaster, 9-11 July, 1969*, edited by A. G. Mackenzie and I. M. Stuart. Lancaster, England: University of Lancaster Library, 1969.

Buckland, Michael K., and Woodburn, I. "An Analytical Approach to Duplication and Availability." *University of Lancaster Occasional Papers*, no. 2. Lancaster, England: University of Lancaster Library, 1968.

Burdick, C. "The Library and the Academic Community." *Library Resources and Technical Services*, 8 (Spring 1964), 157-160.

Burns, R. W., Jr. "A Generalized Methodology for Library Systems Analysis." *College and Research Libraries*, 32 (July 1971), 295-303.

Bush, G. C., Galliher, H. P., and Morse, Philip M. "Attendance and Use of the Science Library." *American Documentation*, 8 (January 1956), 87-109.

Butler, Pierce. *An Introduction to Library Science*. Chicago, University of Chicago Press, 1933.

Carnegie Commission on Higher Education. *The More Effective Use of Resources: An Imperative for Higher Education*. New York: McGraw-Hill, 1972.

Carter, Mary Duncan, and Bonk, Wallace John. *Building Library Collections*. Metuchen, N. J.: The Scarecrow Press, 1969.

Cassata, Mary B., ed. "Book Storage." *Library Trends*, 19 (January 1971), 290-395.

Castagna, Edwin. "Last Rites: Uneasy Business of Disposing of Bookish Remains." *AB Bookman's Weekly*, 40 (October 2-9, 1967), 1191-1194.

Chen, Ching-chih. *Applications of Operations Research Models to Libraries*. Ph.D. thesis, School of Library Science, Case Western Reserve University, September 1974.

——. "Current Status of Biomedical Book Reviewing." Parts I and II. *Bulletin of the Medical Library Association*, 62 (April 1974), 105-119.

——. "Current Status of Biomedical Book Reviewing." Parts III to V. *Bulletin of the Medical Library Association*, 62 (July 1974), 296-313.

——. "How Do Scientists Meet Their Information Needs?" *Special Libraries*, 65 (July 1974), 272-280.

——. "Trends in Biophysical Research and Their Implications for Medical Libraries." *Bulletin of the Medical Library Association*, 61 (April 1973), 214-224.

——. "The Use Patterns of Physics Journals in a Large Academic Research Library." *Journal of the American Society for Information Science*, 23 (July-August 1972), 254-270.

Churchman, C. West. *The System Approach*. New York: Dell Publishing Co., 1968.

Cooper, Marianne. "Criteria for Weeding of Collections." *Library Resources and Technical Services*, 12 (Summer 1968), 339-351.

Council on Library Resources. *On the Economics of Library Operation*. Princeton, N. J.: Mathematica Inc., 1967.

―――. "On the Economics of Library Operations in Colleges and Universities." Unpublished report, prepared for the Council by Mathematica Inc., 1972.

Cox, J. G. "Optimum Storage of Library Material." Ph.D. dissertation, Purdue University, June 1964.

Danton, J. P. *Book Selection and Book Collections: A Comparison of German and American Universities*. New York: Columbia University Press, 1963.

―――. "Subject Specialist in National and University Libraries with Specific Reference to Book Selection." *Libri*, 17 (January 1967), 42-58.

Davis, R. A., and Bailey, C. A. *Bibliography of Use Studies*. Philadelphia: Drexel Institute of Technology, Graduate School of Library Science, 1964.

Dawson, C. S., Aldrin, E. E., and Gould, E. P. "Increasing Effectiveness of the MIT Science Library by the Use of Circulation Statistics." Unpublished report for Operations Research Course 8.75, MIT, January 1962.

De Solla Price, D. J. "Networks of Scientific Papers." In *The Growth of Knowledge*, edited by M. Kochen. New York: John Wiley, 1967.

Deweese, L. Carroll. "A Bibliography of Library Use Studies." Library Operations Research Project, School of Industrial Engineering, Purdue University, 1967 (unpublished).

Dobbyn, M. "Approval Plan Purchasing in Perspective." *College and Research Libraries*, 33 (November 1972), 480-484.

Dougherty, Richard M., and Heinritz, F. J. *Scientific Management of Library Operations*. Metuchen, N. J.: The Scarecrow Press, 1966.

Dougherty, Richard M., and Leonard, Lawrence E. *Management and Costs of Technical Processes: A Bibliographical Review, 1876-1969*. Metuchen, N. J.: The Scarecrow Press, 1970.

Dougherty, Richard M., and Maier, Joan M. *Centralized Processing for Academic Libraries*. Metuchen, N. J.: The Scarecrow Press, 1971.

Drake, Alvin W. *Fundamentals of Applied Probability Theory*. New York: McGraw-Hill, 1967.

Drake, Alvin W., Keeney, Ralph L., and Morse, Philip M., eds. *Analysis of Public Systems*. Cambridge, Mass.: MIT Press, 1972.

Ellsworth, Ralph E. *The Economics of Book Storage in College and University Libraries*. Metuchen, N. J.: The Scarecrow Press, 1969.

Encyclopedia Americana, vol. 20. New York: Encyclopedia Americana, 1973, 757-758.

Ettlinger, J. R. T. "Through a Glass Darkly: Academic Book Selection in Crisis." *APLA Bulletin*, 32 (June 1968), 32-40.

Etzioni, Amitai. *Modern Organizations.* Englewood Cliffs, N. J.: Prentice-Hall, 1964.

Evans, G. E. "Book Selection and Book Collection Usage in Academic Libraries." *Library Quarterly,* 40 (July 1970), 297-308.

Franklin, R. D. "How Many Copies Are Enough?" *Library Journal,* 91 (October 1, 1966), 4573-4578.

Funkenstein, Daniel H. "Tomorrow's Medical Student." Reprinted in *Reader in Medical Librarianship,* edited by Winifred Sewell. Englewood, Colo.: IHS-Microcard ed., 1973.

Fussler, H. H., and Simon, J. L. *Patterns in the Use of Books in Large Research Libraries.* Chicago: University of Chicago Press, 1961.

Gaver, Mary Virginia, ed. *Background Readings in Building Library Collections.* Metuchen, N. J.: The Scarecrow Press, 1969.

Goffman, William, and Morris, Thomas G. "Bradford's Law and Library Acquisitions." *Nature,* 226 (June 6, 1970), 922-923.

Goldhor, H. ed. *Selection and Acquisition in Medium-Sized and Large Libraries.* Graduate School of Library Administration, University of Illinois, 1963.

Gomes, Stella S. "The Nature of the Use and Users of the Midwest Regional Medical Library." *Bulletin of the Medical Library Association,* 58 (October 1970), 559-577.

Goyal, S. K. "Application of Operational Research to Problems of Determining Appropriate Loan Period for Periodicals." *Libri,* 20 (1970), 94-100.

——. "A Systematic Method for Reducing Overordering Copies of Books." *Library Resources and Technical Services,* 16 (Winter 1972), 26-32.

Grant, Robert S. "Predicting the Need for Multiple Copies of Books." *Journal of Library Automation,* 4 (June 1971), 64-71.

Haas, W. J. "Management in Research Libraries." *Library Quarterly,* 43 (October 1973), 369-384.

Haro, Robert. "Book Selection in Academic Libraries." *College and Research Libraries,* 28 (March 1967), 104-106.

Hartley, Harry J. *Educational Planning Programming Budgeting: A System Approach.* Englewood Cliffs, N. J.: Prentice-Hall, 1968.

Harvard University. *Directory of Officers and Students.* 1971-1972 and 1972-1973.

——. *The Francis A. Countway Library of Medicine—Library Guide.* Guide to the Harvard Libraries, no. 9. 1973.

——. Medical School. *Dean's Report.* 1972-1973.

Heinritz, F. J. "Quantitative Management in Libraries." *College and Research Libraries,* 31 (July 1970), 232-238.

Herner, Saul. "Systems Design, Evaluation and Costing." *Special Libraries,* 58 (October 1967), 576-581.

Jacob, Itzhak. "A Report on In-Room Use in the Science Library." Unpublished report for Operations Research Course 8.75, MIT, January 1963.

Jain, A. K. "Sampling and Short-Period Usage in the Purdue Library." *College and Research Libraries,* 27 (May 1966), 211-218.

———. "A Statistical Study of Book Use." Ph.D. dissertation, Purdue University, 1967.

Jenks, George M. "Book Selection: An Approach for Small and Medium-Sized Libraries." *College and Research Libraries,* 33 (January 1972), 28-30.

Johns Hopkins University. Milton S. Eisenhower Library. *An Operations Research and Systems Engineering Study of a University Library.* Final Report (no. 5). Baltimore: Johns Hopkins University Library, December 1968.

Katz, William A. *Introduction to Reference Work.* New York: McGraw-Hill, 1969.

Kilgour, Frederick G. "Recorded Use of Books in the Yale Medical Library." *American Documentation,* 12 (October 1961), 266-269.

———. "Computer-Based Systems, a New Dimension to Library Cooperation." *College and Research Libraries,* 34 (March 1973), 137-143.

Knox, William T. "Systems for Technological Information Transfer." *Science,* 181 (August 3, 1973), 415-419.

Koopman, Bernard O. "The Theory of Search. Part III. The Optimum Distribution of Searching Effort." *Operations Research,* 5 (October 1957), 613-626.

Kosa, G. A. "Book Selection Trends in American Academic Libraries." *Australia Library Journal,* 21 (November 1972), 416-424.

Kraft, Donald H. "Library Operations Research." In *Proceedings of the LARC Institute on Library Operations Research* (January 25-26, 1973, Washington, D.C.), edited by H. W. Axford. Temple, Ariz.: The LARC Association, 1973.

Kraft, Donald H., and Hill, T. W. "A Journal Selection Model and Its Implications for a Library System." *Information Storage and Retrieval,* 9 (January 1973), 1-11.

Kraft, M. "An Argument for Selectivity in the Acquisition of Materials for Research Libraries." *Library Quarterly,* 37 (July 1967), 284-295.

Lane, D. O. "Selection of Academic Library Materials: A Literature Survey." *College and Research Libraries,* 29 (September 1968), 364-372.

Lazorick, Gerald J. *Demand Models for Books in Library Circulation Systems.* Buffalo, N.Y.: School of Information and Library Studies, State University of New York at Buffalo, 1970.

Leimkuhler, F. F. "The Bradford Distribution." *Journal of Documentation,* 23 (September 1967), 197-207.

———. "Library Operations Research: An Engineering Approach to Information Problems." *Engineering Education*, 60 (January 1970), 363-365.

———. "Mathematical Models for Library Systems Analysis." *Drexel Library Quarterly*, 4 (July 1968), 185-196.

Leimkuhler, F. F., and Cooper, Michael D. "Analytical Models for Library Planning." *Journal of the American Society of Information Science*, 22 (November 1971), 390-398.

Levit, E. J. "Trends in Graduate Medical Education and Specialty Certification." *New England Journal of Medicine*, 290 (March 7, 1974), 545-549.

Lister, Winston C. "Least Cost Decision Rules for the Selection of Library Materials for Compact Storage." Ph.D dissertation, Purdue University, 1967.

Lyle, Guy R. *The Librarian Speaking: Interviews with University Librarians*. Athens, Ga.: University of Georgia Press, 1970.

McGaw, Howard F. "Policies and Practices for Discarding." *Library Trends*, 4 (January 1956), 269-282.

McGrath, William E. "Determining and Allocating Book Funds for Current Domestic Buying." *College and Research Libraries*, 28 (July 1967), 269-272.

"Making-Do." *The Francis A. Countway Library of Medicine Newsletter*, September 1973, 1-2.

Martin, Jess A., and Manch, Steven B. "Library Weeds." *Bulletin of the Medical Library Association*, 59 (October 1971), 599-602.

Massman, Virgil F., and Patterson, Kelly. "A Minimum Budget for Current Acquisitions." *College and Research Libraries*, 31 (March 1970), 83-88.

Meier, R. C. "Communication Overload: Proposals from the Study of a University Library." *Administrative Science Quarterly* (March 1963), 521-544.

———. "Systems Analysis and Management." *PNLA Quarterly*, 35 (January 1971), 17-22.

Meyer, B. J., and Demos, J. T. "Acquisition Policy for University Libraries, Selection or Collection?" *Library Resources and Technical Services*, 14 (Summer 1970), 395-399.

Moreland, George B. "Operation Saturation." *Library Journal*, 93 (May 15, 1968), 1975-1979.

Morrison, Perry D. "A Symposium on Approval Order Plans and the Book Selection Responsibilities of Librarians." *Library Resources and Technical Services*, 12 (Spring 1968), 133-139.

Morse, Philip M. *Library Effectiveness: A Systems Approach*. Cambridge, Mass.: MIT Press, 1968.

———. "Library Models." In *Analysis of Public Systems*, edited by A. W. Drake, R. L. Keeney, and P. M. Morse. Cambridge, Mass.: MIT Press, 1972.

———. "Measures of Library Effectiveness." *Library Quarterly*, 42 (January 1972), 15-30.

———, ed. *Operations Research for Public Systems*. Cambridge, Mass.: MIT Press, 1967.

———. "Optimal Linear Ordering of Information Items." *Operations Research*, 20 (July-August 1972), 741-751.

———. *Queues, Inventories and Maintenance*. New York: John Wiley, 1958.

———. "Search Theory and Browsing." *Library Quarterly*, 41 (October 1970), 391-408.

Morse, Philip M., and Chen, Ching-chih. "Using Circulation Desk Data to Obtain Unbiased Estimates of Book Use." *Library Quarterly*, 45 (April 1975), 179-194.

Morse, Philip M., and Kimball, George E. *Methods of Operations Research*. New York: John Wiley, 1951.

Mount, Ellis, and Fasana, Paul. "An Approach to the Measurement of Use and Cost of a Large Academic Research Library System: A Report of a Study Done at Columbia University Libraries." *College and Research Libraries*, 33 (May 1972), 199-211.

Nance, R. E. "Strategic Simulation of a Library/User/Funder System." Ph.D. dissertation, Purdue University, 1968.

Neufeld, John. "Save Our Books." *RQ*, 6 (Fall 1968), 27.

"New Federal Budget Provides Slightly More Money for Medical Research." *Journal of American Medical Association*, 227 (March 4, 1974), 989-990.

Newhouse, Joseph P., and Alexander, Arthur J. *An Economic Analysis of Public Library Services*. Lexington, Mass.: Lexington Books, 1972.

Novick, David, ed. *Program Budgeting*. Cambridge, Mass.: Harvard University Press, 1967.

Parker, T. F. "Missing Stream: Operations Management in Libraries." *Library Journal*, 94 (January 1969), 42-43.

Pings, Vern M. "Development of Quantitative Assessment of Medical Libraries." *College and Research Libraries*, 29 (September 1968), 373-380.

Pings, V. M., Olson, E. O., and Orr, R. H. "Summary Report of Study of Academic Medical Library Statistics." *Bulletin of the Medical Library Association*, 57 (July 1969), 233-238.

Potter, Alfred C. "Selection of Books for College Libraries." *Library Journal*, 22 (October 1897), 39-44.

Raffel, Jeffrey A., and Shishko, Robert. *Systematic Analysis of University Libraries: An Application of Cost-Benefit Analysis to the MIT Libraries*. Cambridge, Mass.: MIT Press, 1969.

Raffel, L. J. "Compact Book Storage Models." M.S. thesis, Purdue University, June 1965.

Raisig, L. M., Smith, M., Cuff, R., and Kilgour, F. G. "How Biomedical Investigators Use Library Books at the Yale Medical Library." *Bulletin of the Medical Library Association,* 54 (April 1966), 104-107.

Ramer, James, and Boykin, Joseph. "Book Budget in Academic Libraries." *Southeastern Librarian,* 16 (Spring 1966), 40-43.

Random House Dictionary of the English Language. New York: Random House, 1966.

Rees, A. M. "Medical Libraries and the Assessment of User Needs." *Bulletin of the Medical Library Association,* 54 (April 1966), 99-103.

Richter, E. A. "Academic Library Acquisition Policy." *New Mexico Libraries,* 3 (Winter 1970), 95-99.

Rider, Fremont. *The Scholar and the Future of the Research Library.* New York: Hadham Press, 1944.

Rolfe, A. J., et al. *In-Room Use of Library Books.* Unpublished report for Operations Research Course 8.75, MIT, January 1962.

Rothkopf, Michael. "The Future Circulation Rate of a Book, and an Application of Queuing Theory to Library Problems." Unpublished report for Operations Research Course 8.75, MIT, January 1962.

Rouse, Roscoe. "Automation Stops Here: A Case for Man-Made Book Collections." *College and Research Libraries,* 31 (May 1970), 147-154.

Roy, Robert, et al., eds. *Progress Report on an Operations Research and Systems Engineering Study of a University Library.* Baltimore: Johns Hopkins University Library, 1963.

Saaty, T. L. "Operations Research: Some Contributions to Mathematics." *Science,* 178 (December 8, 1972), 1061-1070.

Schad, Jasper G. "Allocating Book Fund: Control or Planning." *College and Research Libraries,* 31 (May 1970), 155-159.

Schad, Jasper G., and Adams, R. L. "Book Selection in Academic Libraries; a New Approach." *College and Research Libraries,* 30 (September 1969), 437-442.

Seymour, C. A. "Weeding the Collection: A Review of Research on Identifying Obsolete Stock Monographs." *Libri,* 22 (1972), 137-148.

Shaffer, B., and Ernst, M. "A Survey of Circulation Characteristics of Some General Library Books." Unpublished report for Operations Research Course 8.75, MIT, 1954.

Shaw, Ralph R. "Scientific Management in the Library." *Wilson Library Bulletin,* 21 (January 1947), 349-352.

Shores, L. S. "The Library Arts College." *School and Society,* 41 (January 26, 1935), 110-114.

Simon, Julian L. "How Many Books Should Be Stored Where? An Economic Analysis." *College and Research Libraries,* 28 (March 1967), 92-103.

Snyder, Helen I. "Toward an Optimal Library System for Pennsylvania State University." Paper presented at the annual meeting of the American Society for Engineering Education, June 1965.

Spiller, David. *Book Selection: An Introduction to Principles and Practice.* Hamden, Conn.: Linnet, 1971.

Stearns, N. S., and Ratcliff, W. W. "An Integrated Health Science Core Library for Physicians, Nurses, and Allied Health Practitioners in Community Hospitals." *New England Journal of Medicine,* 283 (December 1970), 1489-1498.

Summers, William. "A Change in Budgeting Thinking." *American Libraries,* 2 (December 1971), 1174-1180.

Swanson, D. R., and Bookstein, A., eds. *Operations Research: Implications for Libraries.* Chicago: University of Chicago Press, 1972. (Also as *Library Quarterly,* 42 (January 1972).)

Totten, Herman L. "The Selection of Library Materials for Storage: A State of the Art." *Library Trends,* 19 (January 1971), 341-351.

Trueswell, Richard W. "A Quantitative Measure of User Circulation Requirements and Its Possible Effect on Stack Thinning and Multiple Copy Determination." *American Documentation,* 16 (January 1965), 20-25.

———. "Some Behavioral Patterns of Library Users: The 80/20 Rule." *Wilson Library Bulletin,* 43 (January 1969), 458-461.

———. "Two Characteristics of Circulation." *College and Research Libraries,* 25 (July 1964), 285-291.

———. "User Behavior Patterns and Requirements and Their Effect on the Possible Applications of Data Processing and Computer Techniques in a University Library." Ph.D. dissertation, Northwestern University, 1964.

Tudor, Dean. "Special Library Budget." *Special Libraries,* 63 (November 1972), 517-525.

U.S. National Academy of Sciences. Committee on Scientific and Technical Communication. *Scientific and Technical Communication.* Washington, D.C.: National Academy of Sciences, 1969.

University of Pennsylvania. Wharton School. *Library Planning and Decision-Making Systems.* Final Report of Project No. 8-0802. December 1972.

Wagner, H. M. *Principles of Operations Research.* Englewood Cliffs, N.J.: Prentice-Hall, 1969.

Winkler, Karen J. "College Library Costs Skyrocket Since '49; Report Predicts Its Major Increases in Future." *The Chronicle of Higher Education,* 7 (August 27, 1973), 3.

Wood, D. N. "User Studies: A Review of the Literature from 1966 to 1970." *ASLIB Proceedings,* 23 (January 1971), 14-20.

Zipf, George K. *Human Behavior and the Principle of Least Effort.* Cambridge, Mass.: Addison-Wesley, 1949. (Also reprinted by New York: Hafner, 1972.)

Index

Accession, 23, 47, 80
  date, 61, 66
Acquisition, 23-24, 44-49, 66, 78, 105, 108, 113
  cost of, 124
  date of, 121
  of multicopy, 110
  of single copy, 68
Acquisition policy, 103; *see also* Book selection policy
Active books, 7, 19, 22, 29, 31-32, 35, 81, 83-84, 105, 112, 120-121, 183-185, 197
  mean circulation of, 31-32, 34, 83, 106, 125, 198
Arrival rate, 11
Attendance, *see* Library attendance

Book
  age of, 9, 12, 16, 115
  call number of, 43, 54, 60, 154
  cost of, 111
  due date of, 28, 42-43, 59-60, 127, 145
  half-life of, 107, 121
  nonuse of, 18
  popularity of, 8, 12, 18, 67, 73, 106, 115
  return of, 27
  use of, *see* Book use
  value of, 66, 67
  weeding of, *see* Weeding; Weeding policy
Book acquisition, *see* Acquisition
Book availability, 115-116, 127
Book budget, *see* Budgetary considerations
Book circulation, *see* Circulation
Book collection, 39-40, 102, 121
  future planning of, 113-114; *see also* Collection development
  minimal nucleus of, *see* Core collection, book
  size of, 61, 63-64, 112, 119
Book core collection, *see* Core collection, book
Book demands, 116
Book duplication, *see* Duplication policy
Book loan, *see* Loan period; Loan policy
Book maintenance, 120
  cost of, 124
Book overdue fine, 42, 128; *see also* Overdue books
Book renewals, 60, 105, 127, 145, 148
  distribution by subject, 147
Book requests, 60
Book selection policy, 104, 110-114; *see also* Collection development
Book use
  data collection of, *see* Data collection
  further studies of, 132
  in-library, 50, 52, 66, 132
  measures of, 52, 66
  types of, 50, 66
Book use data, 22, 50-52, 81, 108, 118, 122, 131, 135
Books
  of almost no circulation, *see* Dead books
  in circulation, *see* Live books
  of high circulation, *see* Active books
  of low circulation, *see* Inactive books
  off shelf, 35, 63-64, 66, 82, 116, 127
  on shelf, 35, 63, 116
  reserved and requested by users, 44, 105, 115, 131-132, 135, 143
Boston Medical Library, 39, 44, 46, 121
Boston Medical Library Classification Scheme, 40, 42, 58, 68, 72
Bradford's law of dispersion, 102, 107
Browsers, 153-154
Browsing, 60, 120, 129-130, 153-154
  rate of, 153, 198
Budgetary considerations, 99-109
Budgetary systems, 99-101, 108

Circulation
  annual total of, 31, 33, 83, 93, 94, 108, 198
  expected mean of, 20, 24-25, 31,

Index   210

Circulation (continued)
    117, 198
  prediction of, 93-95, 180-181
  asymptotic value of, 67
  expected mean of, 10, 12-13, 16,
    18, 22-23, 34, 67, 78-81, 102,
    106, 116, 127, 135, 162-167,
    198
  factor of, 116
  first year, 17-18, 117
  prediction of, 33-34, 83, 85, 101,
    105, 115-116, 125-126, 131,
    180-181
  rate of, 13, 28, 198
  volume of, 68, 103-104
Circulation charge cards, 27-28, 42-
    43, 51, 53, 59-60, 63, 135
Circulation data, 31, 122, 125-126,
    135
  biased, 22-23, 26, 29, 31, 34, 52,
    54, 70-71, 81, 83, 131; see also
    Circulation distribution, uncor-
    rected data
  corrected, 31; see also Circulation
    distribution, corrected data
  unbiased, 34
Circulation date, last, 122
Circulation distribution, 10, 23, 55,
    57, 65-66, 68, 71
  corrected data, 30, 82, 84-92, 172-
    179
  by day of the week, 144
  geometric, 17-19, 22, 26, 30-31,
    81-83, 102-103, 172-179
  by publication date, 107, 109, 135,
    138, 183-184
  by subject, 107, 135-137, 140-142,
    185
  uncorrected data, 30, 84-92, 172-
    179
  by user, 102-103
Circulation history (data), 8, 12, 14,
    23-24, 29, 51-54, 56, 61, 65-68,
    70, 78, 82, 121-122, 131, 161-
    170
Circulation interference, 115-117,
    128
Circulation procedures, 42-44
Circulation records, 28, 43, 51, 56,
    58-61, 135, 154, 157
Circulation rules, 42

Collection development, 47, 102,
    104, 110-111
  factors of, 45, 113-114
Conditional probability, 11, 198
Connectivity of interest, 106, 113,
    130, 154-155, 197
Core collection
  book, 104, 123, 183; see also
    Countway Library of Medicine,
    minimal nucleus of books of
  journal, 132
Correction factor, 22, 26-30, 34, 81
Correction models, 22-35, 81-95,
    105
Cost
  of acquisition, see Acquisition,
    cost of
  of book, see Book, cost of
  of book maintenance, see Book
    maintenance, cost of
  per unit of service, 111
  of processing, 124
  of weeding, see Weeding, cost of
Countway Library of Medicine,
    39-49
  annual book acquisition of, 48
  book circulation statistics of, 135-
    144
  book users of, 60, 157-159
  cataloging statistics of, 48
  library expenditures of, 46
  library hours of, 44
  library users of, 44-53, 102-103,
    114, 120, 145, 157-159
  minimal nucleus of books of, 183-
    196
  statistics on book loan period of,
    145-152

Data collection, 4, 10, 22-23, 50-66,
    68, 82
Date due slip, 28, 43, 51, 61-62, 65,
    68, 82, 123
Dead books, 33-34, 83, 106, 125-
    126, 197
Demand rate, 116
Duplication policy, 107-108, 110,
    114-118, 127-128, 135

Expected mean circulation, see
    Circulation, expected mean of

Future book use, *see* Circulation, prediction of
Future circulation, *see* Circulation, prediction of

Harvard Medical Library, 39, 57, 121
High-circulation books, *see* Active books
High-circulation subject classes, 58-59, 106, 113

Inactive books, 19, 31-33, 72, 105, 108, 111-112, 115, 125, 129, 197

Journal use, 132

Least-square-fit method, 15-16, 70, 72-73
Library activities, 105, 133
 accountability of, 108
 index of, 52, 103
Library attendance, 54-56, 103, 131
Library facilities, use of, 133
Library goals and objectives, 101-102, 105, 111
Library hours, 44-46, 103-104, 135; *see also* Countway Library of Medicine, library hours of
Library nonuse, 129
Library nonuser, 133
Library users, 103-105, 119, 127-128, 154; *see also* Countway Library of Medicine, library users of
 minimal nucleus of, 102, 105
 types of, 133
Linear arrangement of library books, 129, 153-154
Live books, 32-35, 72, 83, 197
 mean circulation of, 33-34, 71, 83, 106, 125, 198
Loan period, 42, 59-60, 115-117, 127, 132, 145, 148-149
 distribution of, 145, 148, 150-152
 mean fractional, 35, 116, 127, 145, 148-151, 198
Loan policy, 127
Low-circulation books, *see* Inactive books

Markov models, 7-22, 53, 58-59, 67, 116, 131-132
 modification of, 20, 22-35
 verification of, 73-81, 161-170
Markov process, 10-16, 67, 71
Massachusetts Medical Society, 44
Models, 3-4, 8-10
Morse-Chen models, *see* Correction models
Morse's books use models, *see* Markov models

National Library of Medicine Classification Scheme, 40-41
New England Regional Medical Library Service, 39
 Newsletters of, 48-49

Old Boston Classification Scheme, *see* Boston Medical Library Classification Scheme
Overdue books, 44, 146

Parameter
 circulation, 31, 33-34, 83, 106, 125, 197
 geometric, 18, 22, 31, 34, 82-84, 198
 Markov, 12, 15-16, 18, 34, 67, 70-71, 73, 77-80, 83, 106, 123, 131, 198
Past book use data, *see* Circulation history
Planning Programming Budgetary System, *see* PPBS
Poisson distribution, 7, 11, 13, 33
Popularity of book, *see* Book, popularity of
PPBS, 99-101

Queuing model, 116, 127, 132

Random circulation in time, 32, 35
Random events, 11
Random process, 10-11, 128, 145, 153-154
Random sample, 23, 51, 72
Remote storage, 119-120, 124-125
Reserve books, 50, 53

Reserves and requests, *see* Books, reserved and requested by users

Sample month, 26, 28, 64, 72, 102-103, 107, 116-117, 122, 135-143, 145, 147-148, 151-152, 161, 183
Sampling period, 27-28, 54-56, 59, 70
 size of, 56-58, 72
 unit of, 54-56
Search theory, 60, 120, 153-154
Shelf-list cards, 62-63
Shelf space, 111, 115
Steady state, 17-18, 106
Symbols, glossary of, 197-198

Time, interarrival, 11, 198
Transition probability, 11, 16-17, 198

User frustration, 66, 103, 112, 115, 120-121, 123-125, 130
User satisfaction, 66, 108, 120, 127
Users, *see* Library users; Countway Library of Medicine, book users of; Countway Library of Medicine, library users of

Weeding
 barriers to, 119
 by acquisition date, 121
 by circulation history, 121
 cost of, 120, 124
 criteria for, 120-122
 disposal, 120
 by publication date, 121, 123
 storage, 120; *see also* Remote storage
Weeding policy, 110, 119-126

Year pair, 13-14, 69-70, 73, 77
 entry form of, 68-69, 71

Zero use book, 7, 18-19, 34